OXFORD WORLD'S CLASSICS

MADHUMĀLATĪ

MĪR SAYYID MANJHAN RĀJGĪRĪ's father was Sayyid Muḥammad ʿAlī Manjhan, who was in turn the son of Sayyid Muḥammad Chakkan of Jaunpur. His mother was Bībī Khunja Daulat, the daughter of the renowned Shaikh Muḥammad Qāzin ʿAlā, who, although reared in both the Mādarī and Chishtī Sufi traditions, later proved to be one of the principal exponents of the Shaṭṭārī way in Bihar. He was therefore born and brought up in the very centre of Shaṭṭārī Sufism in Bihar at what was probably its most active and influential period. His own Shaikh was no less than Shaikh Muḥammad Ġhauṣ Gvāliyārī (d. 1563), one of the major spiritual figures of his age, and Manjhan himself was an authorized teaching shaikh at some point in his life. We know that he was a courtier at the court of Islām Shāh Sūr where he was already a well-established poet. He says in his poem he began to write *Madhumālatī* in 1545. Apart from these few slender details nothing else is known of Manjhan other than his poetry, of which only *Madhumālatī* is extant.

ADITYA BEHL teaches in the Department of South and Southeast Asian Studies at the University of California at Berkeley. He translates fiction and poetry from Hindi, Urdu, and Punjabi into English and is the author of a book on Sufi poetry entitled *Shadows of Paradise on Earth: An Indian Islamic Literary Tradition, 1379–1545*, and the editor of *The Penguin New Writing in India* (1994).

SIMON WEIGHTMAN is the former Head of the Department of the Study of Religions at the School of Oriental and African Studies in London. Working mainly in Persian, Hindi, and Sanskrit, he is the author of *Hinduism in the Village Setting* (1976); *Teach Yourself Hindi* (1989)—with R. Snell; *Mysticism and the Metaphor of Energies* (2000); and numerous research papers. He edited *The Traveller's Literary Companion to the Indian Subcontinent* (1992).

OXFORD WORLD'S CLASSICS

For over 100 years Oxford World's Classics have brought readers closer to the world's great literature. Now with over 700 titles—from the 4,000-year-old myths of Mesopotamia to the twentieth century's greatest novels—the series makes available lesser-known as well as celebrated writing.

The pocket-sized hardbacks of the early years contained introductions by Virginia Woolf, T. S. Eliot, Graham Greene, and other literary figures which enriched the experience of reading. Today the series is recognized for its fine scholarship and reliability in texts that span world literature, drama and poetry, religion, philosophy and politics. Each edition includes perceptive commentary and essential background information to meet the changing needs of readers.

OXFORD WORLD'S CLASSICS

MĪR SAYYID MANJHAN SHAṬṬĀRĪ RĀJGĪRĪ

Madhumālatī

An Indian Sufi Romance

Translated with an Introduction and Notes by
ADITYA BEHL and SIMON WEIGHTMAN
With SHYAM MANOHAR PANDEY

OXFORD
UNIVERSITY PRESS

OXFORD
UNIVERSITY PRESS

Great Clarendon Street, Oxford OX2 6DP

Oxford University Press is a department of the University of Oxford.
It furthers the University's objective of excellence in research, scholarship,
and education by publishing worldwide in

Oxford New York

Athens Auckland Bangkok Bogotá Buenos Aires Calcutta
Cape Town Chennai Dar es Salaam Delhi Florence Hong Kong Istanbul
Karachi Kuala Lumpur Madrid Melbourne Mexico City Mumbai
Nairobi Paris São Paulo Shanghai Singapore Taipei Tokyo Toronto Warsaw

with associated companies in Berlin Ibadan

Oxford is a registered trade mark of Oxford University Press
in the UK and in certain other countries

Published in the United States
by Oxford University Press Inc., New York

First published as an Oxford World's Classics paperback 2000

British Library Cataloguing in Publication Data

Data available

Library of Congress Cataloging in Publication Data

Data available

ISBN-13: 978-0-19-284037-0
ISBN-10: 0-19-284037-1

3

Typeset in Times
by RefineCatch Limited, Bungay, Suffolk
Printed in Great Britain by
Clays Ltd, St Ives plc

For Mujeeb Husain Rizvi

CONTENTS

ACKNOWLEDGEMENTS

THE process of collaborative translation, and of bringing to completion a long project, has necessarily involved many people since its inception. Since we think of academia as a community of friends, it is a pleasure to acknowledge the generosity of the friends and scholars who have encouraged and helped us along the way. Our first expressions of gratitude must go to two senior scholars who kindly assisted us at early stages of this project: Dr Shyam Manohar Pandey of the University of Naples, and Dr Mujeeb Husain Rizvi of Jamia Millia Islamia in Delhi. Dr Pandey, the doyen of Hindi scholars of the Sufi romances, generously collaborated with Simon Weightman to produce the first rough prose translation of the *Madhumālatī*; his contributions as co-author are recognized on the title-page of this volume. Dr Rizvi enthusiastically shared his knowledge of the Hindavī Sufi romances with us, helping Aditya Behl to check the printed edition of the text line by line against a manuscript held in the Rampur Raza Library. We dedicate this book to him as a mark of our affection and respect.

A word about the division of intellectual labour is also in order here. The current blank verse translation was composed by Aditya Behl from his own initial verse translation, Simon Weightman's prose translation, and the manuscript and printed editions of the text. This was subsequently checked line by line against Manjhan's Hindavī verses by Simon Weightman. In addition, Aditya Behl's assistants Sean Pue, Saba Waheed, and Shabana Khan helped with the research for the Introduction, both in Berkeley and in London, and commented on early drafts of the verse translation. In her capacity as graduate research assistant, Adrienne Copithorne painstakingly did the research for some of the factual notes to the text and composed clear and elegant explanations for the unfamiliar customs and terms that occur in Manjhan's poem. Our gratitude to all these assistants is heartfelt; without their help, the *Madhumālatī* would have been a much poorer work in its English incarnation. The financial provision for these invaluable aides came from the University of California at Berkeley; we are obliged to the University for supporting our work materially. Aditya Behl's class on Indian Romances at Berkeley read a penultimate version of the draft translation and were the proverbial intelligent general readers who prompted explanations of the aesthetic resonances and cultural meanings of the poem.

In addition, a number of friends, colleagues, and students generously took time from their busy lives to read drafts of the introduction, notes, and translation. We are much indebted to Lawrence Cohen, Wendy Doniger, Maya Fisher, Robert Goldman, Linda Hess, Padmanabh Jaini, Vijay Pinch, and Frances Pritchett for responding to all or part of the volume. A special debt of gratitude is owed to the late A. K. Ramanujan, who encouraged us to produce a verse translation that recreated the poetic form of the original text. We are also grateful to Simon Digby for his support and knowledgeable guidance at crucial moments. The sympathetic and generous response to our text from friends and scholars has revivified in our minds the Sanskrit notion of the *sahṛdaya* or sensitive reader. We are beholden to the late Akbar Ali Khan Arshizada of the Rampur Raza Library for allowing us to have access to the Rampur manuscript of the *Madhumālatī*, and to the staff of the Bharat Kala Bhavan for allowing Aditya Behl to consult the Benares manuscripts of the text. The Philadelphia Museum of Art graciously allowed us to use a leaf from their *Gulshan-iʿIshq* manuscript for the cover. Judith Luna of Oxford University Press has been an enthusiastic and skilled editor; she has enriched this volume through her interest and efforts. Finally, our sincere thanks to all those who provided warm and considerate hospitality, moral support, and insightful direction at important junctures: Naureen Butt, A. W. Azhar Dehlavi, Yasmin, Shahid, and Mehreen Hosain, the Countess Catherine Raczynska, Jameela Siddiqi, Micaela Soar, Veena Taneja, and the late Begum Sakina of Rampur. Our families have loyally and lovingly stood by us throughout the long period it took us to complete this work; without them, none of this would have been possible.

INTRODUCTION

THE *Madhumālatī* (*Jasminum grandiflorum*, 'Night-flowering Jasmine') is a mystical Indian romance composed in AD 1545, here translated for the first time into a western language. Shaikh Mīr Sayyid Manjhan Rājgīrī, the author, was a Sufi of the Shaṭṭārī order. The Sufis have been termed the 'mystics' of Islam, and Sufism its 'mystical dimension'.[1] A Sufi, a mystic or spiritual seeker, would, through his initiation to a particular Shaikh, a spiritual master and teacher, become affiliated to a particular spiritual lineage or chain (*silsilah*). The lineages, organized around links between Sufi masters and their disciples, focused on prayer, fasting, asceticism, and cultivating the self through music and poetry to attain nearness to Allah. The Shaṭṭārīs were an order founded in India in the fifteenth century by Shaikh ʿAbdullāh Shaṭṭār. Manjhan was the disciple of a major Shaṭṭārī Shaikh, Muḥammad Ġhauṣ Gvāliyārī (d. 1563), and the *silsilah* was powerful and popular at the time Manjhan wrote his romance.[2] Manjhan's name means simply 'the middle brother', the midpoint in a series in Hindavī between Chuṭṭan (the little one) and Buḍḍhan (the eldest one). Manjhan's birthplace Rajgir is in the present-day State of Bihar, not far from Patna in northern India, and the poem itself is written in Awadhi or eastern Hindavī. Along with Maithili, Awadhi has remained a major literary dialect of the spoken language of northern and eastern India ('Bhākhā') since the days of the Delhi sultanate.

Manjhan's poem belongs to that moment in Indian history when the success of the empire established by the early Mughal rulers Bābur and Humāyūn was not yet a historical certainty.

[1] For excellent balanced introductory expositions of Sufism and the Orders, see Annemarie Schimmel, *Mystical Dimensions of Islam* (Chapel Hill: University of North Carolina Press, 1975), and C. W. Ernst, *Sufism* (Boston and London: Shambhala Books, 1997).

[2] For further details about the Shaṭṭārī *silsilah*, see below, Section II.

Northern and eastern India, the territory of Hindustan, was occupied by a number of Afghan warlords and Rajput lineages newly demonstrating their martial prowess and attempting to carve out territories for themselves after the demise of the regional sultanates of Delhi and Jaunpur. The Sūr Afghāns from Bihar seized power after their military leader, the warlord Sher Shāh, had defeated the Mughal emperor Humāyūn and forced him to flee to Iran in 1540.[3] During the short Afghan interregnum, Sher Shāh Sūr set up an administrative and military structure that was later to prove useful to the Mughal emperors. He was killed in 1545, on the battlements of the massive fort at Kalinjar, when the base of a cannon exploded towards Sher Shāh rather than away from him. The date is given by a chronogram in Persian, *z'ātish murd* ('he died by fire'), an event to which Manjhan alludes when giving the date at which he began his poem.

Sher Shāh was succeeded by his son Islām Shāh—also called Salīm Shāh—whom Manjhan praises in his prologue as the king of the time. It is as a poet in residence at Islām Shāh's cultured and multilingual court that we have the only historical description of our author Manjhan. He is mentioned in the *Afsānah-i Shāhān* ('Tale of the Kings'), a chronicle of life in Afghan times that has come to us in the form of the family lore of a Bihari Afghan Shaikh of the early seventeenth century:

Wherever he [Islām Shāh] happened to be, he kept himself surrounded by accomplished scholars and poets. Kiosks [*khūshak*] were set up, scented with *ghāliā* [a compound of musk, ambergris, camphor, and oil of ben-nuts*], and provided with betel leaves. Men like Mīr Sayyid Manjhan, the author of *Madhumālatī*, Shāh Muḥammad Farmūlī and his younger brother, Mūsan, Sūrdās and many other

* This come from F. Steingass, *Persian Dictionary*.

[3] See, *inter alia*, 'Abbās Khān Sarvānī, *Tārīkh-i Śer Śāhī*, tr. B. P. Ambasthya (Patna: K. P. Jayaswal Research Institute, 1974), Iqtidar Husain Siddiqui, *History of Sher Shāh Sūr* (Aligarh: Dwadash Shreni and Company Private Limited, 1971) and Dirk H. A. Kolff, *'Naukar', Rajput, and Sepoy: The Ethnohistory of the Military Labour Market in Hindustan, 1450–1850* (Cambridge: Cambridge University Press, 1990).

learned scholars and poets assembled there and poems in Arabic, Persian and Hindavī were recited.[4]

This rich and interactive mixture of vernacular and classical or, in Sheldon Pollock's phrase, 'cosmopolitan'[5] languages was part of a court-sponsored aesthetic culture. The Turkish and Afghan courts of the fourteenth, fifteenth, and sixteenth centuries fostered the growth of regional literary, musical, and artistic identities. Poets at these courts forged a distinctively Indian Islamic aesthetic culture using models and elements from Persian and Arabic literary and religious traditions as well as from Sanskrit and Indian regional languages.

The historical agents who were part of this Indian Islamic literary culture were, however, not just the courtiers and kings of the Delhi sultanate and the Afghan kingdoms that followed in its wake. They were also disciples in Sufi orders, guided by shaikhs who set themselves up as commanding spiritual jurisdiction (*vilāyat*) over different parts of the territory of Hindustan. The army of prayer (*lashkar-i duʿā*), as it is sometimes called, led by these shaikhs formed one dominant cultural force during the period. Sufi shaikhs played at being kingmakers, and established themselves at a calculated distance from royal courts in hospices (*k͟hānaqāh*s). Here they trained disciples to attain nearness to Allah by teaching them spiritual exercises and cultivating their taste for things spiritual (*ẕauq*) through a ritually controlled exposure to music and poetry. They also wrote romances in Hindavī that describe the ascetic quest of the hero towards the revelatory beauty of a heroine (or God) by linking mortification, fasting, and prayer with a female object of desire. Drawing on the local language of ascetic practice, they made their hero into a yogi, while the heroine is a beautiful Indian woman. Their sensuous romances were recited in different contexts, including

[4] Cited and translated by S. H. Askari, 'Historical Value of Afsana Badshahan or Tarikh Afghani', *Journal of Indian History* 43 (1965). 194 (translation slightly emended). The Persian text with a modern Hindi translation is also given in P. L. Gupta, *Kutubana Kṛta Miragāvatī* (Benares: Viśvavidyālaya Prakāsán, 1967), 39.

[5] Sheldon Pollock, 'The Cosmopolitan Vernacular,' *Journal of Asian Studies*, 57/1 (1998).

royal courts and Sufi hospices, and these diverse contexts for reception each provide us with protocols of interpretation for the poetry. Kings were celebrated in the prologues of the genre as ideal readers sensitive to the multiple resonances of poetry. In the Sufi hospice, the erotic attributes of the heroine and the seductive descriptions of love-play found in the genre were understood logocentrically as referring ultimately to God rather than to a worldly beloved.

I. The Formation of a Literary Genre

Amīr Khusrau, the celebrated poet who died in Delhi in 1325, famed both for his contributions to Indian music and to Hindavī and Persian poetry, was a disciple and close friend of the great Chishtī Shaikh Niẓām al-dīn Auliyā'.[6] Although it is certain that he composed poetry in Hindavī to Maḥbūb-i Ilāhī ('The Beloved of Allah'), as the Chishtī Shaikh was affectionately known, no early written manuscripts survive that testify to Khusrau's literary creativity in the spoken language of Hindustan. The only verses that are available to us come through the oral transmission of generations of singers at Sufi shrines (*qawwāls*), as well as through one eighteenth-century manuscript containing Khusrau's Hindavī riddles and punning verses.[7] The first surviving longer composition in Hindavī is the *Cāndāyan*, the romance of Lorik and Cāndā penned by Maulānā Dā'ūd in 1379. Maulānā Dā'ūd was a highly placed courtier in the retinue of Sultan Fīrūz Shāh Tughlaq, and wrote the poem in attendance at the provincial court of Dalmau in Awadh. His immediate patron was Malik Mubārak, the nobleman assigned to Awadh as the *muqṭa'* or governor of the province (*iqṭa'*).

Maulānā Dā'ūd was also a disciple of Shaikh Zain al-dīn

[6] The standard account of Amīr Khusrau remains Muhammad Wahid Mirza, *The Life and Works of Amir Khusrau* (1935; repr. Delhi: Idarah-i Adabiyat-i Delli, 1974).

[7] Based on a single manuscript in the Sprenger collection in the Berlin Staatsbibliothek and recently edited by Gopi Chand Narang as *Amīr Khusrau kā Hindavī Kalām, ma' Nuskhah-yi Berlin Zakhīrah-yi Sprenger* (Chicago: Amir Khusrau Society of America, 1987).

Chishtī, the nephew of Shaikh Naṣīr al-dīn Maḥmūd 'Chirāgh-i Dihlī' ('The Lamp of Delhi'), the successor to Shaikh Niẕām al-dīn Auliyā'. Shaikh Zain al-dīn was the caretaker of the shrine in Delhi, but his competition with Sayyid Muḥammad 'Gesūdarāz' ('Long Locks'), his uncle's prize pupil, led to a dispute that ended in the interment of his uncle's spiritually charged material relics (*tabarrukāt*) with the body of the great Shaikh. The rivalry was part of a frequent pattern of competition in which the lineal descendants of Sufi shaikhs disagreed with their spiritual disciples over the succession. Possession of the *tabarrukāt* was often the key to making any claims to authority.[8] Shaikh Zain al-dīn took care of the shrine in Delhi after the death of Shaikh Naṣīr al-dīn Maḥmūd and the departure of Sayyid Muḥammad Gesūdarāz on his spiritual conquest of the Deccan. He also instructed disciples, amongst whom was the Hindavī poet Maulānā Dā'ūd.

The generic model that Maulānā Dā'ūd created in the *Cāndāyan* is a composite one, and one which can best be seen as the textual record of the historical interaction of the Chishtī Sufis with Sanskritic, Persian, and regional religious and literary traditions. In his creative engagement with Indian and Persian literary models and conventions, Dā'ūd takes topoi and narrative motifs from diverse sources and refits them into a framework adapted from the Persian *maṡnavī*.[9] Chief among the conventions taken from Persian are the elaborate theoretical prologues that frame these romances within the metaphysics of an Islamic godhead reinscribed in a local language as well as within courtly and Sufi institutional settings with their distinct yet interlinked protocols of reception. The central aesthetic value or linchpin of Dā'ūd's literary creation, however, is a uniquely Indian poetics of *rasa*, the 'juice' or 'flavour' of a literary text, poem, or play. Along with the Hindavī words *kāma*,

[8] For an analysis and detailed account of the rivalry, see Simon Digby, '*Tabarrukāt* and Succession among the great Chishti Shaikhs', in R. E. Frykenberg (ed.), *Delhi Through the Ages* (Delhi: Oxford University Press, 1986), 77–89.

[9] See Section III below.

'desire', and *prema*, 'love', Dā'ūd uses the aesthetics of *rasa* to link the narrative pleasure of listening to love-stories with the erotics of union with an impossibly distant transcendent God. His distinctive literary formula also contains elements taken from Indian regional traditions such as the *bārahmāsā*, the rural songs describing the twelve months of separation from one's beloved.[10]

Rasa itself was defined famously in Bharata's eighth-century Sanskrit aesthetic treatise, the *Nāṭya-Śāstra*, as the juice or flavour of a poem arising from 'the combination of the *vibhāva*s (sources of *rasa*), the *anubhāva*s (actions, experiential signs of *rasa*), and the transitory emotions (*vyabhicāribhāva*s)'.[11] The aim of reading is to have an experience of the dominant *rasa* that animates the poem, and the *sahṛdaya*, or cultivated reader, feels the emotions of the parted lovers in the poem. The *sahṛdaya*'s response is shaped by the sources of *rasa* depicted by the poet. These include monsoon clouds indicating the season of love, the experiential signs of love such as bodies trembling and perspiring from desire, and the transitory emotions that attend the progress of the main emotional mood of a poem: apprehension, envy, contentment, shame, joy, and so on. A reader can approach the poet's vision and the feelings of the characters only because he is a *rasika* or connoisseur.

Dā'ūd approaches these classical conventions and ideas creatively, using them to compose a text that served as a model or formula for an entire regional tradition of Indian Sufi poetry. After the *Cāndāyan* of Maulānā Dā'ūd stands Quṭban's *Mirigāvatī* (1503), composed at the court of Sultan Ḥusain

[10] For examples of these, as well as a sound discussion of the meanings and literary place of the *bārahmāsā*, see Charlotte Vaudeville, *Bārahmāsā in Indian Literature: Songs of the Twelve Months in Indo-Aryan Literatures* (Delhi: Motilal Banarsidass, 1986).

[11] Translated in J. L. Masson and M. V. Patwardhan, *Aesthetic Rapture: The Rasādhyāya of the Nāṭya-Sāstra* (Poona: Deccan College Postgraduate and Research Institute, 1970), i. 46. For a succinct and clear account of Bharata's theory, see David L. Haberman, *Acting as a Way of Salvation: A Study of Rāgānugā Bhakti Sādhana* (Oxford: Oxford University Press, 1988), 13–16.

Shāh Sharqī of Jaunpur. Although there are scattered references to two romances entitled the *Paiman* and the *Jot Nirañjan* from the early sixteenth century, these have not survived.[12] The model of the *Cāndāyan* and the *Mirigāvatī* is emulated most powerfully by Malik Muḥammad Jāyasī, several poems by whom are still extant. Pre-eminent among these is the *Padmāvat* (1540), which tells the story of King Ratansen of Chittaur and his quest for the Princess Padmāvatī. In addition, he composed a version of the life of Krishna called the *Kanhāvat*, as well as a number of shorter poems. These include the *Akhrāvat* ('Alphabet Poem'), an acrostic composed out of the beliefs of a millenarian group of Sufis (the Mahdavīs of Jaunpur), and the *Ākhirī Kalām* ('Discourse on the Last Day') a foreshadowing of the events of doomsday. Finally, there is the *Madhumālatī* (1545) of Mīr Sayyid Manjhan Rājgīrī, the Shaṯṯārī Sufi attached to the court of Islām Shāh Sūrī.[13] Although poets continued to compose romances on this model until the early twentieth century, they did not reproduce the formula of the two heroines or the elaborate Sufi ideology of the earlier works.[14]

What is an ideal romance for the authors and audiences of the Hindavī narratives? All four poets use the same metre and form and all draw on the conventions of the Persian *masnavī* to frame their romances with introductory prologues. In these prologues there is first praise of God, then of Muḥammad and the first four 'righteous' Caliphs, then praise for the king of the time and the author's immediate patron, then praise and thanks to the author's spiritual guide followed by a disclaimer of the poet's own poetic skills. The stories are set in the ambience of the court, with kings and queens, princes and princesses, handmaidens, friends and companions. There are marvellous palaces

[12] S. A. A. Rizvi, *A History of Sufism in India* (Delhi: Munshiram Manoharlal, 1983), ii. 155 n. 2.

[13] For summary accounts of these texts, see R. S. McGregor, *Hindi Literature from its Beginnings to the Nineteenth Century* (Wiesbaden: Otto Harrassowitz, 1984), 26–8, 65–73.

[14] R. S. McGregor, *Hindi Literature from its Beginnings to the Nineteenth Century*, 150–4.

and lush gardens containing mango orchards, canals of cool running water, and picture-pavilions. Demons, heavenly nymphs, wonderful beings, and magical events all add to the imaginative allure of these works. Early in each poem an image of divine beauty is introduced: the heroine's body is described in a formal literary set-piece called a *nakh-śikh-varṇana* ('toe-to-head description') in Sanskrit which parallels the *sarāpā* ('head-to-foot description') in Persian and uses the same symbolism and imagery. In the twenty verses of these set-pieces, the beloved is described from the top of her head to her legs, usually with verses alternating between emphasizing divine grace and beauty (*jamāl*) and divine might and majesty (*jalāl*). This first encounter of the lover and the beloved is treated as a way of conveying the Sufi concept of the first meeting of the soul with divinity in the phenomenal world.[15] After this initial contact with the image of divine beauty, which is then taken away, the hero begins to suffer from *viraha*, the pain of love in separation. The stories of the romances are driven by the urge to transform this desire into a mutually fulfilling love, called *prema-rasa* by the poets.

All the plots have certain formulaic elements that are drawn from earlier canons or common cultural stereotypes about gender and culture and reshaped into a distinctive formula by the Hindavī poets. These include the moment of the awakening of love through a vision, a dream, or a description of the heroine's beauty as a divine manifestation, a convention common to both Persian and Indian romances. The hero and heroine have helpers who commonly exemplify spiritual values such as mystical absorption (*sahaja*) or the abstract quality of love (*pema/prema*). Alternatively, there are demons to fight and trials of strength, which the lovers have to pass through in order to attain each other. The necessary transformation of the hero into a yogi and his ascetic quest draws on the poetry of the Gorakhnāth *panth*. The ordeals on the quest for the beautiful princess and the passage to a heavenly realm are modelled on Persian spiritual quests

[15] Peter Gaeffke, 'Alexander in Avadhī and Dakkinī *Ma<u>th</u>nawīs*', *Journal of the American Oriental Society*, 109 (1989), 528.

like ʿAṯṯār's *Conference of the Birds*.[16] The hero's abandonment of a first wife in order to consummate his love with the divine heroine is a distinctive motif, and ultimately draws on the common cultural stereotype of the jealousy between co-wives (*sautan*) in a harem. This deserted wife then sings a *bārahmāsā*, a description of her suffering from the pain of love in separation in each of the twelve months of the year, which is conveyed to the hero. On hearing it, the hero takes his divine beloved and returns home with her, whereupon the two co-wives quarrel and have to be reconciled. The hero's resolution of the strife between the co-wives, his death and the burning of both his wives on his funeral pyre uses the misogynistic stereotype of the Indian woman's *satī* to signify a mystical annihilation (*fanā*).

II. The Shaṯṯārī Sufi Silsilah

The involvement of the Shaṯṯārīs in this richly creative religious and literary world began with the founder of the spiritual lineage, Shaikh ʿAbdullāh Shaṯṯār (d. 1485), who came to India from central Asia in the second half of the fifteenth century. In the competitive cultural landscape of northern India, it might have been expected that a newcomer would settle in a single place and slowly build up his following and area of spiritual influence, his *vilāyat*. However, ʿAbdullāh Shaṯṯār preferred a rather more martial style of public presentation. He travelled widely with a large retinue of disciples dressed in military uniforms, and, to the beat of drums, in every town or village, he demanded to know if there was anyone who wished to be shown the way to God. Inevitably the Shaikh's claims to spiritual superiority brought him into competition with the Sufis who were prominent in the regional sultanates. Eventually, he settled down in Mandu under the patronage of Sultan Ġhiyāṯ al-dīn Tuġhlaq and was buried there after his death.

[16] See Farīd ud-dīn ʿAttār, *The Conference of the Birds*, tr. Afkham Darbandi and Dick Davis (Harmondsworth: Penguin Books, 1984), and James Winston Morris, 'Reading *The Conference of the Birds*', in Wm. Theodore de Bary and Irene Bloom (eds.), *Approaches to the Asian Classics* (New York: Columbia University Press, 1990), 77–85.

One of the prominent Sufis who both ignored his challenge and made disparaging remarks about the outlandish claims of newly arrived Sufis from Khurasan and Fars, was the Bengali Shaikh Muḥammad Qāẓin ʿAlā, who was the maternal grandfather of our author, Manjhan. His initial hostility was overturned by a miraculous dream in which his deceased father told him his spiritual future was in the hands of Shaikh ʿAbdullāh. He left for Mandu and waited three days outside the Shaikh's house until, moved by his humility, the Shaikh took him on as a disciple, but only after he had promised to give up his previous methods and learn Shaṭṭārī practices. Shaikh Qāẓin ʿAlā (d. 1495) became Shaikh ʿAbdullāh's principal *khalīfa* or successor, and took the Shaṭṭārī method of spiritual practice to Bengal and eastern India. Shaikh ʿAbdullāh Shaṭṭār forged a distinctive spiritual regimen based on fasting, ascetic exercises, practices of visualization, and the Arabic letters that made up the names of Allah.

These practices were passed down in his lineage through the successors of Shaikh Qāẓin ʿAlā, Shaikh Ẓuhūr Ḥājī Ḥamīd (d. 1523) and Shaikh Abu'l Fatḥ Hadīyatullāh Sarmast (d. 1539). These Shaikhs established a Shaṭṭārī presence in Bihar and had many links with local lineages such as the Firdausīs, as well as with the rulers of Bihar. Shaikh Ḥamīd had as disciples the remarkable brothers Shaikh Muḥammad Ġhauṡ and Shaikh Phūl. Under him they learned the Shaṭṭārī method of *ẕikr*, the esoteric science of the invocation of the names of Allah encrypted in the letters of the Arabic alphabet. They also performed forty-day fasts and meditated in the caves and jungles around the town of Chunar. During this period Muḥammad Ġhauṡ composed the most famous work of Shaṭṭārī asceticism, the *Jawāhir-i Khamsah* ('Five Jewels').[17] Arranged in 'five jewels' that ascend from ordinary prayers to the inheritance and realization of divine truth, the work was seen as a *summa* of esoteric Indian Sufi practice and is commonly found in manuscript form in shrine libraries to this day.

[17] We have used the India Office Library manuscript of the *Jawāhir-i Khamsah*, Ethé MS 1875, in preparing this summary account of Shaṭṭārī practice.

The third *jauhar* or jewel, the central part of the book, is focused on the invocation of the divine names. This mode of practice, with elaborate prescriptions for purity and directions for gaining different sorts of powers, implies a Sufi notion of the human body as the site for a divine manifestation in microcosm. Shaikh Muḥammad Ġhauṡ's account of the coming into being of all created things is encoded in the twenty-eight letters of the Arabic alphabet. In Shaṭṭārī letter-mysticism, combinations of letters signified selected names of Allah in sequence as well as places in the Shaṭṭārī cosmology, and each was the abbreviated code for a different Shaṭṭārī practice. Apart from interior visualization, the Shaṭṭārī cosmology had another application: to predict or to influence the future by calling up the angels or spiritual agents of each station in order to make them perform whatever task was desired, or to make an efficacious talisman or amulet.[18] Each of the twenty-eight letters was matched with a numerical value, a name of Allah, a quality, either terrible or benevolent, a perfume or incense, an element, a zodiacal sign, a planet, a jinn, and a guardian angel. These were called up in rituals of invocation that varied with the particular goals of the seeker.

In accordance with the order's tradition of conquering new territory, Shaikh Muḥammad Ġhauṡ went to Gwalior in 1523. After three years, he had acquired a considerable following and was an acknowledged influence on the local population. This enabled him to intervene in the political and military struggle over Hindustan between the Afghan rulers and the Mughals in the 1520s. Although the received Sufi wisdom was to avoid having anything to do with kings, in sixteenth-century India Sufi

[18] A detailed account of this practice, as well as an extensive table containing all the stations and all their corresponding elements, is given in Thomas Hughes, 'Daʿwah', in *Dictionary of Islam* (1885; repr. Calcutta: Rupa, 1988), 72–8. For more details about Shaṭṭārī magical practices, see Jaʿfar Sharīf, G. A. Herklots, and William Crooke, *Islam in India or the Qānūn-i Islām: The Customs of the Musalmāns of India* (1921; repr. New Delhi: Oriental Books, 1972), 218–77. For a review of the scholarship on Indo-Muslim esoteric practices, see Marc Gaborieau, 'L'Ésotérisme musulman dans le sous-continent indo-pakistanais: un point de vue ethnologique', *Bulletin d'Études Orientales*, 44 (1992), 191–209.

lineages like the Chishtīs, the Naqshbandīs, and the Shaṭṭārīs took sides with Mughals or Afghans in their struggles for sovereignty over northern India. The Chishtīs, for example, had longstanding historical connections with local Afghan sultans and nobility and did not back the Mughals in their fight for supremacy. On the other hand, Shaikh Muḥammad Ġhauṡ, the poet Manjhan's spiritual guide, was instrumental in the Mughal emperor Bābur's capture of the fort of Gwalior from the Afghans. By passing privileged information to the leader of the Mughal forces and exhorting him to establish a token presence in the city, the Shaikh enabled Bābur's army to seize this key strategic fortress through a covert night attack. He was rewarded with a considerable land-grant on which he built his hospice in Gwalior. His establishment became a favoured site for aristocratic patronage during the reigns of Bābur and Humāyūn. Shaikh Muḥammad Ġhauṡ and his brother Shaikh Phūl were so highly influential in the Mughal court that many Sufis of other lineages took Shaṭṭārī affiliation in addition to their own existing connections, simply in order to acquire patronage and position.

The emperor Humāyūn in particular was extremely interested in occult and mystical matters and was especially favourably disposed to the Shaṭṭārīs. One imperial chronicle relates that Shaikh Muḥammad Ġhauṡ and his brother Shaikh Phūl taught the emperor occult sciences and were very much in favour at court. Humāyūn's younger brother Mirzā Hindāl eventually had Shaikh Phūl murdered in 1539 when the Shaikh attempted to dissuade him from making his own bid for power. Shaṭṭārī fortunes suffered a further reversal when Sher Shāh Sūrī defeated Humāyūn in 1540. When Humāyūn went into exile in Iran, Manjhan cultivated the Afghan court, almost certainly with the encouragement of his spiritual guide Shaikh Muḥammad Ġhauṡ. The Shaikh himself, on the other hand, fled from Afghan reach to the sultanate of Gujarat, whence he conducted a secret correspondence with Humāyūn. In this way, the Shaṭṭārīs had both possible outcomes covered. The author of the *Madhumālatī*, Shaikh Manjhan, with impressive pedigrees as the grandson of Shaikh Qāẓin ʿAlā and as the spiritual disciple of Shaikh Muḥammad Ġhauṣ̤, was at the very centre of the Shaṭṭārī Sufi order when it was at its most vigorous and influential. When his presence was noted as a courtier at the court of Islām Shāh, it would have been both as a poet and as a Sufi Shaikh, almost certainly by then authorized to give spiritual instruction to others.

A person wishing to set out on the spiritual path would first find a Shaikh, either one personally impressive or one belonging to the chosen Sufi lineage, who was willing and authorized to accept him or her as a pupil. Along with the authorization, *ijāzat*, went the *barakat*, the grace, blessing, spiritual power which derived from the spiritual founder of the lineage and was passed from one Shaikh to another down the chain, the *silsilah*. Thus a lineage was a chain of blessings and authority, and the different orders were distinguished one from another by the pedigree of the Shaikhs who were members. A spiritual lineage was also known as a *ṭarīqah*, a path or way, and a disciple on the path was known as a *sālik*, a traveller. Each lineage had its own path of spiritual training and development, although all included such spiritual practices as prayer, fasting and other privations, periods of seclusion, attendance at the Shaikh's talks, collective and private formulaic repetitions, self-observation and self-awareness exercises. What is important for the understanding of Shaikh Manjhan's poem is how the Shaṭṭārī *ṭarīqah* differed from those of other orders.

The Shaṭṭārīs, probably more than any other spiritual lineage, appropriated Indian yogic practices into their regimen. Among Shaikh Muḥammad Ġhauṣ̤'s many compositions is the Persian *Baḥr al-Ḥayāt* ('The Water of Life'), a translation of the *Amṛtakuṇḍa* ('The Pool of Nectar'), a now-lost Sanskrit text on yoga.[19] In accordance with the order's competitive stance, it should

[19] For a detailed study of this text, see Carl Ernst's translation and introduction to the text, in *The Arabic Version of 'The Pool of the Water of Life' (Amṛtakuṇḍa)* (forthcoming), as well as Yusuf Husain, 'Haud al-Hayat: La Version arabe de l'Amratkund', *Journal Asiatique*, 113 (1928), 291–344. For a listing of the numerous manuscript versions of the Persian and Arabic versions of the text, see Richard M. Eaton, *The Rise of Islam and the Bengal Frontier, 1204–1760* (Berkeley: University of California Press, 1993), 78 n. 23.

come as no surprise that the Shaikh represented his efforts as liberating useful practices for cultivating spiritual awareness from the shackles of false belief. These practices included: using exercises for breath control, using yogic postures for sitting, maintaining ritual purity of place and person, assimilating the Indian yogic chakras and their tutelary deities into the Shaṭṭārī cosmology, controlling diet strictly to exclude flesh and liquor, and using certain Hindavī words in the *z̤ikr* (repetition of names and attributes of Allah, often done in conjunction with physical exercises to accomplish spiritual transformation). In addition, the Shaṭṭārīs claimed their method of spiritual development to be swifter than the methods of other lineages in effecting the spiritual transformation of its disciples. 'According to the Shaṭṭāriyya technique, the neophyte at the very beginning of his training is required to consider himself in the presence of Being and then descend step by step from the realm of Self-manifestation of the Absolute to the phenomenal world. Then step by step he re-ascends and reaches the Divine sphere, effacing all traces of the stages of ascent. In contrast to this method, the other Sufis direct their disciples to ascend step by step from the realm of humanity to *Waḥdat al-Wujūd* [the unity of all existence].'[20]

Shaṭṭārī self-transformation was thus focused on realizing the human being's link with Allah and seeing oneself as part of a larger universe that has its source in Allah and refracts the divine essence through the many veils of existence. The circular structure implied by the initial taste of *jaz̤bah* or mystical absorption and the eventual return to Being can be seen to have its impact on the plot-structure of the *Madhumālatī*. Thus, the hero Manohar ('Heart-enchanting') meets his divine beloved Madhumālatī through supernatural agency, falls in love with her, is separated, and then has to climb back step by step to the joys that he first tasted in a midnight encounter. In addition, as one scholar has pointed out, 'The Shattars did not have to pass through the stage of *fanā* [evanescence] or the final stage of *fanā al-fanā* [extinction in evanescence]. Their intuitive perception of Allah in their own beings was permanent. This state was

[20] Rizvi, *A History of Sufism in India*, ii. 151–2.

described as *baqā al-baqā*, the everlasting reintegration of the spirit with Allah. Mystics of other *silsilah*s were either conscious of their love for God or experienced ecstasy while the Shattars transcended these two states as separate conditions producing a new combination of their own.'[21] The Shaṭṭārī poet Manjhan eschews the generic pattern of the two co-wives of the hero and their final annihilation on a funeral pyre. As we shall see, his romance ends with the everlasting and blissful union of the two pairs of happy lovers.

III. The Prologue to the Story

Despite these broad correspondences between Shaṭṭārī cosmology and poetic meaning, we should emphasize that there is no single or flat allegorical scheme to be found in the events and imagery of the story. Rather, when these works were performed in Sufi hospices and royal courts, different protocols of interpretation were used to explain the poem's mystical or erotic meanings and allegorical moments. In the elaborate prologue to the romance, the poet establishes a set of historical and theoretical frameworks that enable us to delineate these different understandings of his poem. These are modelled on the panegyrical conventions of the Persian *masnavī* or verse romance, which begin with the praise of God (*ḥamd*), the Prophet Muḥammad (*na'at*), the ruling king, and the author's commissioning patron, frequently a highly placed nobleman or courtier.[22] In common with the other poets of the genre, Manjhan extends these conventions to create a set of distinctive Hindavī metaphysical and aesthetic terms. He begins his prologue with six verses in praise of Allah. Manjhan links the Creator first with 'love, the treasure-house of joy' (*prema prītī sukhanidhi*), the

[21] Rizvi, *A History of Sufism in India*, ii. 160.

[22] For a concise definition of the Persian *masnavī*, a heroic, historical, didactic, or romantic poem composed in rhyming couplets (*aa*, *bb*, *cc*, etc.), see Jan Rypka *et al.*, *History of Iranian Literature* (Dordrecht: D. Reidel, 1969), 98 *et passim*. For an example of the genre translated into English with a good introductory discussion, see Niẓāmī, *Haft Paykar: A Medieval Persian Romance*, tr. Julie Scott Meisami (Oxford: Oxford University Press, 1995).

central value of the love-story. Then he sketches out the attributes of the ruler of the universe: the Creator (*vidhātā*), Lord (*gosā'īṉ*), King (*rājā*) of the three worlds (heaven, earth, and the nether world, the *tribhuvana*) and the four ages (*juga*). In constrast to all of these stands the poet, whose tongue is not equal to the praise of the glorious Creator. When all those who came before him have failed in the task, how can the poor poet Manjhan succeed in conveying Allah's true stature?

Manjhan answers his rhetorical question by asserting that his poem can only go 'as far as the bird of knowledge can fly, as deep as the mind can fathom . . . beyond that point, where are the means?' Despite this metaphysical and poetic assumption of Allah's ineffable nature, the poet goes on to find Hindavī approximations for the widespread Sufi theory of *waḥdat al-wujūd* or the unity of all existence, playing on the Lord's unity (*waḥdat*) and his multiplicity (*kas̱rat*). Manjhan expresses his amazement at the contrast between the oneness of the Creator and the multiplicity of created forms behind which God is hidden. Manjhan represents the Lord as unqualified, yet singular, hidden, yet manifest, formless, yet many-formed. Manjhan refers to the Names of Allah, which are so important as prototypes of all things in existence. In the Sufi cosmogony, these form the patterns or models through which divine light is refracted into the veils of existence. Manjhan's use has a special referent, though, because the Shaṭṭārīs formulated an elaborate system of letter mysticism and cosmology based on the Names of Allah. The divine Names were used extensively by the Shaṭṭārīs to inculcate God's qualities or attributes in the practitioner.

Next, he uses the convention of the *na'at* (praise of the Prophet) and the praise of the 'companions' of the Prophet elegantly to suggest Muḥammad's true nature. Muḥammad is not simply the Prophet but rather the cosmic principle of the Creator within creation, the reason for creation and the light within it. Manjhan uses the paradoxical logic of the Sufi theory of the refraction of divine light into the forms of this world to declare the sole substantial reality of Muḥammad's body (*sarīra*) and the shadowiness of the concrete, sensible world: 'He is the substance, and the world his shadow.' Further, he uses the Hindavī word *rūpa* ('form, beauty') to skirt the language of incarnation dangerously. Allah is *alakh*, the invisible one, but the form that can be seen is that of Muḥammad. The true meaning of this beautiful form is God; significantly, *rūpa* is also used extensively in the erotic encounter in the romance to refer to the divine and human aspects of the love that blossoms between the hero and heroine. He ends his *na'at* with the standard words of praise for the first four 'righteous' Caliphs, expressed simply and beautifully.

There follows the traditional address of obeisance (*khitāb-i zamīnbūs*) to the ruling sultan, Salīm Shāh, which is couched in terms of conventional extravagance. Modelled on Persian prologues that themselves draw on the inflated claims and rhetoric of Islamic texts on polity and statecraft ('mirrors for princes'), the address to Salīm Shāh waxes eloquent in praise of the king's generosity, bravery, and justice. Manjhan uses the standard tropes of the lion and cow playing happily together, of lamb and wolf grazing together in peace, to describe Salīm Shāh as an ideally just king and his state as a 'garden come to flower without any thorns'. He also refers to kings famed for their greatness and nobility in Indian mythology and history: the eldest of the Pāṇḍavas from the *Mahābhārata*, Yudhiṣṭhira, the generous Karṇa, and the cultivated patron of poetry and the arts, King Bhoja of Ujjain. Manjhan also praises the Afghan nobleman and military commander Khizr Khān Turk,[23] a regional governor of Bengal who may have patronized the poet and supported him in his entourage.

The balance of spiritual over temporal is then redressed by no fewer than eight verses in praise of Manjhan's spiritual guide, Shaikh Muḥammad Ġhauṣ Gvāliyārī. As we have seen, Shaikh Muḥammad was intimately involved in politics at the Mughal courts of Gwalior and Agra. The verses addressed to him emphasize his long years of asceticism and his importance in defining Sufi practice for seekers at his hospice. He is described

[23] For more details about Khizr Khān Turk, see Iqtidar Husain Siddiqui, *History of Sher Shāh Sūr*, 107.

as a great Shaikh, 'profound in knowledge, matchless in beauty'. The poet focuses on two crucial aspects of the Shaikh's power: the transformative power of his gaze (*disṭi*), and the figurative kingship of even a disciple of his. The first of these refers to the power of the gaze of the spiritual guide, which can reach within a disciple's being and change his way of being in the world. The disciple can then triumph over 'death', a reference to the Sufi experience of *fanā*, self-annihilation on the path. The triumph over death refers to the stage of subsistence after annihilation, *baqā*. Here the poet uses the Hindavī *disṭi* to approximate the Persian *tavajjuh*, the absorbed attention of the Shaikh which transforms the consciousness of the disciple, awakening him to the unseen mysteries of the Shaṭṭārī spiritual cosmos. Such a disciple becomes not merely an earthly king like the one the poet has been praising, but king over all the ages of the world.

Having completed the conventional and historical proprieties, Manjhan now comes to defining some theoretical terms that are important for a fuller understanding of his poem. He elevates *prema-rasa* to the *rāja-rasa*, the royal *rasa*, and sketches out three key elements of his aesthetic: the ideology of love (*prema*), the importance of ascetic practice, and the privileged status of language in disseminating the truth embodied in poetry. To begin with Manjhan's view of love, the topos can be traced back to Persian *mas̱navī* prologues, which frequently include short philosophical reflections on love or poetry. These ordinarily emphasize that the world has its foundation in love, without which the human being is just an aggregate of clay and water. Similarly, in Manjhan's *Madhumālatī*, the very first word is love, and the final couplet is again devoted to love. Love is thus both the beginning and the consummation of his work. For Manjhan, love is much more than the feeling human beings sometimes have for one another; it is a cosmic force which pre-exists creation, which drives creation and which permeates creation. Particularly beloved by Sufis with regard to the causes of creation is the tradition attributed to God: 'I was a hidden treasure and longed that I should be known'. While one understanding of this tradition is that God created the universe because he wished to be known, another understanding emphasizes that it is only through love that God can be known. For Manjhan, then, love is the most precious property in the universe. Along with love goes suffering, particularly the pain felt of being separate from one's beloved, whether human or divine. This pain of love in separation, *viraha*, is both an intense sorrow and a great blessing because it is the very means by which the human soul becomes self-conscious.

Love and beauty are central to the aesthetics of the *Madhumālatī*, in which the heroine becomes an exemplification of the process of the self-disclosure of the divine. Her beauty arouses love within the seeker, while *viraha*, the condition of being separated from his beloved, drives him onwards along the Sufi path. The path of asceticism involved, among the Shaṯṯārī Sufis, an intensive regimen of fasting and vegetarianism, supererogatory prayers, and a programme of yogic exercises and letter-mysticism. As we have seen, the Arabic letters of the Names of Allah encoded a system of visualization and interior discipline. Manjhan also refers to the unique Shaṯṯārī engagement with the Indian practices of yoga, exhorting the seeker to 'abandon consciousness, wisdom, and knowledge' in order to focus on meditative practice. He describes as a void (*sūnā*) the place where the seeker can remain absorbed in the attributeless Allah. Allah is the Absolute, the ground for revealing the self to itself. In this ascetic regimen, all created forms are refractions of divine essence but need spiritual practice in order to realize their identity-in-difference with divinity.

In addition, the poet uses the term *sahaja-samādhi*, the 'mystic union of Sahaja'. In Kabir and the other north Indian devotional poets of the fifteenth and sixteenth centuries, *sahaja* refers to the soul's 'spontaneous or self-born' unity with the attributeless or *nirguṇa* Rāma, the transcendence in immanence to which the seeker has to awaken.[24] Among the Sufi poets the term represents the internalization of the Sufi paradox of the identity, yet radical difference, of the being of divinity and human beings. This carries through into Manjhan's view of language, which

[24] See Charlotte Vaudeville, *A Weaver Named Kabir* (Delhi: Oxford University Press, 1993), 115.

encapsulates the paradox. As he points out, 'if words arise from mortal mouths, then how can the word be imperishable?' Further, 'if man, the master of words, can die, then how does the word remain immortal?' Language becomes the currency of immortality for the poet, since it encompasses the divine and the human. Words endure, although humans pass away. The answer to this paradox, of course, is that the word, like divinity, is perpetually alive because it is refracted in every heart.

In itself this topos is directly traceable to Persian prologues, which contain frequent reflections on poetry or verbal discourse (*sukhan*).[25] These focus on the creative power of the word *Kun* or 'Be', with which Allah created the heavens and the earth. This is approximated in the Hindavī text to the mystic word Oṃ, which Manjhan borrows from Indian religious systems to express the might and majesty of Allah in the Qur'ānic cosmogony. Manjhan makes the word the foundation of creation, as well as of all poetic discourse. As he puts it, 'If the Maker had not made the word, how could anyone hear stories of pleasure?' The poet resolves the paradox of identity-in-difference through his claim that divinity is manifest (*pargaṭa*) in the word, an incarnationist view that would be heretical to express in Persian. Language, in Hindavī poetics, becomes the ground for understanding and representing the revelation of divinity to humans.

Language thus embodies poetic pleasure, but it also becomes the medium for another sort of embodiment: the refraction of the divine essence in visible form. For the Hindavī Sufi poets, the body of the heroine provokes a blinding flash of revelation in the eyes of the seeker. The revelatory flash pushes the seeker on to his quest for love, to realize the union that he has only glimpsed in his vision. To savour *prema-rasa* is to understand the secret of the shared identity-in-difference between the seeker and the sought, the subject and object of mysticism. Manjhan asks his audience to cultivate the taste for this royal *rasa* at the end of his prologue:

[25] See, for instance, Niẓāmī, *Haft Paykar: A Medieval Persian Romance*, tr. J. S. Meisami, 22–3.

A story sweet as nectar I will sing to you:
O experts in love, pay attention and listen!
Such juicy matters only connoisseurs know,
tasteless stuff is tossed out by them.
Termites run away from wood without juice;
will camels eat cane without any sugar?
Whatever has *rasa*, is enjoyed as such,
and the man who does not have the taste
will find even the tasteful tasteless.
Many tastes are found in the world, O connoisseurs!
But listen: I shall describe love, the royal savour of savours.
[43.1–6]

Rasa is the pleasure which listeners or readers take in stories as well as the lovers' consummation of desire in the savour or juice of love (*prema*). The Sufi cosmology within which this aesthetic of *prema-rasa* is set allows the Hindavī Sufi poets to refer suggestively to the relation of mirrored desire between God and creatures. It is in this sense that the Hindavī romances are susceptible to interpretation in multiple ways, whether as sensuous ornate poetry in courtly performance, or as mystical verses referring ultimately to God within the context of Sufi shrines.

IV. Manohar and Madhumālatī

After this elaborate prologue, the poet begins the story of Manohar and Madhumālatī in earnest. Many of the narrative motifs that he uses will be instantly recognizable to readers of Indian and Islamic story literatures. For instance, the story opens with King Sūrajbhānu (Light of the Sun) who has everything conceivable except a son, for whom he longs and hopes. For twelve years he serves an ascetic, who finally gives his Queen a small morsel of magical food which results in her giving birth to a son, a motif common to many Indian epic, literary, and folk traditions. The major device used to order the plot is the initial night meeting between the lovers orchestrated by flying nymphs, after which the lovers must wander in pain until they are able to regain that first flush of felicity. This motif occurs also elsewhere, most famously in the *Arabian Nights*, in the tale of the

Prince Qamar al-Zamān.[26] In that story, the lovely Princess Budur is carried to the bedroom of Qamar al-Zamān by flying jinns, who cannot decide which of the two is more beautiful. They leave them there overnight while they go to play. The Prince and Princess awaken, look at each other and fall in love. When they go to sleep again, the jinns carry the Princess back to her father's palace, and the Prince spends the rest of the story on a quest for the beautiful maiden who captured his heart in a midnight encounter. In the same way, the plot of the *Madhumālatī*, in common with those of the other Hindavī Sufi romances, draws the reader into the story by arousing his or her desire and constantly deferring that desire till the lovers attain erotic, narrative, and spiritual consummation.

Once the hero is born, astrologers are summoned who name the child Manohar. Foreshadowing the central narrative themes of desire (*kāma*), separation (*viraha*), and love (*prema*), they also predict that in his fourteenth year he will meet his beloved and fall in love. The two will then be separated and he will wander as a yogi for a year suffering the pain of love in separation. After that he will be King in all his births. The Prince is brought up and properly educated so that at the age of 12 he is crowned King. When he reaches the age of 14 some passing nymphs, attracted by his good looks, resolve to find a Princess for him of matching beauty. They debate the matter and decide on Madhumālatī, the daughter of King Vikram Rāi. The King rules the city of Mahāras, the great *rasa*, suggesting the ultimate aesthetic and spiritual value of *prema-rasa*. To compare the lovers, the nymphs transport Manohar to Madhumālatī's bedroom and put his bed next to hers. Astonished at the resulting loveliness they pronounce them a perfect match and go off to play. Manohar wakes up and is amazed by Madhumālatī's beauty, which the poet describes in the twenty verses of a head-to-foot description of the heroine's body.

[26] Richard F. Burton (tr.), *A Plain and Literal Translation of the Arabian Nights Entertainments, Now Entitled the Book of the Thousand Nights and a Night* (Benares = Stoke Newington or London: Kama Shastra Society, 1885–6), iii. 212–348, iv. 1–29.

When Madhumālatī wakes up she becomes extremely alarmed, but as they talk, love, coming from a former birth, is born between them. They pledge themselves to eternal fidelity and make love—though not fully—and then fall asleep. The nymphs return and are horrified at their dishevelled state and quickly carry back Manohar to his palace. When he awakes, the pain of separation overwhelms the Prince and he tells his nurse Sahajā (the simple or spontaneous mystery or mystical state) what has happened. Various kinds of doctors are called but they fail to cure him because they do not know love. Eventually Manohar resolves to set out against his parents' wishes to find Madhumālatī in Mahāras. He disguises himself as a saffron-clad yogi and sets out with a large retinue, but as they cross an ocean a storm sinks the ship. All are destroyed except Manohar who is washed up on a foreign shore, 'alone save for the name of Madhumālatī and the mercy of God'.

Manohar sets off inland and reaches a plantain forest, the *kadalī vana* that signifies the place of self-mortification and spiritual attainment in Tantric practice and devotional poetry in the north Indian languages.[27] As he is wandering through this dark wood, he finds a pavilion in which a young and innocent Princess, Pemā (Love), is imprisoned. She is the beloved daughter of King Citrasena of Citbisarāuṉ (Forgetfulness or Ease-of-Mind). She was out playing with her girlfriends when they had to take shelter in a gallery or pavilion painted with pictures (*citrasārī*) to escape a swarm of bees. The pictures painted on the walls of the pavilion suggest the realm of images (*ʿālam-i imṣāl*) in Sufi cosmology, one step closer to the world of concrete phenomena than the place of the divine Names. As they came out of the picture-pavilion a demon seized her and brought her to the dark forest where she is an unhappy prisoner. Manohar introduces himself and tells her about Madhumālatī. Pemā, in reply, says she is a childhood friend of Madhumālatī's and that Madhumālatī visited her parents' home with her mother every month. When he hears this, Manohar resolves to save Pemā by

[27] See David Gordon White, *The Alchemical Body: Siddha Traditions in Medieval India* (Chicago: University of Chicago Press, 1996), 113.

confronting the demon. When the demon returns, Manohar wounds it, but the demon miraculously recovers.

Pemā explains that there is a tree whose ambrosial fruit grants immortality, and that in it resides the demon's life. Hearing this, Manohar knows that Allah would give him victory if he could but destroy the tree. He is hesitant to commit the sin of killing a living tree, but is persuaded by Pemā's unfortunate plight. By cutting down the tree and uprooting the trunk, he leaves the demon no source from which to renew his life. Once the demon is dead, Manohar takes Pemā back to her parents, who are so grateful they offer him their kingdom and Pemā's hand in marriage. He declines, since his heart is pledged to Madhumālatī. He becomes increasingly impatient to set off on his quest again, when Pemā informs him that Madhumālatī and her mother are coming the next day. He waits in the picture-pavilion, restless with the pain of separation. Pemā brings Madhumālatī there, leaving them together as she guards the door. Manohar moves in and out of consciousness in her presence. She is initially angry at his cruelty in deserting her, until their former love reawakens. They renew their vow not to make love fully until they are married and fall asleep together. Madhumālatī's mother, meanwhile, worrying about her daughter, descends on the pavilion and finds them there together. Overcome with shame and rage, she has Madhumālatī taken back to Mahāras, where she utters a spell and turns Madhumālatī into a bird. When Manohar wakes up he finds Madhumālatī gone; he is cast down once more in his own bedroom at Kanagiri. He resumes his yogic disguise and sets off again on the quest for his beloved.

Madhumālatī, transformed into a bird, flies all round the world in search of Manohar. This motif is found commonly in Islamic mystical literature, in which the divine in the form of the Universal Spirit moves through the world in the form of a dove after creation.[28] She suffers horribly from *viraha*, the pain of love in separation. Despairing, she sees a Prince who looks like Manohar and allows herself to be caught. He is Prince Tārācand

[28] See, for instance, Muhyī'ddín Ibn al-ʿArabí, *The Tarjumán al-Ashwáq: A Collection of Mystical Odes*, tr. R. A. Nicholson (London: Royal Asiatic Society, 1911), 20, 72–3.

of Pavanerī (Wind City, a reference to the airs or winds of the subtle yogic body) who, hearing her story, leaves his kingdom to serve her and bring her back to her family and native land. Madhumālatī's mother is full of remorse and quickly restores her to her former self. She offers Tārācand Madhumālatī in marriage but he refuses, knowing she could only be happy with Manohar. Madhumālatī's parents meanwhile write to Pemā telling her what has happened. Madhumālatī encloses a *bārahmāsā*, a song describing her suffering through the twelve months using exquisite natural and seasonal imagery. The letters reach Pemā just as Manohar reappears still disguised as a yogi. Further letters are exchanged and a marriage is arranged between Manohar and Madhumālatī. After the wedding ceremony, they consummate their long love-affair in full, much to the amusement of Madhumālatī's girlfriends. Tārācand stays with them both and one day he sees Pemā swinging in the picture-pavilion and falls in love with her although he does not know who she is. Madhumālatī realizes it must be Pemā he has fallen for and tells Manohar. Manohar says that since Pemā had been offered in marriage to him there was no difficulty in her being married to Tārācand. The marriage of Pemā and Tārācand takes place and after a while they all decide that they must return to their respective kingdoms. After an elaborate leave-taking, Manohar and Madhumālatī finally reach his kingdom where, amid great rejoicing, he is reunited with his happy parents.

This outline of *Madhumālatī* reveals an entertaining and sensuous love-story that is both Indian and Islamic in terms of narrative motifs, in common with the other texts of the genre. The plot moves through successive stages of deferred desire, driving the lovers and the audience along to the narrative, metaphysical, and erotic satisfaction of desire in the final union. The poet ends with a rhymed couplet that serves to round off the story and to justify its continued circulation, translation, and dissemination:

The elixir of immortality will fill love's sanctuary, wherever it is found.
As long as poetry is cultivated on earth, so long will our lovers' names resound.

Since poetry is still cultivated on earth, the sensitive reader (*sahṛdaya*) will recognize that the *Madhumālatī* is a Sufi romance full of delightful imagery and narrative symmetry. Both pairs of lovers come together happily at the end to produce a beautifully balanced conclusion. The only two formal literary conventions in the story are the head-to-foot description of the heroine and the *bārahmāsā*, the rest being told with a lightness and sensitivity in keeping with the theme. The poem fully justifies Manjhan's claim that it is pervaded with *prema-rasa*, the evocative *rasa* of love that is above all the *rāja-rasa*, the royal *rasa* or savour fit to be enjoyed by kings.

V. Mystical Meanings and Symbolism

The various Sufi *silsilah*s that composed Hindavī poetry in north India were fully steeped in the conventions and symbolism of the various genres of Persian poetry, both lyric (*ġhazal*) and narrative (*mas̱navī*). At the same time, the Sufis were fascinated by the poetics and alluring imagery of Indian classical and regional poetry as they encountered it in musical and dance performances and in poetic recitation. The cultural history of sultanate and Mughal India is in part the history of the enthusiastic participation of Sufis and other Muslims in the formation of the canons of Indian poetry, art, and music. The genre of the Hindavī Sufi romance should be read against this larger historical background of cultural appropriations, comminglings, and creative formulations. Thus, the Hindavī Sufi poets used Indian *rasa* theory and the conventions of Persian poetry to create a romantic genre centred around the various meanings of *prema-rasa*, the juice or essence of love. As we have seen, *rasa* means taste or essence, and was used in Indian poetic theory to refer to the property in a poem that evokes a trans-subjective emotional response in the hearer or reader. *Rasa* has at least two other meanings. At its core, the word means the physical juice, sap, or semen that runs through humans as well as the natural world. Secondly, this liquid essence or semen can be manipulated through certain yogic practices to produce mystical bliss.

When the Hindavī Sufi poets appealed to their readers as *rasikas*, they were able to combine the notion of the *sahṛdaya*, a person of literary taste, refinement, and sensibility, with the notion of the *ʿāshiq*, the lover, and the *sālik*, the seeker on the mystical path. There is a constant assertion through the prologues of the genre that these poems have multiple layers of significance. They are multivalent and multilayered, containing as many levels of meaning as there are levels in the soul of the reader to apprehend. Rather than straightforward allegory, which requires a point-to-point correspondence between levels of meaning, these works are full of multiple suggestions and resonances. As J. R. R. Tolkien notes in his introduction to his verse translation of the Middle English *Pearl*,

> A clear distinction between 'allegory' and 'symbolism' may be difficult to maintain, but it is proper, or at least useful, to limit allegory to narrative, to an account (however short) of events; and symbolism to the use of visible signs or things to represent other things or ideas . . . To be an 'allegory' a poem must *as a whole*, and with fair consistency, describe in other terms some event or process; its entire narrative and all its significant details should cohere and work together to this end. There are minor allegories within *Pearl* . . . But an allegorical description of an event does not make that event itself allegorical. And this initial use is only one of the many applications of the pearl symbol . . . For there are a number of precise details in *Pearl* that cannot be subordinated to any general allegorical interpretation, and these details are of special importance since they relate to the central figure, the maiden of the vision, in whom, if anywhere, the allegory should be concentrated and without disturbance.[29]

The *Madhumālatī* is 'allegorical' and 'symbolic' in this precise sense, containing a variety of suggestive incidents, an allegorical centrepiece in the form of the seductive divine heroine, a genuine poetic commitment to a range of poetic meanings, and a sense of the poem *as a whole* suggesting and evoking

[29] J. R. R. Tolkien, 'Introduction', in his translation of *Sir Gawain and the Green Knight, Pearl, and Orfeo* (London: Unwin Paperbacks, 1975), 6–7.

rasa. It is clear from the text of the *Cāndāyan*, the first surviving Hindavī Sufi romance, that the poet was familiar with the technique of suggesting non-literal and non-figurative meanings, called *dhvani* (resonance) or *vyañjana* (suggestion) in Sanskrit literary criticism.[30] The later poets of the genre, especially Malik Muḥammad Jāyasī and Mīr Sayyid Manjhan Shaṭṭārī Rājgīrī, used these techniques to suggest and to evoke spiritual levels of meaning, the fleeting 'scent of the invisible world'.

Manjhan thus wrote against a background of presuppositions and expectations that was far wider than the conventions of his genre. He used both the poetics of *rasa* and suggestion in the works of Indian poets and the poetics of mystical symbolism found in Sufi poetry, particularly in Persian. The Persian, Sanskrit, and vernacular poets most relevant to Manjhan's time and place form a set of horizons against which one can measure the extent and effect of his own poetics of *prema-rasa*. The works of Persian poets were understood to be delicate, full, and richly suggestive poems, but lacking the graphic allure and frank eroticism of Hindavī. Comparing the *Madhumālatī* to the Sanskrit and vernacular poets of the period opens up new horizons of understanding. Thus, the Sanskrit, middle Indic, and new Indo-Aryan poetry to the god Kṛṣṇa from the period contains a fully worked out theology and aesthetics aimed at savouring the juice or essence of love. In the incarnationist theology of the poets who address a personified divinity (*saguṇa*), the seeker or devotee transforms his subjectivity by imagining himself in an embodied relationship with divinity. On the other hand, Kabir and the *nirguṇa* poets imagine a formless godhead, but their

[30] The sophisticated and brilliant *magnum opus* that best systematizes the *dhvani* theory is the *Dhvanyāloka* ('Light on Dhvani') of Ānandavardhana along with the commentary of Abhinavagupta, the *Locana* or 'Eye'. For these texts, see *The Dhvanyāloka of Śrī Ānandavardhanāchārya with the Lochana Sanskrit Commentary of Śrī Abhinavagupta*, ed. with a Hindi trans. by Jagannāth Pāṭhak (Benares: Chowkhamba Vidyabhawan, 1965). Both texts have been translated into English by D. H. H. Ingalls, J. M. Masson, and M. V. Patwardhan as *The Dhvanyāloka of Ānandavardhana with the Locana of Abhinavagupta* (Cambridge: Harvard University Press, 1990).

version of *prema* is focused on self-recognition through the meditative practice of the divine Name.

The Hindavī Sufi poets fall somewhere in between these two poles. In their poems, the erotic body of the heroine signifies divinity in a temporary revelation that is intended to draw the seeker out of himself and on to the ascetic path. Since their metaphysics is focused on a transcendent principle that cannot be embodied, it is the journey of self-transformation and the balancing of this world and the hereafter that is central to their aesthetics. Since the Sufis believed in a notion of ordinate love, in which each object of desire is loved for the sake of the one higher to it, their poetry requires narrative stages in which the seeker advances towards the highest object through a series of ordeals. This is embodied in the erotic body of the heroine, allegorically understood to contain the concentrated blinding flash of Allah's divine revelation. Savouring the *rasa* of the events and imagery of the story involves picking up these multiple resonances and allowing them to transform one's subjectivity.

Thus, the aesthetics of the Hindavī Sufi romances was aimed at suggesting and awakening love between a transcendent godhead and the human world through the circulation of love between human lovers. In this poetry there is an interplay between profane and divine love, where divine love is considered *ʿishq-i ḥaqīqī*, love of God, and human love is just a reflection of this spiritual or true love, being described as *ʿishq-i majāzī*, metaphorical or profane love. This set of distinctions, often referred to as ordinate love and defined as a ladder or progression in Sufi treatises, is apparent to us from the brief and scattered interpretative comments on the Hindavī romances in the Persian sources of the sultanate period. The beloved in Sufi poetry, as well as the lover, demons and ordeals, can all have at least a double reference but they cannot be understood schematically or allegorically. The symbolism is altogether more subtle, using suggestion and allusion to hint at symbolic levels which are co-present with the literal, so that in any one context, in any particular verse or passage, one level might be applicable, or two or several. The heroine is not always God, the beloved, sometimes she is simply a beautiful woman, and sometimes she is both. Similarly the hero is sometimes a lovelorn young man, sometimes the human soul, sometimes a spiritual traveller, sometimes the created world, sometimes any two or three of these together. The richness of the symbol is measured by the number of levels of understanding and response it can evoke in the reader or hearer.

The text of the *Madhumālatī* is richly allegorical and symbolic, outrunning the precise details of its allegory by the beauty and multivalence of the symbols used. In order to understand how this complex set of literary techniques, anchored in a poetics of *rasa*, is properly mystical, we need to turn the lens on another facet of the poem. In evoking the 'scent of the invisible world', the poet uses both allegorical events and symbolic excess. The classic writer on the theory of mysticism, Evelyn Underhill, defines symbols and their meanings very usefully: 'The greater the suggestive quality of the symbol used, the more answering emotion it evokes in those to whom it is addressed, the more truth it will convey. A good symbolism, therefore, will be more than a mere diagram or mere allegory: it will use to the utmost the resources of beauty and passion, will bring with it hints of mystery and wonder, bewitch with dreamy periods the mind to which it is addressed. Its appeal will not be to the clever brain, but to the desirous heart, the intuitive sense, of man.'[31] When Manjhan addresses himself to the *rasika* it is precisely this desirous heart and intuitive sense to which he is appealing. In her analysis, Underhill identifies three major classes of mystical symbols: that of the pilgrim or traveller on the way, the *sālik*; that of the lover searching for his Beloved, the *ʿāshiq*; that of the seeker of inward transformation, the *sādhak*.[32]

In the *Madhumālatī*, Manjhan employs all three allegorically and intertwines them into a beautifully constructed narrative. The first level of symbolism is that of the *sādhak*, here the yogic level. In the genre of the Hindavī Sufi romance, the hero ordinarily disguises himself as a yogi when he sets off in search of the

[31] Evelyn Underhill, *Mysticism* (New York: Doubleday, 1990), 126.
[32] See Underhill, *Mysticism*, 125–48.

beloved. A number of key yogic terms are used to suggest the ascetic level of meaning through a coded vocabulary. The highest state is referred to as *sahaja*, the state of spontaneous bliss, wherein is experienced *mahārasa*, the great *rasa*, the name of Madhumālatī's city. Manohar has a nurse called Sahajā, and Tārācand's city is called Pavanerī, which can be taken as indicative of *pavana*, breath. Pemā's city is called Citbisarāuṉ, which means peacefulness or forgetfulness of mind, the objective of meditation. Pemā means love and the release of Pemā from the clutches of the demon could be taken as the hero's liberation of the abstract quality of love from the darkness of the phenomenal world into which she has fallen. In terms of the yogic system of self-mortification, it could also signify the release of *śakti* from the base of the spine so that it can rise up the psychic channel *suṣumṇā* to union with Śiva and thus bring about immortality. Finally, when Manohar tells Madhumālatī that he is the sun and she is the moon this too would be taken to refer to the two psychic channels, the *iḍā* and *piṅgalā nāḍīs* that run on either side of the *suṣumṇā*. This yogic level of imagery and terminology is as explicitly a disguise as is the yogic appearance that Manohar adopts when he sets off on his search. The assumption of Gorakhnāthī garb is as surely an indication of the translation of Islam into an Indian landscape as it is an allegorical sign of the seeker's self-transformation by the end of his quest. Manohar has always shed his yogic guise, his *desī* version of Islam, by the time he meets Madhumālatī. In the final fairy-tale union, he is Islam internally and externally transformed into an Indian religious and literary world. The hero is the *ʿāshiq*, the lover, and the *sālik*, the Sufi traveller on the path, conventional symbols of Sufi poetry which can now be examined.

Underhill further analysed the various stages of the mystical path, mainly on the basis of Christian mystics, although she does show some acquaintance with Muslim mystics as well. Her analysis is suggestive in that it creates a generalized scheme with four major phases that she called awakening, purification (*via purgativa*), illumination (*via illuminativa*), and union (*via unitiva*). While there is no historical connection between the Shaṭṭārī Sufis and the Christian mystics, the scheme helps us to focus on the narrative stages of the awakening, purification, illumination, and consummation of desire in the *Madhumālatī*. Manohar must be understood as the human soul which is granted a foretaste of divine beauty in the form of Madhumālatī, whereupon love is born between them coming from a previous life. This is certainly a familiar situation in Indian poetry, where reincarnation is a presupposition, but in Islamic terms it must refer to a pre-existent state of love between the soul and God which is reawakened. This portion of the story, until the nymphs separate the couple, is the first stage, and could be said to correspond to the awakening of love.

The second stage, purification, begins when Manohar is overwhelmed by the pain of love in separation and becomes ill. Doctors, often symbolic of learning and rational thought (*ʿaql*), fail to cure him because they do not understand love. All Manohar's tribulations and sufferings are part of this purgation of the lower forces in his nature. This culminates in the moment when he is able to slay the demon and set love, Pemā, free, after which love becomes his guide, *murshid*, and leads him to his second meeting with Madhumālatī. This second encounter marks the third stage, that of illumination or gnosis, called *maʿrifa* in Sufi schemes of spiritual advancement. It takes place, significantly, in the picture-pavilion which is symbolic of the world of imaginal forms (*ʿālam-i imsāl*). Here Manohar invites her to draw back the veil of her locks and Madhumālatī, for the first and only time, indicates that her beauty is something more than human beauty and cannot be seen with one's ordinary eyes.

As we have mentioned, the poets of the genre use a coded vocabulary to suggest multiple levels of symbolism and meaning. For example, the location of Citbisarāun as a halting place (*maqām*) on the spiritual path is interesting, since the word can mean not only peace of mind but also forgetfulness. There is a sense in which this stage on the path is the point of greatest risk. Forgetfulness can translate as *ġhaflat*, negligence, which is one of the greatest problems the Sufi traveller faces. When Manohar reaches Pemā's home he is offered everything, including Pemā, but he resists the temptation because of his pledge to Madhumālatī; that is, he remembers his primary loyalty. A further temptation occurs in his meeting with Madhumālatī which they both recognize and reject, namely to make love fully as if they were married. They remember their former vow not to do so until they are married. Symbolically this signifies the recognition that illumination, *ma'rifa*, is not final union, that there is further to go on the path. Forgetfulness can also be taken as transcending the ordinary consciousness of the empirical world and enjoying ecstatic states, as Manohar does in their second encounter. Citbisarāuṉ is therefore an excellent choice of name for the location of illumination since it is charged with symbolic potency, indicative of both the high risk and the high reward of the traveller on the mystical path.

The transition between illumination and union, famously called 'the dark night of the soul' by St John of the Cross, is usually a barren despairing period in which both lover and beloved are not sure of the final outcome. The lovers are separated by Madhumālatī's angry mother, who transforms her delinquent daughter into a bird by the use of a magic spell. The bird Madhumālatī, formerly the image and experience of God, flies about the world in a desperate quest for her lover Manohar. After a year, she allows herself to be caught by Tārācand, a Prince who resembles Manohar. At the yogic level of symbolism Tārācand is suggestive of breath, but in a Sufi sense he is representative of selflessness and disinterested service (*k̲h̲idmat-i k̲h̲alq*). In the spirit of selfless service to Madhumālatī, he deserts his kingdom and does not expect any return for his devotion since the lovely and magical bird is already pledged to another. It was through love, Pemā, that Manohar was able to reach Madhumālatī, and now it is through the selflessness and devoted service of Tārācand that Madhumālatī is able to reach Manohar. Manjhan departs from the conventions of the genre at this point. He puts the *bārahmāsā*, the song of the pain of love in separation through the twelve months, in the mouth of Madhumālatī. The other romances usually have the *bārahmāsā* as a song sung by the deserted wife, who is usually taken to symbolize the lower self, the *nafs*, or the world, or both. In giving the *bārahmāsā* to Madhumālatī, Manjhan is able to demonstrate in a strong way—in that it departs from the convention—the love and yearning of God for the human soul.

Manjhan handles the final stage of the consummation of desire, the ultimate savouring of *prema-rasa*, through a double denouement that uses the conventions of traditional Indian marriage. In the practice of child marriage, it was usual for the bride to remain with her parents after the ceremony until she reached the age of puberty. After this there was a second ceremony, the *gavana* or 'going', in which all goodbyes were said and she set out for her husband's home after the ritual of consummation as a sexually mature woman.[33] Union itself, as in other mystical literatures, is described in terms of both mystical marriage and of sexual union. After describing the grand marriage ceremony and the first night of union, Manjhan uses the time spent at her parents' home to allow Pemā and Tārācand to fall in love and get married so that all four live together in perfect harmony. The second ceremony, the *gavana*, then takes place with leave-taking and goodbyes. In Madhumālatī's case, this long goodbye includes her parents, relatives, friends and retainers, as well as the walls and ramparts, the bed, her clothes and her toys, that is, the entire conditioned world of materiality and relationship. All four set off, but, after a while, Pemā, human love, and Tārācand, selfless love and service, separate from the other two, since they cannot enter the totally unconditioned world to which Manohar and Madhumālatī are heir. Eventually Manohar reaches the kingdom from which he set out and becomes king in all his births. The cycle is complete; as the Sufis would say: 'From God we come and to God shall we return.' For Manohar and Madhumālatī, as spiritual travellers and Sufi lovers, this return is represented in life and not in death.

Underneath this generalized Sufi symbolism, which can be understood as allegorical moments or stages along a mystical

[33] See S. W. Fallon, *A New Hindustani–English Dictionary, With Illustrations from Hindustani Literature and Folklore* (Benares: Medical Hall Press, 1879), 1015–16, and William Crooke, *A Rural and Agricultural Glossary for the North West Provinces and Oudh* (Calcutta: Thacker, Spink, and Co., 1888), 104–5.

progression as well as a weaving together of levels of symbolism, it is possible to detect a specifically Shaṭṭārī set of resonances. The attentive reader will recall from our summary account of the Shaṭṭārī path that the neophyte tastes mystical absorption in the divine essence at the very beginning of his ascetic practice. In the poem at hand, this is signified by Manohar's initial communion with Madhumālatī, the image of God and divine beauty in both its gentle (*jamālī*) and its terrible (*jalālī*) aspects. The episode with the heavenly nymphs and the first meeting in which a pre-existent love is reawakened, which Manohar describes as both real and unreal at the same time, describes just this process. Thereafter, Manohar, suffering from *viraha* and with only the name of Madhumālatī, descends, step by step, to the phenomenal world where he finds the Princess whose name is love detained by the evil demon. The Name of God proves to be his salvation because Pemā, love, recognizes it as the name of her childhood friend. Through his victory over the demon, he is able to begin his ascent back up from this low point on the upward arc of the circular Shaṭṭārī regimen. With love as his guide, he is reunited with God but in the imaginal world of the picture-pavilion.

Up to this point the story has been that of Manohar, but now it is told from Madhumālatī's point of view. It is as if the human soul can only hope to reach as far as illumination through its own efforts. Thereafter, only through selfless love and service is God able to reach the human soul and take it to union. In the other Sufi romances written within this genre, the heroes all die and their co-wives all commit *satī* on their husbands' funeral pyres. This implies that men sacrifice women on the mystical path after spiritual self-transformation. In the cultural logic of the period and among the Sufis, the final sacrifice is taken as referring to *fanā*, the annihilation of self, a necessary process for every mystic. In the *Madhumālatī*, however, nobody dies. The Shaṭṭārī path reaches beyond *fanā*, the annihilation of egotistical selfhood, to *baqā*, subsistence in God, and finally to *baqā al-baqā*, everlasting reintegration in God, which is the culmination of Manjhan's story. In this, as in the other ways that have been shown, the Shaṭṭārī path is distinctive. In going beyond *fanā* and using this unique double denouement, *Madhumālatī* transcends the other poems of this genre.

It should be remembered that the yogic, Sufi, and Shaṭṭārī levels of signification are not really discrete elements since the different symbols are all intertwined and perfectly merged with the literal imagery and narrative. The allegorical and complexly symbolical aesthetics of *prema-rasa* necessarily involve a communication of desire between lover and beloved, human and divine, and reader and text. Savouring the juice of love meant, for the authors and audiences of the Hindavī Sufi romances, bringing all three relationships to consummation. Sufi authors considered that the form, shape, and potentiality for analogy of a story or situation had the power to settle in a reader and transform human understanding and consciousness. From all that has been said, it will be apparent that in the *Madhumālatī*, Manjhan composed a beautifully balanced and enchanting poem rich in its suggestive power and potential for mystical interpretation. It is hoped that this brief introduction will contextualize the work and its author and permit a more informed appreciation of the poem. We would like to emphasize, however, that the poem should be read and enjoyed as a *rasika* would read it, with an open heart, a discerning mind and a sensibility open to the poem's suggestive power.

NOTE ON THE TEXT

A FAMOUS dictum has it that one can never translate a poem, only rewrite it. Our work with Manjhan's *Madhumālatī* has aimed at recreating the poetic form of the text as closely as possible in English while conveying the lexical sense of the poetry accurately. Each verse of the poem consists of five short rhymed couplets, followed by a longer rhymed couplet summing up the point of the verse, somewhat reminiscent of the insistent 'bob and wheel' verse-structure of the Middle English poem *Sir Gawain and the Green Knight*.[1] The second verse of *Madhumālatī* is transcribed below to show the structure and patterns of the poetry and its metres and rhymes:

eka aneka bhāva paramesā *eka rūpa kāchẽ bahu bhesā*
tīni loka jahvā̃ lagi ṭhāi *bhoga kai anabana rūpa gosāī̃*
kartā karai jagata jeta cāhai *jamu thā jamu rahai jamu̧ āhai*
bāju thā̃va berasai sabha ṭhāī̃ *nirguna eka oṁkāra gosāī̃*
guputa rūpa pargaṭa sabḣa ṭhāī̃ *bājhu rūpa baḣurūpa gosāī̃*
tribhuvana pūri apūri kai, eka joti sabha ṭhā̃va
jotihi anabana mūrati, mūrati ȧnabana nā̃va

The first line scans as follows:

–∪∪–∪–∪∪∪––, –∪–∪––∪∪––.

The line consists of two half-lines or *ardhālīs*, each having sixteen *mātrās* or metrical instances and usually ending in a spondee (–). A short syllable, indicated by ∪, is one *mātrā*, and a long syllable, indicated by –, counts as two *mātrās*. This metre, in which there are two rhyming half-lines of sixteen *mātrās* each, is called *caupāī.* Every verse of *Madhumālatī* is of five couplets in the *caupāī* metre followed by a longer rhyming couplet called a *dohā*. A *dohā* is two rhyming lines of twenty-four *mātrās* each, with a pause or caesura, indicated above by a comma, after the first thirteen *mātrās*. The first line of the *dohā* scans as follows:

∪∪∪∪–∪∪–∪–, –∪–∪∪∪–∪.

[1] See *Sir Gawain and the Green Knight*, ed. J. R. R. Tolkien and E. V. Gordon, (Oxford: Oxford University Press, 1925).

Manjhan exercises considerable metrical licence with regard to both metres, but never with regard to the rhyme. *Madhumālatī* consists of five hundred and thirty-eight verses, each containing the five couplets of the *caupāī* followed by a *dohā*. The last verse, five hundred and thirty-nine, consists solely of one *dohā*.

In our translation of the *Madhumālatī*, every attempt has been made to represent the poetic form of the original through blank verse. As far as possible, each half-line or *ardhālī* is translated by a line of English, as are also the longer lines of the *dohā*. In the translation each verse is represented by ten or twelve short lines in blank verse, followed by a longer two-line version of the *dohā*. Occasionally the imagery and the meaning is so packed that the translation has to spill over into an extra line, but overall the format remains the same as in the original. No attempt is made, however, to rhyme, or to reproduce the metrical pattern. There is one further departure from the original. In order to break the text up for the reader, headings have been put in at appropriate places. This does not happen in Manjhan's poem, although it was a convention taken from Persian romance that the other Hindavī Sufi poets used fully. Beyond this, since the texture of Manjhan's verse is polished, sweet and straightforward, the English used in the translation is equally light and unpretentious. Where it has been felt that an explanation was needed, this is given in a note. This type of annotation is particularly necessary as far as the prologue is concerned but thereafter the comments are sparser.

It remains only to say something about the poem itself and the present translation. The text used throughout for the translation is the critical edition of Mataprasad Gupta.[2] Four manuscripts of the text are extant: Rā, the Nawab of Rampur's manuscript, housed in the Rampur Raza Library, was written in the Persian script in AD 1719. It is well preserved and written on *faux* Chinese paper with wide brush strokes of gold wash interspersed through the text. It lacks only the first page containing the *sar-i lauḥ* or frontispiece and the first verse. The remaining manuscripts are housed in the Bharat Kala Bhavan at Benares

[2] *Editio princeps, Madhumālatī* (Allahabad: Mitra Prakāśan, 1961).

Hindu University. Bhā, the first Benares manuscript, is written in Persian script. It is badly damaged and lacks 1–35, 41–78, 107–10, 538, and 539. Mā, the oldest manuscript, was copied by the scribe Mādhodāsa in AD 1587. It is severely damaged and lacks verses 1–276 and 343–422. E, the Ekadala manuscript, comes from the town of Ekadala in Fatehpur district in Awadh. It is a complete manuscript, written in Devanagari script in AD 1687, and was used as the basis of an edition by Dr Shiv Gopal Mishra.[3] Critical analysis establishes that there are two manuscript traditions: the first represented by Bhā and Mā, the second represented in Rā. E is a mixture of the two traditions and has more verses. Having two independent traditions permitted the editor a comparative treatment, but this revealed very few minor divergences or variants. The existence of two textual traditions can be accounted for either by the normal processes of textual transmission, or by the possibility that Manjhan himself may have produced more than one version of the actual poem. Both traditions use Persian Nastaliq script, while Devanagari occurs in only one group of manuscripts. This suggests that the earliest scribes and compositors in Hindavī used Nastaliq as well as an older version of Devanagari, probably depending on whether the authors or copiers were Persian-speakers or not. Analysis has suggested, however, that the editor used a modern handwritten transcription of the Nawab of Rampur's manuscript to establish Rā. Although few variants were found, this has been taken into account in the present translation; we have used both the Rampur manuscript and the critical edition in deciding the text that has been translated.

[3] (Benares: Hindī Pracārak Pustakālaya, 1957).

SELECT BIBLIOGRAPHY

Concerning Madhumālatī and its author, Manjhan

ʿĀqil Khān Rāzī, 'Mihr-o-Māh', Ethé MS 1636 (London: British Library).

Askari, S. H., 'A Fifteenth Century Shuttari Sufi Saint in North Bihar', *Journal of the Bihar Research Society*, 37 (1951), 66–82.

—— 'Gleanings from the Malfuz of the 17th Century Shuttari Saint of Jandaha', *Current Studies* (1963), 1–26.

Avalon, Arthur [Sir John Woodroffe]. *The Serpent Power: The Secrets of Tantric and Shaktic Yoga* (1919; repr., New York: Dover, 1974).

Banārsīdās, *Ardhakathānaka*, ed. and trans. Mukund Lath (Jaipur: Rajasthan Prakrit Bharati Sansthan, 1981).

Mañjhan, 'Madhumālatī', Hindi MS 6 (Rampur: Raza Library).

—— *Madhumālatī*, ed. Śivagopāl Miśra (Benares: Hindī Pracārak Pustakālaya, 1957).

—— *Madhumālatī*, ed. Mātāprasād Gupta (Allahabad: Mitra Prakāśan, 1961).

Muḥammad Kabīr, 'Afsānah-i Shāhān', MS Add. 24409 (London: British Library).

Sirhindī, Nāsir ʿAlī, 'Qiṣṣah-i Madhumālatī', MS Add. 6632 (London: British Library).

Weightman, S. C. R. 'Symmetry and Symbolism in Shaikh Manjhan's Madhumālatī', in Christopher Shackle and Rupert Snell (eds.), *The Indian Narrative: Perspectives and Patterns* (Wiesbaden: Otto Harrassowitz, 1992).

—— 'Shaikh Manjhan's Madhumālatī Revisited' in L. Lewisohn and D. Morgan (eds.), *The Heritage of Sufism*, vol. iii: *Late Classical Persianate Sufism (1501–1750): The Safavid and Mughal Period* (Oxford, One World Publications, forthcoming), 464–92.

Concerning the genre of the Sufi Romance in Hindi

Abidi, S. A. H. (ed.), *ʿIsmat Nāmah yā dāstān-i Lorik va Maina* (New Delhi: Markaz-i Taḥqīqat-i Zabān-o Adabiyāt-i Farsī dar Hind, 1985).

—— 'The Story of Padmavat in Indo-Persian Literature', *Indo-Iranica*, 15 2, 1–11.

Ahmad, Aziz, 'Epic and Counter-epic in Medieval India', *Journal of the American Oriental Society*, 83 (1963), 470–6.

Askari, S. H., 'A Newly Discovered Volume of Awadhi Works Including Padmawat and Akhrawat of Malik Muhammad Jaisī', *Journal of the Bihar Research Society*, 39 (1953), 10–40.

—— 'Avvalīn musalmān aur desī bhāshā'en̲, *Patna University Journal* (1954), 59–80.

'Attar, Farīd ud-dīn, *The Conference of the Birds*, trans. Afkham Darbandi and Dick Davis (Harmondsworth: Penguin Books, 1984).

Bilgramī, 'Abdul Vāḥid, *Haqā'iq-i Hindī*, Ahsanullah Collection MS 297.7/11, Aligarh: Maulana Azad Library; trans. into Hindi by S. A. A. Rizvi (Varanasi: Nāgarīpracārinī Sabhā, 1957).

Briggs, George W., *Gorakhnāth and the Kānphaṭa Yogis* (1938; repr. Delhi: Motilal Banarsidass, 1989).

Chaturvedī, Parashurām, *Bharatīya Premākhyān* (Allahabad: Bharatī Bhār, 1985).

Dāūd, Maulānā. *Cāndāyan*, ed. Parameshvarilal Gupta (Delhi: Hindī Granth Ratnākar, 1964).

—— *Cāndāyan*, ed. Mataprasad Gupta (Varanasi: Viśvavidyālaya Prakāśan, 1967).

De, S. K., *History of Sanskrit Poetics* (Calcutta: Firma K. L. Mukhopadhyay, 1960).

Gerow, E., *Indian Poetics* (Wiesbaden: Otto Harrassowitz, 1977).

Grierson, Sir George Abraham, *The Modern Vernacular Literature of Hindustan* (Calcutta: Royal Asiatic Society of Bengal, 1889).

Holbrook, Victoria Rowe. *The Unreadable Shores of Love: Turkish Modernity and Mystic Romance* (Austin: University of Texas Press, 1994).

Jāyasī, Malik Muḥammad. *Jāyasī Granthāvalī*, ed. Ramchandra Shukla (repr. Varanasi: Nāgarīprācanī Sabhā, 1950).

—— 'Padmāvat', Hindi MS 1 (Rampur: Raza Library).

—— *Padmāvat*, ed. and trans. George A. Grierson and Sudhakar Dvivedi (Calcutta: Royal Asiatic Society of Bengal, 1896–1911).

—— *Padmāvat*, ed. V. S. Agravāl (Cirgānv, Jhānsī: Sāhitya Sadan, 1955).

—— *Padmāvat*, ed. Mātāprasād Gupta (Allahabad: Bhāratī BhaṆḍār, 1973).

—— *Padmāvat*, trans. A. G. Shirreff (Calcutta: Royal Asiatic Society of Bengal, 1944).

Khandalavala, Karl, 'The Mṛgāvat of Bharat Kala Bhavan as a

Social Document and its Date and Provenance', in *Chhavi: Golden Jubilee Volume* (Varānāsi: Bhārat Kalā Bhavan, 1971).

McGregor, R. S., *Hindi Literature from Its Beginnings to the Nineteenth Century* (Wiesbaden: Otto Harrassowitz, 1984).

Meisami, Julie Scott, 'The World's Pleasance: Hafez's Allegorical Gardens', *Comparative Criticism*, 5 (1983), 153–95.

—— 'Allegorical Gardens in the Persian Poetic Tradition: Nezami, Rumi, Hafez', *International Journal of Middle Eastern Studies*, 17 (1985), 229–60.

—— *Medieval Persian Court Poetry* (Princeton: Princeton University Press, 1987).

Millis, John, 'Malik Muhammad Jayasī: Allegory and Religious Symbolism in his Padmavat', Ph.D. diss., University of Chicago, 1984.

Morris, James Winston, 'Reading The Conference of the Birds', in Wm. Theodore de Bary and Irene Bloom (eds.), *Approaches to Asian Classics* (New York: Columbia University Press, 1990).

Nagendra and Gupta, S. (eds.), *Hindī Sāhitya kā Ithihās* (NOIDA: Mayur Paperbacks, 1991).

Pandey, Shyam Manohar (ed.), *Loka Mahākāvya Loriki* (Allahabad: Sāhitya Bhavan, 1979).

—— *Madhyayugīn Premākhyan* (Allahabad: Lokbhāratī Prakāśan, 1965).

—— *Sūfī-kāvya Vimarśa* (Agra: Vinod Pustak Bhaṇḍār, 1968).

—— 'Maulana Dāūd and His Contributions to the Hindi Sūfī Literature', *Annali dell'Istituto Orientale di Napoli*, 38 (1978), 75–90.

—— *The Hindi Oral Epic Canaini* (Allahabad: Sahitya Bhavan, 1982).

—— 'Kutuban's Mrigavatī: Its Content and Interpretation', in *Devotional Literature in South Asia: Current Research* (1985).

—— *Hindī aur Fārsī Sūfī Kāvya* (Allahabad: Sāhitya Bhavan, 1989).

Pritchett, Frances W., *Marvelous Encounters: Folk Romance in Urdu and Hindi* (New Delhi: Manohar, 1985).

Quṭban, *Mṛgāvatī*, ed. Parameśvarilal Gupta (Varanasi: Viśvavidyālaya Prakāśan, 1967).

—— *Mṛgāvatī*, ed. Mātāprasād Gupta (Agra: Pramaāik Prakāśan, 1968).

—— *Mṛgāvatī*, ed. D. F. Plukker, Academisch proefschrift, University of Amsterdam, 1981.

Rakeśagupta, *Studies in Nayaka Nayika Bheda* (Aligarh: Granthayan, 1967).

Schimmel, Annemarie, *Classical Urdu Literature from the Beginning to Iqbal* (Wiesbaden: Otto Harrassowitz, 1975).
Shukla, Ramchandra, *Hindī Sāhitya kā Itihās* (Varanasi: Nāgarīpracāriṇi Sabhā, 1957).
Vaudeville, Charlotte, *Bārahmāsa in Indian Literatures: Songs of the Twelve Months in Indo-Aryan Literatures* (Delhi: Motilal Banarsidass, 1986).

Concerning Sufism and the Shaṭṭārī Order

ʿAbdullāh Shaṭṭār, 'Shajarat-ut-Tauḥīd', Persian MS (Phulwari Sharif: Khanqah Mujeebia).
Aḥmad, Masūd, *Shāh Muḥammad Ġhauṣ Gvāliyārī* (Mirpur Khas: Aftab Press, 1964).
Ahmad, Qazi Moinuddin, 'History of the Shattari Silsilah', Ph.D. diss., Aligarh Muslim University, 1963.
Arberry, A. J., *Sufism: An Account of the Mystics of Islam* (1950; repr. New York: Harper and Row, 1970).
Auliya', Shaikh Niẓam-al-dīn, *Favā'id al-Fu'ād*, trans. by Bruce Lawrence as *Morals for the Heart* (New York: Paulist Press), 1992.
Austin, R. W. J., *The Bezels of Wisdom* (New York: Paulist Press, 1980).
ʿAlavī, Shaikh Wajīhuddin, *Sharḥ-i Jām-i Jahān Numā* Persian MS 1302 (Calcutta: Asiatic Society of Bengal).
Chittick, William, *The Sufi Path of Knowledge* (Albany: State University of New York Press, 1989).
Corbin, H., *Creative Imagination in the Sūfism of Ibn ʿArabī*, trans. Ralph Manheim (Princeton: Princeton University Press, 1969).
Digby, Simon, 'The Literary Evidence for Painting in the Delhi Sultanate', *Bulletin of the American Academy of Benares*, 1 (1967).
—— 'Abd al-Quddūs Gangohī (1456–1537 A.D.): The Personality and Attitudes of a Medieval Indian Sufi', *Medieval India: A Miscellany*, 3 (1975), 1–66.
—— 'The Sufi Shaikh as a Source of Authority in Mediaeval India', in Marc Gaboriean (ed.), *Islam et Société en Asie du Sud: Collection Puruṣārtha 9* (Paris: École des Hautes Études en Sciences Sociales, 1986).
—— 'Tabarrukāt and Succession among the great Chishtī Shaikhs', in R. E. Frykenbuerg (ed.), *Delhi Through the Ages* (Delhi, Oxford University Press, 1986), 77–89.

Eaton, Richard M., *Sufis of Bijapur, 1300–1700: Social Roles of Sufis in Medieval India* (Princeton: Princeton University Press, 1978).

Ernst, Carl W., 'Sufism and Yoga according to Muḥammad Ghawth', paper presented at the American Academy of Religion Conference, Anaheim, 1989.

—— *Sufism* (Boston: Shambhala Books, 1997).

Farḥī, Isma'īl, 'Makhzan-i Da'vat', Curzon MS 437 (Calcutta: Asiatic Society of Bengal).

Ghauṣī Shaṭṭārī, Muḥammad, 'Gulzār-i Abrār', Persian MS 259 (Calcutta: Asiatic Society of Bengal).

Gvāliyārī, Shaikh Muḥammad Ghauṣ, 'Kalīd-i Makhāzin', Persian MS 912 (Rampur: Raza Library).

—— 'Jawāhīr-i Khamsah', Ethé MS 1875 (London: The British Library).

Haq, M. M., 'The Shuttari Order of Sufism in India and Its Exponents in Bengal and Bihar', *Journal of the Asiatic Society of Pakistan*, 16 2 (1971), 167–75.

Hughes, Thomas, *Dictionary of Islam* (1885; repr. Calcutta: Rupa, 1988).

Husain, Yusuf, 'Haud al-Hayat: La Version arabe de l'Amratkund', *Journal Asiatique*, 113 (1928), 291–344.

Izutsu, Toshihiko. *Sufism and Taoism: A Comparative Study of the Key Philosophical Concepts* (Berkeley: University of California Press, 1984).

Maghribī, Muḥammad Shīrīn, 'Jām-i Jahān Numā', Persian MS 1326 (Ahmedabad: Pirmohammedshah Library).

Nizami, K. A., 'Early Indo-Muslim Mystics and Their Attitude towards the State', *Islamic Culture*, 22 (1948), 387–98.

—— 'The Shattari Saints and Their Attitude Towards the State', *Medieval India Quarterly*, 1 2 (1950), 56–70.

—— *Some Aspects of Religion and Politics in India During the Thirteenth Century* (Delhi: Idarah-i Adabiyat-i Delli, 1961).

Rashīd, Shaikh, 'Davā'ir-i Rashīdī' (cat. no. 3269, Hyderabad: Salar Jung Museum and Library).

Rizvi, S. A. A., 'Sufis and Natha Yogis in Mediaeval Northern India (XII to XVI Centuries)', *Journal of the Oriental Society of Australia*, 7 1–2 (1970), 119–33.

—— *A History of Sufism in India*, 2 vols. (Delhi: Munshiram Manoharlal 1978–83).

Schimmel, Annemarie, *Mystical Dimensions of Islam* (Chapel Hill: University of North Carolina Press, 1975).

—— *As Through a Veil: Mystical Poetry in Islam* (New York: Columbia University Press, 1982).
—— *A Two-Colored Brocade* (Chapel Hill: University of North Carolina Press, 1992).
Sells, Michael, 'Bewildered Tongue: The Semantics of Mystical Union in Islam', in Moshe Idel and Bernard McGinn (eds.), *Mystical Union and Monotheistic Faith: An Ecumenical Dialogue* (New York: Macmillan, 1989).
Sharīf, Ja'far, Herklots, G. A., and Crooke, William, *Islam in India or The Qānūn-i Islām: The Customs of the Musalmans of India* (1921; repr. New Delhi: Oriental Books, 1972).
Takeshita, M., *Ibn ʿArabī's Theory of the Perfect Man and Its Place in the History of Islamic Thought* (Tokyo: Institute for the Study of the Languages and Cultures of Asia and Africa, 1987).
White, David G., *The Alchemical Body: Siddha Traditions in Medieval India* (Chicago: University of Chicago Press, 1996).

Concerning the history of the period

Alam, Muzaffar, 'Competition and Co-existence: Indo-Islamic Interaction In Medieval North India', *Itinerario*, 13 1 (1989), 37–59.
Bābur, Zāhiru'd-dīn Muḥammad Pādshāh Ghāzī, *Bābar-Nāma*, trans. Annette S. Beveridge (1921; repr. Delhi: Low Price Publications, 1989).
Eaton, Richard M., *The Rise of Islam and the Bengal Frontier, 1204–1760* (Berkeley: University of California Press, 1993).
Ghorī, Gulab Khan, *Gvāliyār kā Rājnaitik aur Sanskritik Itihās* (Delhi: B. R. Publishing Corporation, 1986).
Habib, Muhammad, *Politics and Society During the Early Medieval Period: Collected Works of Professor Muhammad Habib*, ed. K. A. Nizami. 2 vols. (Delhi: People's Publishing House, 1981).
Pandey, A. B., *The First Afghan Empire in India* (Calcutta: Bookland Limited, 1956).
Roy, Asim, *The Islamic Syncretistic Tradition in Bengal* (Princeton: Princeton University Press, 1984).
Saeed, M. M., *The Sharqi Sultanate of Jaunpur* (Karachi: University of Karachi Press, 1972).
Siddiqui, I. H., 'Shaikh Muhammad Kabir and his History of the Afghan Kings', *Indo-Iranica*, 19 4 (1966), 57–78.
—— *History of Sher Shāh Sūr* (Aligarh: Dwadesh Shreni and Company Private Limited, 1974).

—— 'Social Mobility in the Delhi Sultanate', In Irfan Habib (ed.), *Medieval India I: Researches in the History of India, 1200–1750* (Delhi: Oxford University Press, 1992).

Dictionaries and reference works

Apte, V. S., *The Practical Sanskrit–English Dictionary* (Kyoto: Rinsen Book Company, 1986).

Crooke, William, *A Rural and Agricultural Glossary for the North West Provinces and Oudh* (Calcutta: Thacker, Spink, and Co., 1888).

Dowson, John, *A Classical Dictionary of Hindu Mythology and Religion, Geography, History, and Literature* (London: Kegan Paul, Trench, Trubner and Co., Ltd., 1928).

Fallon, S. W., *A New Hindustani–English Dictionary, With Illustrations from Hindustani Literature and Folklore* (Benares: Medical Hall Press, 1879).

McGregor, R. S., *The Oxford Hindi–English Dictionary* (Oxford and Delhi: Oxford University Press, 1995).

Platts, John T., *A Dictionary of Urdū, Classical Hindī, and English* (Oxford: Clarendon Press, 1884).

Shyamsundardas *et al.*, *Hindī Shabdsāgar*, vols. 1–11 (Benares: Nagari Pracharini Sabha, 1965–75).

Steingass, F., *A Comprehensive Persian–English Dictionary* (New Delhi: Oriental Books Reprint Corporation, 1981).

Further reading in Oxford World's Classics

Niẓami of Ganja, *Haft Paykar*, ed. and trs. Julie Scott Meisami.

The Pañcatantra, ed. and trs. Patrick Olivelle.

CHRONOLOGY

1379	Composition of *Cāndāyan* by Maulānā Dā'ūd.
1485	Death of Shaikh ʿAbdullāh Shaṭṭār, the founder of the Order.
1495	Death of Manjhan's maternal grandfather, Shaikh Qāẓin ʿAlā.
1503	Composition of *Mirigāvatī* by Quṭban in the Sharqī court of Jaunpur.
1523	Shaikh Muḥammad Ġhauṣ goes to Gwalior.
1526	Bābur proclaimed Emperor.
1530	Death of Bābur; accession of Humāyūn.
1540	Defeat of Humāyūn by Sher Shāh Sūrī, and his flight to Iran.
1540	The date at which Malik Muḥammad Jāyasī began to write *Padmāvat*, which is said to have taken eighteen years to complete.
1545	Death of Sher Shāh Sūrī. Manjhan begins to write *Madhumālatī*.
1553	Death of Islām Shāh Sūrī.
1554	Restoration of Humāyūn; enthronement of Akbar as Emperor.
1555	Death of Humāyūn.
1556	The end of the pretensions of the Sūr dynasty.
1563	Death of Shaikh Muḥammad Ġhauṣ Gvāliyārī.

MADHUMĀLATĪ

THE PROLOGUE

In Praise of God

1. God, giver of love, the treasure-house of joy
Creator of the two worlds in the one sound Oṃ,*
my mind has no light worthy of you,
with which to sing your praise, O Lord!
King of the three worlds* and the four ages,*
the world glorifies you from beginning to end.
Sages, the learned, thinkers on the Absolute,*
all have failed to laud you on earth.
How can I accomplish with a single tongue
what a thousand tongues could not in four ages?
    Manifest in so many forms, in all three worlds, in every heart,
    how can my senses glorify you with one tongue alone?

2. In every state the Supreme Lord is One,
a single form in many guises.
In heaven, earth, and hell, wherever space extends,
the Lord rejoices in multiplicity of form.
The Maker makes the universe as He wills.
He came as Death, comes still, will always come.*
Placeless, He is present everywhere.
Unqualified, He is Oṃ, the singular sound.
Hidden, He is manifest everywhere.
Formless, He is the many-formed Lord.
    One Light there is which shines alone, radiant in all the worlds.*
    Countless are the forms that Light assumes, countless are its names.*

3. If gods, men, and serpents, as many as there are,
were to praise the Lord for a million years,
still all would give up, saying in shame,
'We did not know You as You are.'
If the mind were to wander for a million years,
how could its poor intelligence reach God?

Giver of bread, He feeds the world,
Creator, Destroyer, and sole Sustainer,
alone in the three worlds and the four ages,
He plays, Himself, in multiple forms.
Invisible, untainted,* the one Creator is a single shape in many disguises.
Here, He is in beggar's rags; there, in the robes of the primordial king.

4. How can I describe the One
who pervades the universe in so many forms?
In the three worlds, all know His Being,
whatever exists, exists in Him.*
Though manifest, not hidden, in all four ages,
yet rarely can anyone know His mystery.
Manifest, He is luminous in ten directions,*
immanent in all things, yet always transcendent.
To the one who applies his mind to Him,
the Creator shows His hidden nature.*
He hides, He plays openly, He permeates all things,
No other exists, nor ever did, nor ever will!

5. The one born on earth never to know You,
lives uselessly and dies repentant.
He has lived his earthly life in vain
who seeks from life anything but You.
Lord, I have a wish in my heart,
that I may love You for Yourself.
My tongue cannot express the certainty
with which my soul knows You.
When every epithet that comes to mind fails,
how can I sing Your praises?
As far as the bird of knowledge can fly, as deep as the mind can fathom,
thus far one can go: beyond that point, where are the means?

ing of the beginning, end of the end,
orms but only One Essence,

He is One, there is no other.
He has neither beginning nor end.*
Through Him my heart has realized this truth:
in all three worlds, there is One alone.
No match for You exists anywhere.
Creation itself is the mirror of Your face.*
Only the man who forgets his self
can find You by searching, losing his all.
    Knower of all mysteries, Enjoyer of all joys,
    behind all of creation, You are the One Lord!

In Praise of Muḥammad

7. Listen now while I tell of the man:
separated from him, the Maker became manifest.
When the Lord took on flesh, He entered creation.
The entire universe is of His Essence.
His radiance shone through all things.
This lamp of creation* was named Muḥammad!
For him, the Deity fashioned the universe,*
and love's trumpet sounded in the triple world.
His name is Muḥammad, king of three worlds.
He was the inspiration for creation.
    The moon split in two at the pointing of his finger;*
    from the dust of his feet the cosmos became stable.

8. Muḥammad is the root, the whole world a branch,
the Lord has crowned him with a priceless crown.
He is the foremost, no other is his equal.
He is the substance and the world his shadow.
Everyone knows the Maker, the hidden mover,
but no one recognizes the manifest Muḥammad!
The Invisible One, whom no one can see,
has assumed the form of Muḥammad.
He has named this form Muḥammad,
but it has no meaning other than the One.
    I shout it out loud, let the whole world hear:
    'Manifest, the name is Muḥammad; secretly, you know
      it is He!'*

In Praise of the Four Caliphs

9. Now listen while I tell of his four companions,*
the givers of doctrine, truth, and justice.
The first was Abū Bakr,* the Proof,
who accepted as truth the words of Muḥammad.
The second was ʿUmar,* the king of justice:
he left father and son for the work of God.
The third, ʿUs̱mān,* knew the secrets of scripture.
The fourth was the Lion ʿAlī,* the virtuous,
who conquered the world by the grace of his sword.
They held the original scripture as truth, accepting nothing else.
Visibly, they focused on actions, inwardly walking the path of God.

*In Praise of Salīm Shāh**

10. Salīm Shāh has become a great king in the world,
he takes pleasure in the earth through his power.
When he is angry and presses down his stirrup
Indra's throne* in heaven trembles.
Through the nine regions and the seven continents*
there is fear and confusion at the sound of his name.
When he took the universe as his kingdom
no warrior remained on earth to oppose him.
All ten directions fear his might,
and even in Laṅkā* there is consternation
from the brilliance of his sword.
Lord of the earth, he appreciates virtue: he is a treasury of the fourteen sciences.*
A true man who can break his enemy's arm, he is a strong, wise king.

11. Through Salīm's ascetic power, his momentous birth,
the doors of Kabul and India are one.
In the north, snowy mountains attest his authority.
Southwards, Hanumān's bridge* limits his power.
Syria and Rome are his western frontier;

eastwards, he is famous till the ocean shore.
All nine regions are happy, for Salīm is
a Yudhiṣṭhira* in virtue, a Harīścandra* in truth.
In creation's three worlds, I cannot recall anyone
equal to him in the grace of his sword.
> The nine regions all bless him, 'May you rule in the world
> as long as moon and sun endure, as long as the pole-star
> shades the earth!'

12. The fame of his justice resounds high and clear,
lamb and wolf graze together at peace.
I cannot describe his just rule, where the lion
plays with a cow's tail in its paw.
Through his austerities his kingdom is strong,
a garden come to flower without any thorns.
His policy in the world ensures
the strong cannot oppress the weak.
Right is known from wrong as milk from water.
The man who knocks on his door, finds it open.
> Joy and happiness, enthusiasm and delight: everyone
> accepts these virtues here.
> Poverty, grief, oppression, and fear have left the land and
> fled away.

13. How can I describe the wonders of his kindness?
He grants robes and crowns to monarchs.
When the doors of his generosity are opened
Karṇa* comes calling with outstretched hands.
When the trumpet-call of his gifts reaches heaven,
Ḥātim,* Karṇa, Bhoja* and Bali* are all ashamed.
In truth he is Harīścandra, in almsgiving Bali,
Yudhiṣṭhira in virtue, incarnate in the age of Kali.
King Bhoja cannot equal his merits or knowledge;
in valour, Vikrama* cannot compare.
> Joy rules the seven continents, the nine regions are happy.
> Save for the pain of separation, there is no grief in all the
> land.

*In Praise of Shaikh Muḥammad Ġhauṣ̱**

14. There is a holy man great in the world,
a Shaikh beloved of God,
profound in knowledge, matchless in beauty.
Whoever comes to touch him, calling on his name,
is cleansed from sin and gains enlightenment.
Whomever the Shaikh loves in his heart,
he calls to him gently and crowns him king.
The one whom his gaze touches is protected,*
and the stain of his body is washed away.
The disciple who seeks out this Guru's glances
and fosters them, washes out the stain of death!*
A sight of the Guru washes away sorrow—bless those who cherish that vision!
The disciple whom the Guru nurtures is the king of all four aeons.

15. Shaikh Muḥammad is a matchless guide,
he is the steersman over seven oceans.*
Whoever comes in contemplation of his feet,
sees his face and is filled with joy.
All hopes are fulfilled, for now and hereafter.
The man who bends and touches his feet
destroys his sins. From the Shaikh's mouth
comes only knowledge. He teaches the fourteen sciences
and the secret syllables of spiritual power.*
In his heart, there's no pleasure, nor grief.
He meditates constantly, absorbed in union.
Shaikh Muḥammad is generous and appreciates virtues.
In both the worlds, he is pure and true, a preceptor profound and deep.

16. As the sun's rising illumines the world,
his light radiates from east to west.
Some people's eyes are lit by that sun,
like stars, which he lights with ultimate knowledge.
For those who are born as blind as bats,
even that rising sun is dark.

In this Kali age,* the man who takes courage
gains perfection through courage alone.
Shaikh Muḥammad is a matchless adept,
he grants spiritual power even to cowards.
    Like a magic stone, his touch transforms base metal to
        gold.
    Even I, irresolute, came to be realized through a
        glimpse of Shaikh Muḥammad.

17. The man absorbed in the Absolute knows,
he understands the alphabet of the soul.
The letters of the soul are difficult, unfathomable,
only the Guru can take you through them.
If you want to know these syllables,
simply lose your self, it's simplicity.*
If you want the Guru's grace,
leave aside all the mind's arguments; know him!*
Everyone sees his manifest form,
but few recognize his secret nature.*
    The Lord has made mighty kings and saints who steady
        the world,
    but Shaikh Muḥammad Ġhauṡ transcends the
        attainments of both.

18. Shaikh Muḥammad is an ocean of knowledge,
fathomless and profound. The man who serves him
crosses over to the farthest shore.
Some dip their heads in, others wash their limbs,
some wash only their hands and faces,
and some come to drink at this ocean shore.
Others look and just come back,
but all obtain the blessings of life.
Others remain bereft of this ocean's waters,
only a few have earned enough merit.
    As one resolves, so does one perfect oneself. In this age
        of Kali,
    the Shaikh is a fathomless ocean, a hoard of knowledge
        and virtue.

19. The man who comes, desire in his heart,
    and sees his face, attains his goal.
    Ultimate knowledge enters his heart,
    deep in meditation, he is shown the way.
    The man who sleeps and loses the day,
    loses his bag in the market-place.
    Who knows what one's fate will hold?
    The harder you practise, the further you get.
    And if your forehead has the line of fate,
    you'll see Shaikh Muḥammad in this life.
        God makes some as seeing men; in their hearts, the
            trumpet blows.
        Those He creates as sightless bats live in total darkness.

those that question & search Vs live up

20. All the pandits in the age of Kali
    shaved their heads to learn from him.*
    As his disciples, they attained perfection.
    Many too are the madmen born on earth,
    but to all he gave the knowledge of salvation.
    He does nothing but meditate, absorbed in knowledge,
    and makes kings of seekers, whether clothed or naked.
    The man who stays with him four days,
    rejects both worlds and just stays on.
    Those he looks at with compassion
    turn aside from now and hereafter.
        The Shaikh's heart shines, more dazzling than a million
            suns,
        for he has swallowed up pride and transcended the triple
            world.

x Shaikh

21. Twelve years he stayed alone in a place
    which sees neither sun nor moon.
    A horrible, rugged, difficult place,
    called Dhundha Dari in this age of Kali,
    with impassable mountains on all four sides
    where no human had gone before.
    There he went to meditate on God.
    He ate only leaves and berries in the forest.
    In subduing his soul, he killed a mad elephant,

and imbibed the nectar of pleasure, enlightenment.*
Controlling his self with great austerities, he attained perfection.
Twelve years in mountain and wasteland he stayed absorbed in God.

*In Praise of Khizr Khān**

22. Now listen while I tell of Khizr Khān the brave,
invincible in battle, intelligent and wise.
He is a man of knowledge, virtue and courage,
learned and wise, yet a hero in battle.
He is the King's mighty right arm,
wherever he stands, retreat is impossible.
When he gives his word, he does not waver,
like the pole-star, he is firm and unmoving.
He is bounteous like the billowing ocean.
Never does an untruth cross his lips.
War incarnate, he is brave, yet knowledgeable and refined.
By the grace of his sword
he is courageous and true, a treasury of the fourteen sciences.

23. 'In the whole army, there's only one man
who worships the sword,' said Salīm Shāh in praise.
His blade is thirsty for red blood and booty,
and when his spear moves, everyone flees like mice.*
Enemies hear his pledges and tremble,
thunder and lightning strikes at their hearts.
When his army attacks, all the warriors praise him,
and rush into battle on his left flank.
He is the bravest in the world,
purest gold in all twelve parts.
No rival for his sword in the Kali age, no connoisseur to match him.
When he takes up sword in hand, enemies hear him and quake.

*In Praise of the Word**

24\. Word, O word, where is your home?
From where did your light shine forth?
Where were you born? My mind cannot fathom it.
My mind has puzzled over this,
and no one can say what it means:
if words arise from mortal mouths,
then how can the word be imperishable?
If man, the master of words, can die,
then how does the word remain immortal?
    Reflect on my words, and you will see:
    the word is alive in every heart, like Him.

25\. If the Maker had not made the word,
how could anyone hear stories of pleasure?
Before the beginning, before first creation,
the word was incarnate in Hari's mouth.*
First, word, one word, the sound of Oṃ,
good and bad, it pervaded the cosmos.
The Creator gave the word a high place in creation,
it distinguishes man from beast.
Everyone knows about the word,
God is incarnate within it.
    No one has seen You, no one knows Your home,
    Master of the triple world, You are manifest in the word.

26\. Words came into the world as precious pearls,
through them the Guru taught enlightenment.
The Maker fashioned the four holy Vedas,
and the word became manifest on earth.
Words came down from heaven to earth,
sent down by the Lord Himself.
Had He found anything to equal the word,
He would have sent that in its place.
Through man, immortal word became flesh,
undying through all four ages.
    word is too precious to be described or sketched.
    word belongs to God, who has neither form nor line.

In Praise of Love

27\. Love made an entrance at the beginning,
then the world came into existence.*
From love all creation sprang:
love filled each created form.
Only he enjoys life's reward on earth
in whose heart is born love's anguish.
The man whose soul does not know love,
does not know the simple mystery.*
Fate gives some the pain of separation,
gives them the crown of the triple world.
> Do not think separation is pain; from it, joy comes into the world.
> Blessed is the man whose sorrow is the sorrow of love-in-separation.

28\. Love is the costliest jewel in existence.
The man whose soul knows love is blessed.
God made the world only for love.
Through love, God Himself is manifest.
Love's radiance lights up all of creation.
No rival to love exists anywhere.
Rare are those who have the luck
to gain the good fortune of love.
The word rings out in all four ages:
'He alone is the king,
who gives his head on the path of love!'
> The market of love is open to all. O people, buy what you need.
> Buyers, look at profit and loss; don't lose a chance like this!

importance of love.

29\. The root of creation, separation's anguish,
brought into being the whole world.
A man needs previous merit to feel this pain.
Know this in your soul, that love
is the dearest thing in all the world.
Whatever I've seen and heard tells me:
for love's sake, nothing is forbidden.

Hearts in which love's lamp is lit,
see the beginning and end of all things.
Hearts which are tortured by separation,
remain immortal, never die.
No scripture, no wisdom, no magic power, can teach the lesson of separation.
This treasure goes only to those on whom God's grace falls, compassionate.

30. The man whose soul is marked by love,
sees the Unseen One wherever he looks.
And then if insight is born in his heart,
he sees himself in all other selves.
If the tree of knowledge blooms and bears fruit,
he abandons everything, eats of nothing but this tree.
No duality remains in the world for him,
wherever he looks is eternal joy.
You are the lamp in the house of creation.
Never mistake the body for the soul.
All the joys and sorrows of the world happen exactly as God wishes.
When they touch you, know that it is God no one else.

*To the Soul**

31. O soul, you are an ocean of treasures.
Why do you destroy yourself with pride?*
All of creation is the mirror of your face,
from it the triple world shines with light.
In heaven, earth and the nether world,
your radiance gives light to all.
You alone are manifest in all creation,
everything is You, there is no other.
Whoever loses his self can find himself.
Wh[illegible] can he find who has not lost himself?
[illegible] light of the triple world, what place is there where you are not?

Look hard, you are everywhere, at play in all that comes to be.

*Some Spiritual Advice**

32. Now listen, here's some practical advice:
sit in meditation and focus on the Absolute form.
Seize the upward breath in your body,
blow at the fire within your heart.
When the flame rocks, it showers sparks,
and burns the blackness off your body!
Then sound* will vibrate through your body,
while you can barely hold yourself in!
That is the light of your inner heaven,*
live in that mystic sound!
Among millions of beings, a solitary man enjoys this heaven.
He dwells like fragrance in the circle of emptiness,* in the abode of bliss.

33. Abandon consciousness, wisdom and knowledge,
focus on meditation, not on your body.
When you reach the state of union,
there you will find your own true self.
In the place of the Absolute, the Pure,
the Void, will be your self without any selfhood.
Beyond all knowledge, unknowing rules,
where your self will lose all knowledge of itself.
There, in the mystical, self-born union of Sahaja,
your own true self will be revealed.
Stay in absorption in the deep cave, motionless as if in sleep,
in the union where there is no you, no other, and no action.

*In Praise of Carnāḍhi**

34. The city of Carnāḍhi is a peerless fort,
built like invincible Laṅkā in this age of Kali.

A river runs around it to the east,
and the Gaṅgā is its moat to the north and west.
I cannot describe the Gaṅgā which flows
within its walls. It must be seen to be appreciated.*
A thousand kings with forces joined
and laying siege, would retreat in shame.
Above, its roofs are built in many shapes,
while down below the divine river surges and swells.
The city is matchless in beauty, the fort impregnable and strong,
Impossible to acquire, just like hard-earned merit.

35. The fort is beautiful, its king, godlike and wise,
its people are happy and intelligent.
Enlightened all and devotees of God,
themselves joyful, they feel the pain of others.
Generous and kind and dutiful are they,
deeply absorbed in the savour of love.
All are nobly born, and enjoy every good fortune.
Think of it as the shadow of paradise on earth,
for I cannot adequately sing its praises.
In every lane and every house, there is excitement and joy.
Heaven has come down to earth, and made its dwelling here.

A Warning

36. Kali, the age of degeneration, is black as a cobra.
A tricky old virgin, she charms the triple world.
Old and young, she deceives them all,
she devours everyone who is born on earth.
Many have fallen for this pretty girl, Kali.
She is engaged to many men, but marries none.
This wicked sinner cheats the whole world,
men who lust for her come to no good.
Don't fall for her, she's fickle and treacherous,
or you will lose both capital and interest.
O lustful parrot, leave the silk-cotton tree, for it has trapped many birds!*

Only those whose hearts are blind could possibly enjoy this evil sinner.

37. She's tricky; no man who falls for her
ever profits from it, but loses his capital.
Like a palm tree's useless shade,
she offers much but quickly slips away.
She's a mean bitch, no good to anyone.
She sticks to you for just a few days,
never is she a faithful wife until death.
The man she nurtures she certainly kills,
whomever she picks up, she always abandons.
High or low, she visits everyone's house,
but she never stays forever.
She's an enchanting whore, and black-faced, a fraudulent ancient virgin.
She beguiles the whole world and then devours it, this restless little imp of a girl.

38. No spring has ever come to the world
that did not suffer a fall of leaf.
No moon has ever grown to fullness
that was not lost in the dark of the month.
O wise people! Do not forget this Kali:
she is like water in a pitcher of air.
Do not wilfully deceive yourselves,
or you will have much to repent of at leisure.
In this age of Kali, no one is born immortal.
Everyone is sorry in the end.
She never stays for anyone, so don't go falling in love with her!
Do not be taken in by a world ten times trickier than you!

To the Reader

39. In the year nine hundred and fifty two,
the man of truth abandoned this Kali age.*
Then a desire arose within me
to weave a tale in language full of feeling,

using the sweetest, most powerful words
that ever I had heard or stored in my heart.
All who aspire to love should hear me,
for I will speak in words sweet and tender.
I offer you a delightful story in verse,
cease all arguments and enjoy the tale.
Listen to this sweet and moving story, full of feeling and love!
And if you hear a line with a flaw, I beg you spare the poet's blushes.

40. God inspired this tale in my heart:
listen and I will tell it to you.
The connoisseur who relishes the savour of love
will expertly reckon every flaw and excellence.
For when a poet strings his words together,
poetic excellence hides defects of verse.
In just this way did God make humans deficient.
He made the human spirit pure,
but placed it in a body prone to sin.
Mankind, which was defective at creation,
will surely so remain until the end of time.
God alone is flawless and free from the taint of sin.
If we find faults in man's imperfection, why should we be amazed?

41. Scholars, hear this plea of mine:
I fold my hands, bow down to your feet.
If you cannot admire the virtues of my poem,
I beg you not to be mean, spiteful critics.
If, when you read my poem, you like it,
then you can criticize it and destroy the flaws.
Where the words do not flow, improve them.
Be generous when you criticize, consider good and bad.
What is the good of writing bad poetry?
What can one do with such stuff?
If madmen find fault with my work, that does not worry me.

Blessed is the man who accepts my faults to grasp the deeper meaning.

42. I am sure no scholar will condemn me,
but one cannot expect anything from fools.
If the learned do not stand against me,
what harm is there in madmen's rants?
From the day our forefathers left paradise,
our very nature has been home to fault.
O people, hear my words with understanding.
Unless you understand, you have no right to criticize!
Even if one word in ten is bad,
do not launch into an attack, let it go!
Only a fool hears exquisite verse with head bowed in silence;*
only if he finds a word out of place, does he run to catch it out.

43. A story sweet as nectar I will sing to you:
O experts in love, pay attention and listen!
Such juicy matters only connoisseurs know,*
tasteless stuff is tossed out by them.
Termites run away from wood without juice;
will camels eat cane without any sugar?
Whatever has *rasa*, is enjoyed as such,
and the man who does not have the taste
will find even the tasteful tasteless.
Many tastes are found in the world, O connoisseurs!
But listen: I shall describe love, the royal savour of savours.

The End of the Prologue.

THE STORY OF MANOHAR AND MADHUMĀLATĪ

The Birth of Manohar

44. A story first from the age of Dvāpar*
I now recount in words in the Kali age.
The fort of Kanaigiri, fair 'city of gold',

was the shadow of paradise on earth.
Its King was Sūrajbhānu, 'light of the sun',
famed through the nine regions and the seven continents.
Countless were his horses and elephants,
matchless his grain, his wealth, his pomp and splendour.
But now his life's sunlight grew pale and weak,
no son of his rose to shed new light.
God's grace had given him plenty: grain, treasures, horses, and elephants.
But day and night his heart and mind were filled with longing for a son.

45. In the age of Kali, a son is a man's second life.
Without a son, life and birth are destroyed.
A mother and father can enjoy the world
only if a son carries on their name.
Without a son, who recalls them after death?
Without a son, who gives rice-balls for the ancestors?*
Worldly life is a waste without a son.
A son is a lamp to dispel the world's darkness.
All this is true for a good son.
May God preserve families from bad sons!
A bad son is like a sixth finger growing on one's hand:
keep it and it is infamous, cut it off and it pains.

46. To Kanaigiri came a great ascetic,
people went to pray at his feet.
After them, came the King himself,
washed his feet, raised the water to his head.
'The Creator is kind to have let me meet you.
Whatever I have asked for, God has always granted.
All my prayers have now been answered.
I have only one wish in my heart
which you may well be able to fulfil.'
When the holy man was deep in meditation, all the people went back home.
Only the King stayed on in the forest, serving faithfully at his feet.

47. Day and night the King served him devotedly.
He stayed awake all night, did not sleep by day.
He forgot hunger, thirst, and the ease of sleep,
and stood always in the holy man's service.
When fully twelve years had passed,
the ascetic opened his eyes and saw him.
'Who are you, in the form of a human?
Why are you standing here?'
'I am the King of this city.
I have served you all of twelve years.
Treasure, horses, and elephants I have, queens and riches and stores of arms.
But God did not grant me a son: I cannot cross to the farther shore.'

48. When he heard the King's entreaty,
the holy man was happy and blessed him,
'Listen, O protector of the earth!
The Lord has granted you a son.'
He cooked some food and with great joy,
gave to the King a chosen morsel.
'Give this to your favourite rani,
the one you love the most.'
The King raised the morsel to his head,
touched the ascetic's feet and went home.
The King went to his favourite Queen and told her, 'Eat this,
bathe and purify yourself, then withdraw from here.'

49. In his old age, the King's despair
became transformed into hope.
To the royal house the Lord gave new hope,
and the King rejoiced, expecting his heir.
In the Queen's tenth month,
when the Twins had entered Aries,
the mighty birth took place.
The sun was in the seventh house
and the moon was in the fifth.
Venus was stationed in the tenth,

while Jupiter was in the ninth.
When, on the tenth night, he was born,
Saturn looked down at the baby's face.
He was the image of the God of Love,* his parents' support and born fortunate.
The Prince was the shining light of his clan, born at an auspicious conjunction.

The Astrologers' Prediction

50. With the dawn, the pandits came,
to count the planets and cast his horoscope.
They thought hard and assessed his qualities,
predicted that he would be a great king,
'Gods and sages will salaam at his door,
all the kings of the world will serve him.
He will be talented, intelligent, and generous,
a hero in battle, powerful and proven.
He will be kind, profound and merciful,
and will understand the suffering of others.
The auspicious line of Rudra is on his neck, head, and feet; his sign is Leo.
He will be the shining lamp of his line. Name him Manohar, 'heart-enchanting'.

51. 'In his fourteenth year, on the ninth day
of the bright half of the eleventh month,
when the sun is in his birth sign
and the moon is in the seventh house,
he will meet his beloved, the love of his life.
On the night between Wednesday and Thursday,
the pain of love will be born in his heart.
The lovers will be parted and the Prince,
suffering the pain of love-in-separation,
will wander as a yogi for one whole year.
After that he will be a king in all his births,
thus do the stars predict.
His horoscope has auspicious signs, but some of the planets are hostile.

At the age of fourteen, the Prince's heart will be consumed with grief.'

The City Celebrates

52. On the sixth night after the Prince's birth,*
trumpets sounded in celebration.
Every house in the city rejoiced.
Joy and enthusiasm filled every home,
in every alley, the drums of happiness rang out.
People heard the news and ran to the palace,
all thirty-six serving castes* congratulated the King.
Maidens sang songs in ecstasies of joy,
fair young women with musk on their brows,
bodies anointed with sandal and aloes,*
adorned with necklaces on their breasts,
lips stained with betel,* vermilion on their heads;*
everywhere there was tumult, celebration.
In every house and every lane, the city rang with happiness.
Everyone sang Dhrupada and Dhruva* verses, in voices sweet and fine.

53. Joy and festivity filled the royal house.
Every subject received a gift of clothes.
To all his kin the King sent horses and silken robes,
and all the farmers in the land
were freed of taxes for the year.
And all who were unhappy in city and country,
the King made happy again through his gifts.
All the different kinds of celebrations
defy description with the poet's tongue.
Shops were hung with rare silks. Musk, incense, and camphor
perfumed the streets; young women adorned their heads with vermilion.

54. On the twelfth day, a great feast was held,
to which the whole city was invited.

The King himself seated and fed the poor,
and horses were sent as presents to his kin.
Many were the beggars who came to his door,
grew fat on the feast served on plaintain leaves.
To the citizens of the thirty-six castes,
the King gave out the birthing gifts.
Bards returned home with fine horses,
their wives with silken saris.
To celebrate the Prince's birth, the King made gifts of gold and silver,
food, riches, horses, elephants, jewels and pearls, until his treasury was bare.

The Prince Grows Up

55. The King found five well-born nurses,
and seven maids to play with the baby.*
Five times a day they cooked ambrosial food,
and day by day the royal Prince grew tall.
Like a flowering branch in spring,
he blossomed on a diet of warm milk.
The King and Queen rejoiced over the baby,
a greater joy than either heart could bear.
Every second, the King hugged the baby.
He gave away endless wealth for his sake.
The King revelled happily over his son, the joy of his declining years.
The days were spent in fun and frolic, the nights in joyous celebration.

56. The Prince grew older, delighting
in pleasures both day and night.
When he was five, he began to walk.
The King appointed a pandit as his teacher
at whose feet he was to learn.
Putting much wealth before the pandit,
the King said: 'This child is yours
as much as he is my son.

Give him knowledge, do not stint,
and if I feel you accomplish this,
I will serve you every day myself.'
    The King fell at the pandit's feet, entreating him, 'Make no mistakes,
    Nurture him with the love you and I have known since childhood.'

57. The pandit taught the Prince well
that each word had several meanings.*
He taught him yoga and the science of sex,
drew pictures and explained their meanings.
Soon the Prince became so clever
he could explain many levels of mystery in scripture.
He taught him the true meanings*
of the *Yogasūtra** and the *Amarakośa*,*
poetics and prosody and the *Kokaśāstra*.*
Who could match the Prince
in grammar, astrology or the *Gītā*,*
in the arts of meaning, poetry or song?
    The Prince studied many other books of knowledge and practice,
    he became so skilled that no one could defeat him in debate.

58. The Prince was occupied with learning and the arts
until he reached the age of twelve.
Then he took up the science of war,
in all the forms the world had known.
He was adept at sword and shield,
dagger, spear, and the skill of wrestling.
At bow and arrow he had no equal.
He could shatter a pearl tied on one's hair.
When he took up his bow of horn,
the celestial rainbow hid itself in shame.
    A hero in battle, full of knowledge and virtue, adept in all the fourteen sciences,
    he was great in fortune and wisdom, the image of the maddening God of Love.

Manohar Become King

59. Now do I sing of the events of his twelfth year.
Spontaneously this thought arose within the King:
'I am old and cannot keep my health for long.
Let me take the Prince and crown him king.'
He summoned his subjects and close family,
as many relatives as lived within the city,
and took counsel with them all:
'I am pale and yellow with age
like the rays of the setting sun.
If the council agrees today, I shall entrust
the running of this kingdom to the Prince.
A man's begetting a son in old age, a woman's fresh youth without a husband—
who can control them? They are like springtime in a barren land.

60. 'What use have I for property now?
If you agree, I will make the Prince your king.
I would be free of the worries of the world.
My son can delight in the pleasures of kingship.
If you allow it, I will crown him King.
Then I can chant the name of Hari,
and seek to cross to the further shore.'
The populace, his relatives, his vassals and courtiers,
all were overjoyed to hear the Prince's name.
Everyone was delighted by the King's address,
and began to celebrate with great enthusiasm.
Festivities resounded in all directions, through the seven continents and the nine regions,
when the King announced that he would grant Prince Manohar the realm.

61. On Thursday, in the sign of the Twins,
in the bright half of the month of Caitra,*
when the moon was cool and clear,
the King called the Prince to him.
When the Prince arrived the King stood up,
and the Prince bowed and touched his feet.

The King embraced him, then seated him on the throne.
His father was first to pay him homage,
and then the entire kingdom bowed to him.
　　The King took off his crown and placed it on Manohar's head.
　　The city erupted with joy and enthusiasm; the whole world blessed the new King.

62. All the nobles and vassals there assembled,
at royal command bent their heads to the Prince.
The news was heard in the seven continents
and the nine regions of the earth,
from sunrise to sunset his fame resounded.
The word rang out through the circle of the earth:
by throne and realm he was the ruler of the world.
The triple world followed his orders,
and acknowledged him as their Lord.
The Prince's writ ran throughout
the length and breadth of the Creator's universe.
　　From east to west, the entire earth—gods, men, sages and celestials—
　　obeyed all of the Prince's commands and served him constantly.

The Prediction Fulfilled

63. The Prince lived happily for a long time,
all the days of happiness his horoscope foretold.
After fourteen years and eleven months
came the dawn that destroyed his pleasure and play.
Then the sad days ruled by hostile planets
came and engulfed the Prince.
The sun was bright in the sign of Leo.
The moon, decked out with the sixteen adornments,*
had entered the circle of the heavens.
on a night between Wednesday and Thursday
as the Creator had written in the book of fate,
the fatal blow fell on the Prince.

lines of loss and gain and sorrow written on one's
orehead
not be erased by all three worlds, even acting all
together.

64. Now listen to the origin of love's savour,
and how the Prince became mad with the wine of love.
One day, dancers came from a foreign land,
who performed the amazing dances of the south.
The Prince had always loved dancing,
and had them dance at his court day and night.
When he saw their bewitching performance,
he sent silken robes and invited them to his assembly.
Sūrajbhānu came and took his seat,
together with all the nobles of the realm.
Midnight fell as they watched the dancing, and the old
King grew sleepy.
The company rose, the beautiful dancers left, and the
Prince retired to bed.

65. Who could describe the Prince's bed or couch?
I must tell only the tale that's to be told.
The moment the Prince was united with his bed,
drowsiness descended, sweet sleep overcame him.
Sleep seized his eyelids which had stayed apart.
Like yogis who practise sexual union,
or parted lovers, his lashes came together.
God created sleep to be the greatest comfort,
for eyes which are free from the grit of love.
How could the Maker in his wisdom call love happiness
and ease?
How can I describe love, that lodges in the eye, except as
painful grit?

66. The happy are intoxicated with happiness,
while the sad grieve in their sorrows,
but pleasure and pain both fly away
from eyes which are visited by sleep.
Sleep can be both good and bad:

he alone is awake who knows the difference.*
The world should not criticize sleep, my friend,
many have attained perfection through it.
Only the man who knows truly how to sleep,
can taste the joy of the wine of love.
  The true sleeper behaves alike in sleep and when he is awake.
  I do not praise that sleep, however, which kills a man as he lives.

67. O ignorant man, sleep not that sleep
that makes a man lifeless while yet he lives.
Sleep to the world is a lesser death,*
but excessive sleep is truly death itself.
Just as the delights and kingdoms of our sleep
amount to nothing when we wake,
just as the inspirations of our dreams
prove false on awaking,
both sleeping and waking within this world
should be regarded as unreal.
  A raging fire is this world's sleep, a flame which destroys all it touches.
  Sleep not that sleep, you fool, which will destroy all your capital.

68. O God, where did I get to, where am I?
I was telling you one thing, but said another instead.
I was about to tell the story of the Prince,
but sleep intervened and carried me away.
I return now to the story, so listen to how
the Prince was overwhelmed by sweet sleep,*
and how some nymphs chanced to gather round
the Prince's bed as he lay there sleeping.
The nymphs were amazed to see in him
the precious, beautiful form of a celestial.
  'We are heavenly nymphs, and he is a man, so he is no concern of ours,
  but let us marry him to the loveliest bride between the east and the west.'

69. 'From east to west, to the world's edges,
what place is there that we have not seen?
We know the whole world well.
We must find a match worthy of this Prince.'
One praised Saurāṣṭra and Gujarāt,
while another told of the Isle of Singhala.*
They went through all three worlds,
but could not find a beauty to match him.
Then one nymph stood up and said:
'There is a maiden worthy of this Prince.
Vikram Rāi, the valiant king of the city of Mahāras,*
has a virgin daughter
named Madhumālatī, 'night-flowering jasmine', whose
beauty eclipses the sun and moon.'

70. When they heard her, the nymphs were delighted,
but one said the Prince was more beautiful than she.
Thinking it over together, they announced
that the Prince and Princess should be compared.
One nymph said: 'Let's take the Prince there.'
Another said: 'Let's bring the Princess here.'
A third pointed out that these comings and goings
would take up the entire night.
So, they cast the Prince into a charmed sleep,
and lifted his bed up into the air.
They took him to her as she lay happily asleep, the light of
the triple world.
His bed they placed next to hers, to see side by side their
beautiful bodies.

71. Words cannot describe the sight before them:
shamed, the sun hid in the daytime,
and the moon hid herself by night.
In the face of such astonishing beauty
the nymphs were struck dumb, overcome by shame.
Looking at the one, they saw such loveliness!
But when they glanced at the other,
they found beauty beyond compare.
Both were perfect and complete in beauty.

Neither was less lovely than the other.
The Prince was fair without blemish,
while the face of that most alluring maiden
displayed all sixteen attributes of beauty.
  The more the nymphs looked at them, the lovelier they appeared.
  God had made them perfectly, matchless in the triple world.

72. The nymphs then declared that both
were perfect in beauty,* and neither
was more excellent than the other.
'If God should let them come together,
the three worlds would echo with celebration.
To look upon them is to taste the joy
of yogis in the state of mystical union.*
Lord, life of the three worlds,
please grant that they come together in love.
We have searched creation's three worlds,
and nowhere is the equal of these two.
  He is the sun and she the moon. She is the sun and he the moon.*
  If love were born between them, the last trump would sound through the triple world.*

73. 'God Himself incarnated these two*
as darlings and true lovers in this world.
Since we have come at foot's pace to this city,
let's go and play in the marvellous mango-grove,
and visit the garden of a thousand trees
while these two remain here fast asleep.'
At this the nymphs set off for the garden.
The Prince awoke and stretched lazily.
He saw a bed placed beside his own
on which a beautiful princess lay.
  The sun was not more brilliant, nor the moon her match in beauty.
  Perfect in beauty's sixteen qualities, youth herse head resting on her arm.

The Prince's Vision

lace, silken drapes were hung all around,
between golden pillars studded with gems.
The chamber was like the heavens:
the maiden's face shone like the moon,
and the precious stones were stars.
Her band of handmaidens were the Pleiades,*
her couch a heavenly swinging cradle.
She slept naturally and peacefully,
as if her form were moulded to the bed.
To describe her bed is beyond my powers,
so I must continue this juicy tale of pleasure.
    The maiden was adorned in all the sixteen ways, and lay in sweet and tranquil sleep.
    When the Prince saw her, his senses fled, and the light of his intelligence left him.

75. When the Prince looked again at her,
lying asleep so naturally, peacefully,
he awoke and returned to consciousness.
Astonished, he looked all around in amazement:
'O Lord, whose city is this? Whose this palace?
Who is this that sleeps here so tranquilly?
Blessed is the man for whom the Creator
cast this maiden in bodily form.'
The moment that he saw Madhumālatī
she possessed his heart completely.
His soul bowed down to her beauty.
Seeing her lying in sweet sleep,
the fire of love engulfed his body,
consuming him utterly, from top to toe.
    Like a lotus opening towards the sun, he blossomed as he saw her face.
    Primeval love, like a new green shoot, sprouted in the Prince's heart.

76. As he beheld the loveliness of her form,
he fainted away every second,

only to collect himself the next.
He was astonished to see such beauty:
'O God, who is she? Where am I?
Such a beautiful form, and so adorned!
A glimpse of this maiden's face,
would confound the greatest sages.
How can I describe her form and features?
She has entered my heart in a thousand ways.
Her beauty has thrown my soul into confusion.
My life flies from me like a restless leaf from a tree.'
As the Prince observed her lovely form and adornments, he found fulfilment,
yet his thirsty eyes could not leave the contemplation of her beauty.

Madhumālatī Described

Her Parting

77. Let me first tell of the parting in her hair,
difficult of ascent as the path to heaven.
As he looked at her parting and her flowing locks
he kept straying from the path and returning to it.
Strikingly lovely was the parting on her head,
like the keen edge of a sword stained with blood.
Who could traverse the path of that parting?
At every step, ringlets and curls set snares for the traveller.
All who passed were killed outright,
and therefore the path appears red with blood.
Of all who saw the parting of this blessed girl, so like a sword's keen edge,
who is left to describe it, since she cleaves all who look on in two?

78. A ray of sunlight was her beautiful parting.
When it had won all the world, it moved heavenwards.
It was not a parting, but the market-place of heaven,
the path of the sun's and moon's rising and setting.
Where did this stream of nectar flow from,
the source for her moon-face's inexhaustible radiance?

The Prince lost his soul when he saw her lovely parting,
he was drawn to it like moths to the lamp-flame.
Did not the Creator himself place it on her head?
To what then shall I compare it?
    In the dark night it shone like lightning against the blackest clouds,
    as if fallen from the sky and come to rest on the maiden's head.

Her Hair

79. Her scattered locks were poisonous serpents
gliding easily over the pillows in excitement,
gem-bearing snakes,* moving so quickly,
viciously, full of deadly venom.
Just as the night grew radiant
when she revealed her face,
the day darkened as she let down her locks.
They were not tresses but the sorrows of lovers
become the adornments of her head.
Whoever in this world saw her locks,
lost all awareness of his own condition.
    When this blessed virgin let loose her hair, the world was shrouded in darkness,
    the God of Love spread out his net to snare the souls of grieving lovers.

80. Did you know why the world
was filled with such sweet fragrance?
Did the musk deer open its pod?
Or did Madhumālatī let loose her hair?
Did you know why the breeze from the south
blew in the world with the scent of sandal?*
One day this lovely girl set free her hair,
and all the wind gods came to dance attendance.
From that day the southern breeze
has wandered sadly, longing for her,
yet even today his hope is unfulfilled.
    Ever since he blew around Madhumālatī's fragrant dark locks,

the southern breeze remains constantly sad, grieving day
and night.

Her Forehead

81. Her forehead was spotless as the moon
on the second night of a month,
shining through nine regions and three worlds.
Beads of perspiration shone brilliantly on her face,
as if the Pleiades had engulfed the moon.
A black spot of musk adorned her brow,
as if the moon had fallen into the demon Rāhu's power.*
So beautiful was her alluring brow,
the moon in shame retreated to the heavens.
Brilliant in a thousand aspects, her brow
shone splendidly, radiantly, above the world.
Her moon-face below, her dark locks above: what an
image of passion!
Night locked in embrace with the moon, with the night
surmounting.

Her Eyebrows

82. Love happily took in his hands his bow.*
Using his strength, he broke it into two halves.
Without any alchemy, he put them point to point,
arranging them as Madhumālatī's eyebrows.
How beautifully her eyebrows graced her face,
as if Love's bow had been embodied on earth.
Had this enchanting maiden arched her brows,
Indra would have unstrung his rainbow in shame.
Love conquered the triple world with his bow;
then he brought it as a gift to Madhumālatī.
Vanquishing the triple world, the bow came to rest
when no warrior remained.
Who could have won against a glance which pierced the
heart right through?

Her Eyes

83. Her intoxicating eyes, black, white and red,
pierced the heart when her glances struck.

Large lively eyes, keen, crookedly seductive,
with eyelids covering them like wagtail's wings.*
Her eyes were hunters who took countless lives,
then lay at rest, their bows beneath their heads.
They were like fish playing face to face,*
or two wagtails fighting on the wing.
Her eyes were murderous, thirsty for life,
yet on seeing them one wished to die.
They were a wondrous paradox that could not be resolved:
her eyes were does that lay fearlessly, each one beneath a hunter's bow.

Her Eyelashes

84. Her eyelashes were arrows steeped in poison.
When a glance struck, venom overcame the heart.
The man who confronted the arrows of her lashes,
reduced the pores of his body to a sieve.
When her glance and lashes pierced a heart,
it turned both blood and heart to water.
When another's glance met hers,
two knives were sharpened blade on blade.
Who could win against the arrows of her lashes?
With every glance, she let off a hundred shafts.
Pierced by her charming glances, who could protect his life any more?
Seeing the lashes of this blessed girl, who could wish for anything but to die?

Her Nose

85. The beauty of her nose defies description.
I searched the three worlds, did not find its likeness.
A parrot's beak, a sword's keen edge,
a sesamum flower: these do not describe it.
Nor could it be Udayācala,* the eastern hill.
Her nose is the channel for the sun and moon.*
No one could approach her nose in loveliness.
Sweet scents sustained it day and night.

To what shall I compare her nose
which the sun and moon themselves fanned with air?
With what qualities shall I describe this blessed maiden's nose?
Day and night it was fanned with cool air by sun and moon alike.

Her Cheeks

86. Two cheeks adorned her lovely face,
rich in colour, full of rare delight.
I am bereft of reason, words fail me.
How can I describe her cheeks?
Who could practise austerities harsh enough
to enjoy such priceless treasures?
Her beautiful cheeks were fashioned by God.
What simile could describe their loveliness?
What can we poor humans accomplish?
Even the gods bow down before her cheeks.
Gods, men, sages, and celestial of musicians—all lose their reason before her cheeks.
On seeing their loveliness, even Lord Śiva's* concentration strays.

Her Lips

87. Her lovely lips dripped with nectar.
Inflamed by love, they thirsted for blood.
They were tender, juicy, red in colour,
*bimba** fruits placed against the moon.
No, no, this simile does not suffice:
God squeezed the moon's nectar to form them.
Her lips, full of nectar, were yet untasted.
When the Prince saw them, he felt
his life drain away, and cried aloud:
'When will the Lord grant my life be restored?'
Her lips, flame-coloured, were known as a sea of nectar by the world.
Seeing nectar and flame together, marvellous, set fire to one's life breath.

…nt teeth defied description,
their shining dazzled the glance.
When she smiled slightly in sleep,
lightning flashed from the heavens.
When her lips parted, her teeth shone:
the sages of the triple world were blinded
and lost all recollection of themselves.
Mars, Venus, Jupiter, and Saturn
were stunned by the radiance of her teeth.
They all disappeared, who knows where,
and hid themselves within the moon.
    If someone describes this as God's self-disclosure, then understand the nature of God:
    the Lord is hidden in this world, and no one has ever seen Him.

Her Mole

89. The lovely mole upon her face
could not be described by any simile.
The Prince's eyes were enamoured of its beauty.
They became transfixed, and would not leave it.
'It is not a mole, but the reflection of my eye,
in which her face appears ever more lovely.
Her face is a clear, unblemished mirror,
in it my eye's shadow appears as a beauty-spot.
The pupil of my eye is soft and dark.
On her pure and spotless face it has fallen as a mole.'
    The maiden's lovely face was a stainless, shining mirror
    in which the reflection of the Prince's eye appeared as a mole.

Her Tongue

90. Sweet as nectar was the tongue
within the maiden's mouth.
It spoke in tones of pleasure and delight.
Even the dead would savour with joy

her words as sweet as nectar.
Whoever heard her priceless gems of words,
themselves spoke sweetly in the world.
Who has performed such severe austerities
to be able to touch his tongue with hers?
Her sweet tongue, so rich in all delight,
moved languidly within the maiden's mouth,
as if it had passed between two hostile foes,
and reached the abode of pleasure.
Sweet as nectar, full of pleasure and delight, was the tongue within her alluring mouth.
Within her moon-like radiant face, her tongue was an intoxicating spring of nectar.

Her Ears

91. Her lovely ears were shells of limpid pearl,
the heavenly planets were her earring studs.
Her pendants were encrusted with diamonds and gems.
On one ear she had hung the sun,
on the other, the sphere of Jupiter.
With two luminous orbs on either side,
her face rose like the moon between two stars.
What man did God make fortunate enough
to hold the attention of those ears, to speak to her?
The demon planet Rāhu had been split in two,
and placed as ears to protect her moon-face.
Her orb-like pendants shone luminously, radiant with Viṣṇu's* light.
If Rāhu had not been afraid of them, he would surely have devoured this moon.*

Her Neck

92. What simile best describes her neck?
It was surely turned on the All-Maker's wheel.
Who bears the mark of high destiny,
to sacrifice his life on the saw at Prayāg?*
For whom did the Creator fashion her neck?
Blessed the man who knows the joy

of embracing Madhumālatī's lovely neck.
How auspicious the life, how blessed the birth,
of the man for whom the Lord created her neck.
After looking at the triple crease of her neck,*
how could anyone's body stay conscious?
The three lines looked exquisite on the blessed maiden's neck—
for which great ascetic was her beautiful neck made by the Lord of the worlds?

Her Arms

93. Viśvakarman, the All-Maker,*
shaped her graceful arms himself.
For all my searching, I found no equal.
Her arms were lovely, strong, and powerful—
on seeing them mighty heroes sacrificed themselves
for this beautiful, powerless woman.
Her wrists were unique, matchless,
the God of Love formed them on his lathe.
Beneath them were her flawless palms,
pure as crystal filled with deep red vermilion.*
So many grieving lovers had she killed
that all ten fingernails shone red with blood.
Her lovely arms, so strong and graceful, vanquished all three worlds.
Blessed the man whose fortunate neck her beautiful arms embraced.

Her Breasts

94. So shapely were her precious breasts,
seeing them threw the triple world into confusion.
Her breasts were firm and hard to the touch
for the Lord had put them near her stony heart.
When another heart should touch her heart,
their nipples would rise up to honour him.
Youth herself plucked for her two wood-apples,*
new fruit, perfect, as yet unripe, from the tree.
When the lord of her life entered her heart,

her nipples rose up shyly and came out.
Her lovely firm breasts, with dark-tipped nipples, too proud to bow before anyone,
were like two kings sharing a boundary line who would never come together.

95. Pointed, sharp and unscrupulously seductive,
her breasts entered lovers' hearts on sight.
Lovely they looked, with darkened arrows on their tips.
Famous as brave fighters through the three worlds,
they wanted to dispute the boundary line in war,
but then a necklace came between them.
Her breasts were mighty warriors in war.
When they heard of battle or slaughter,
at once they came to adorn the battlefield.
Their nature was to strike, crooked or straight.
In battle they always advanced, never retreated.
Her breasts' perverse cruelty does not astonish the poet; they pained
not her on whom they grew, but those who looked on their loveliness.

Her Waist

96. The line of hair on her navel
was a venomous serpent released
from its lair, roaming dangerously.
When it fell into her navel's pool,
it curled around, unable to climb out.
Her slender stomach was graceful, alluring,
the Lord created it without an inside.
Seeing the narrowness of her waist,
one feared the buttocks' weight would make it snap.
So slender and fine was her waist,
that hands could not grasp it at all.
It was so delicate it would break at a touch.
Had not the three folds of her stomach supported it, her waist
would surely have snapped from the weight of her hips below.

Her Thighs and Legs

97. The triple fold on her waist suggested
the Maker held her there while shaping her.
For fear of immodesty before my elders,
I shall not describe her intoxicating treasury of love.
The sight of her hips aroused the mind,
excited passion in the body in an instant.
Seeing her thighs plunged one's being
into utter confusion, struck one dumb.
Pink and white, softly blooming,
lotuses could not equal her legs.
Her legs were well-shaped like a plantain tree, golden, upside down,
or the trunk of an elephant, but truly I feel ashamed to offer a likeness.

Madhumālatī Awakes

98. Who could describe her sleeping on her couch,
without ornament, coquetry, or sidelong glances?
Matchless women the Lord has made in the past,
beautiful by nature and needing no adornment,
but here was creation's auspicious symbol of womanhood.
Shyly, her body met Love's mad promptings.
Seeing her sleeping so peacefully on her bed,
the pain of restless passion awoke in the Prince's body.
Spontaneously his consciousness was freed of all attachments;
separation came and overwhelmed his soul.
Seeing Love's bow in splendour on her brow, his senses left him instantly.
'Blessed is that man's life for whom love is born in this maiden's heart.'

99. I am sorry to describe her as she sleeps.
Why don't I wake her up to recount her beauty?
Let me awaken her and have her speak words of *rasa*
so I may take pleasure in hearing her sweet speech.
The maiden raised her arms above her head.

Lazily she yawned and stretched her limbs.
Her eyes awakened and became alert
like a hunter's arrows raised in ambush.
When a natural frown appeared upon her brow,
it seemed the God of Love had drawn his bow.
    Her eyebrows were arched like the drawn bow of Kāmadeva,
    and the triple world trembled in anticipation of her arrows.

100. That darling Princess awoke and looked about, astonished.
She became alert and glanced around her,
a doe alarmed, sensing lions and tigers on the hunt.
Then the Princess, looking more carefully,
saw another bed spread out beside her.
She saw a mighty Prince lying upon it.
She was astounded when she saw his form
and, though confused, gathered up her courage.
    Though that beautiful, excellent maiden was still extremely overcome,
    she composed herself and, sitting up, took courage to address the Prince.

101. The lovely maiden opened her matchless lips
to speak words as sweet as nectar.
In pleasant and delightful tones she asked:
'Who are you, O god-like Prince?
Tell me your name, my lord.
Through what power did you come here?
For where this maiden dwells
even the wind is not allowed to enter.
I adjure you speak the truth about yourself.
    Are you a god from Indra's heaven? Are you a serpent from Hell?
    Or are you a human from this mortal world? Tell me and resolve my confusion.

102. 'Are you a demon or some ghostly apparition?
Can this body of yours be human?

Did you get miraculous power through a guru's words?
Or did you apply magic kohl to your eyes?
Is it a spell which has given you this power?
Did your guru make you drink some special herb?
How did you come so silently to my chamber,
were you borne on a vehicle by the winds of the mind?
On all four sides the doorways are impassable
and countless guards lie awake all around.
Seven circular paths lead to this chamber.* Many brave men stay awake to guard them.
How have you come to this place to which even the wind has no access?

103. 'By God I adjure you speak the truth:
tell me how these things have come to pass.
Did someone bring you here by force,
and so confuse you that you cannot speak?
I see that you are human in every way.
On your forehead shines the jewel of fortune.
But why are you so silent? Will you not speak?
Seeing you here has quite bewildered me.
My soul is overcome with astonishment at seeing you.
Gather your courage and sit up; do not be afraid.
Tell me, I beseech you, the truth about yourself.'

104. When he heard these words sweet as nectar,
the Prince's body became immortal.
When he saw her he was perplexed and astonished,
and lost all consciousness of himself.
His heart was struck by pointed arrows,
as though her glances had been sharpened on a stone.
As sugar instantly dissolves in water,
so did the Prince's soul surrender its selfhood.
So lovely was her form he could not look on it directly,
and the doors of his two eyes would not stay open.
Seeing her beauty his eyes were confused, unable to look at her directly.
From his eyes flowed tears of blood, and his eyelids refused to open.*

Prince Manohar Explains

105. 'Listen, best of maidens, and I will tell you
what you have so naturally asked.
The city of Kanaigiri is a wonderful place.
The whole world knows my father, King Sūrajbhānu.
My own name is Prince Manohar.
I am of the Rāghava line.* I belong to Kanaigiri.
I had scarcely closed my eyes in sleep,
and now I see I've woken up here.
I do not know who brought me here
for there to occur a meeting of glances.
My two eyes are captivated by your beauty, and I do not see any release for them.
For the more an elephant struggles in the mud, the deeper he sinks in the quagmire.

106. 'Sleep has only just left and I'm awake.
The sight of your beauty has robbed me of my life.
It must be merits previously earned
that have brought me to see your face.
Maybe in a former birth I sacrificed my life,
and that merit has brought me here
to see this vision of your beauty.
Or else it was my good fortune to fulfil
my soul's desire by pilgrimage to Prayāg,*
or even to give my head to the saw.
I have found you, a woman,
as the result of my good actions.
Blessed are those merits of my previous birth.
The arrows of love have entered my heart and my eyes have become enraptured.
Body and mind, my soul, my youth, all love you and will never leave you.

107. 'I look at the full moon of your face today
as the effect of merits from a former life.
The arrows of love have struck my heart.
My soul is caught in the net of separation.

aiden, only the man whose forehead has
e mark of fortune earned in a former life
will be rewarded with a sight of you.
Impelled by love, O Princess, I beseech you:
who is the King whose darling child you are?
Tell me your name. Who is your father?
Of what land is he the sovereign?
For my eyes, which see your dazzling beauty, I sacrifice myself.
For my ears, which hear your sweet wondrous words, I lay down my life.'

Madhumālatī Replies

108. Then that blessed maiden opened her mouth
to speak in her delightful nectar-like voice.
As she delivered words full of *rasa*,
her teeth shone with astounding brilliance.
In the three worlds, everyone was dazzled.
Hearing her words, the Prince fainted:
consciousness left him and intelligence fled.
The sight of her lips plundered his senses,
but her words revived the lover again.
I cannot describe the power of her mouth:
even if one were yearning to die,
her words would bring one back to life.
How can I describe her lips? No words come to my mouth.
They can kill the living if they wish, or restore the dead to life.

109. When the unconscious Prince revived,
one moment he was conscious,
the next he'd faint away again.
His soul could not be contained one moment,
the next it would return fully aware to his body.
hours his soul re-entered his body.
uickened to full consciousness.
, with heart aware,

to his ears came her words, sweet as nectar.
As he heard his darling's words of pleasure,
joy spread through his body's eight limbs.*
When that passionate maiden began to speak her words, full of *rasa* and delight,
all eight parts of the Prince's body became ears to listen to them.

110. The Princess began her story, full of savour,
like a night lotus blossoming for love of the moon.
'Mahāras,' she said, 'is a city without equal.
Vikram Rāi, my father, is its mighty king.
My name, Madhumālatī, is radiant
both in this world and the hereafter.
I, a maiden, am my father's only child.
In this palace I am the darling of the King.'
But of all the words the maiden spoke,
not one remained within the Prince's mind.
Although he tried to understand, her words robbed him of intelligence.
Like salt dissolving easily in water, he spontaneously lost his selfhood.

111. When awareness and intelligence returned,
the Prince sat up but found he'd lost his self.
The arrows of love entered his eyes.
He fell unconscious at the Princess's feet.
Then that most lovely of maidens fanned him,
and sprinkled nectar water on his face.
As she looked at the Prince's face,
compassion overcame her, and with her sari's border,
she wiped the tears from the Prince's eyes.
She felt pity and love was born in her heart.
From her feet she raised his head up high.
When the Prince again sat up and his consciousness steadied,
the blessed maiden in tones of nectar asked him how he was.

112. The King's dear daughter gently asked the Prince:
'Now that you're restored, collect yourself and speak.
Without fear, tell me why your body shakes?
Say why your spirit is distressed,
and why your body trembles so?
Why do you keep on losing consciousness?
I beg you by your father, tell me the truth.
Be not afraid: do not fear anyone,
but tell me why you keep on fainting.
I ask you naturally, out of love: who has deprived you of intelligence?
I have revived you with nectar, why are you not conscious of yourself?'

Manohar Declares his Love

113. 'Listen, dearest one!' the Prince then said,
'In a former life God created love between you and me.
Now that he has brought us into the world,
I have given you my soul in exchange for sorrow.
It is not just today that I grieve for you:
I have known this sorrow from the first creation.
The grief I feel separated from you was revealed
the day the Creator fashioned this body of mine.
Into my body's clay, O most alluring of women,
God mixed the pure water of your love.*
From my former lives I have known the water of your love,
since, kneading it into my clay, the Creator formed this body.*

114. 'I lost my all when I took on the pain of your love.
My soul is yours and yours is mine.
Before life even entered my body
God revealed this sorrow to me.*
If I do not speak the truth,
may God increase in me the pain of loving you.
I have given myself to this pain completely.
For this grief I would sacrifice a thousand pleasures.

How can my tongue call this suffering
when the forms of sorrow give so much joy?
  The pleasures of four aeons cannot equal even a moment of this grief.
  Who can tell what bliss I may enjoy through the blessing of sorrow?

115. 'Suffering overwhelmed mankind
at the very beginning of creation.
The lotus of Brahma* was the home of grief.
The day that sorrow entered creation,
the soul learnt of its own existence.
The pain I feel for you was not born today,
but has been my companion from the beginning.
Now I carry the burden of this grief,
sacrificing all the pleasures of now and hereafter.
I have given myself to you and accepted this pain.
Through dying I have tasted immortality.
  O Madhumālatī, the pain of love for you brings happiness to the world.
  Blessed is the life of the man in whose heart is born the pain of love for you.

116. 'I have heard that on the day the world was born,
the bird of love was released to fly.*
It searched all the three worlds
but could not find a fit resting place.
So it turned and entered the inmost heart,
favoured it and never flew elsewhere.
The three worlds asked it then:
"Why are you attached to the human heart?"
"Suffering", it replied, "is the only hope for humans.
Where there is sorrow, there I dwell."
  Wherever there is grief in the world, love has its dwelling.
  What can a poor man know of love whose heart does not know pain?'

117. 'You and I have always been together.
Always we have been a single body.
You and I both are one body,

ps of clay mixed in the same water.
e water flows in two streams,
p alone lights two homes.
One soul enters two bodies,
one fire burns in two hearths.
We were one but were born as two:
one temple with two doors.
We were one radiant light, one beautiful form, one soul and one body:
how can there be any doubt in giving oneself to oneself?

118. 'You are the ocean, I am your wave.
You are the sun, I the ray that lights the world.*
Do not think that you and I are separate:
I am the body, you are my dear life.
Who can part us, a single light in two forms?
I see everything through the eye of enlightenment.
Who knows how long we have known each other?
Today, O maiden, you do not recognize me.
Think back in your memory—
we knew each other on creation's first day.
When two lives are entwined together in the snare of love,
they recognize each other instantly when they take on bodily form.

119. 'Till now I have lived a soulless life,
but today, on seeing you, I have found my soul.
I knew you the moment that I saw you,
for this is the beauty that had held me in thrall.
This is the beauty that before was concealed.*
This is the beauty that now pervades creation.
This is the beauty that is Śiva and Śaktī.*
This is the beauty that is the soul of the three worlds.
This is the beauty that is manifest in many guises.
This is the beauty found alike in king and beggar.
This same beauty lives in all the three worlds: earth, heaven, and the world below.
This very same beauty I now see manifested, radiant upon your face.

120. 'This is the beauty revealed in countless forms.
This is the beauty unique in its myriad modes.
This is the beauty that is the light of every eye.
This is the beauty that is the pearl in every ocean.
This is the beauty of the fragrance of flowers.
This is the beauty of the pollen the bees enjoy.
This is the beauty of the sun and the moon.
This is the beauty that pervades the entire universe.
This is the beauty of the beginning,
this is the beauty of the end and beyond.
Contemplation of this beauty is true meditation.*
This beauty is manifest in countless states: in water, land, and on the earth's surface,
but only he can look on it who loses himself when he sees it.'

FEMALE METAPHORS FOR GOD

Madhumālatī's Reaction

121. As she listened to his words,
full of love's savour and feeling,
the maiden's soul was at once intoxicated.
Her heart delighted in the tale of love she heard,
and the love of a previous life
was kindled again in her memory.
Just as fragrance mingles with the breeze,
so did the two merge and become one body.
So powerful was the love that engulfed them
that the two came together as one life's breath.
Spontaneously, their souls united and could not be told apart.
When the image of that love from a former life entered into their inmost souls,
both sighed deeply from the heart, recalling their previous acquaintance.

122. Then, moved by love, the maiden smiled and said:
'You have made me mad with this talk of love.
I was so overcome I could not speak.
Hearing your words I tasted love's joys.

Certainly there is no difference between us:
we are one body, reflected twice.
My soul has found its place in your body,
and, through me, your name is manifest.
Mine is the beauty and your body is its mirror.*
I am the sun, you are its light in the world.
As lustre is to precious gems and jewels, so I am your essence and you are mine.
You and I are like brilliance and jewel, who can ever separate us?

123. 'Now, O Prince, listen to my words.
With love you have captured my life's light.
Your love, like the fragrance of the musk-deer,
permeates my heart and cannot be hidden.
Your words of love have confused me utterly.
Casting a spell upon my mind
you have robbed me of my soul.
There was only one soul in this body,
which you stole away from me.
Just as your soul is drunk with my love,
so is mine for you—only four times as much.
Do not think that men have greater claim to true love,
know that a maiden's true feeling is four times that of a man!'

Manohar is Roused but Madhumālatī is Prudent

124. The Prince heard her words so full of feeling.
Kāmadeva awakened and permeated his being.
Desire spread throughout his body.
Lust for worldly pleasure aroused him.
Passion engulfed him and his body trembled.
The lord of passion revealed himself,
as the Prince heard her words full of *rasa*.
His eyes grew red and shameless
as Kāmadeva arranged his army on two fronts.
Who in this world can win against
the conqueror who humbled Śiva?

When youth is fresh and desire intoxicates, when beauty is new and matchless,
when the loved one is near, tell me, how then can virtue be preserved?

125. The Prince turned pale and rampant was his desire.
His pulse raced and from his body came a sigh.
Pierced by the arrows of the God of Love,
he could contain himself no longer.
His hands reached out to the maiden's breasts.
Leaving his finely adorned bed,
the Prince sat on the lovely one's couch.
That excellent maiden stopped his hands
and rose and moved to the Prince's bed.
'O Prince,' she said, 'why should we sin?
Why should we disgrace our parents?
Who would destroy everything for one fleeting moment of pleasure?
In this world the slightest indiscretion brings disgrace upon a woman.

126. 'If a woman seeks to commit a sin,
in vain she destroys herself completely.
Womankind is the abode of sin.
But if a woman has a family,
then they will keep her from sinning.
Otherwise, who can contain her?
The clan is the only obstacle to sin.
Why become a sinner for a moment's pleasure?
Why sin and lose everything forever?
By sinning, who would himself wipe out
the gathered merits of former lives?
By doing acts of virtue everywhere one keeps one's good name clear.
Who would blacken his face pointlessly by entering the house of sin?

127. 'Listen, O Prince! I have one thing to say.
The right path is radiant in both worlds.

How can one whose heart is righteous
fall into the raging fire of sin?
Family and righteousness are both custodians,
I cannot disgrace my mother or father.
He who succumbs to a moment's temptation
has already reserved his place in hell.
But the man who stands by the truth,
even if he is on the path of sin,
will taste the heavenly fruit of immortality.*
> Those who love truth above all else give up this world and its worldly life.
> They abandon everything but never leave truth. Listen, Prince, to the essence of truth!*

128. 'The Lord, who brought you to this place
and ordained that our glances should meet,*
will steer us through our lives.
God will free us of sin, and give us
the treasure of right action.
Why commit sin and destroy our virtue?
Truth abandoned will only cause us regret.
Improper conduct brings disgrace;
to one's family, shame, to one's parents, abuse.
You and I must swear a true oath,
calling on Rudra, Brahma, and Hari as witnesses.
> Swear to me that you will be eternally true in love and I will swear the same.
> Then will the Lord protect our love constantly, in every birth, in every life.'

An Oath is Sworn

129. 'O royal Princess, hear my words.
I give you my word, I will be true.
Without you I have no life in this world,
fo[illegible] are the body and I am its shadow.
[illegible] the life and I am your body.
[illegible] the moon and I am your radiance.

As life sustains the body, and as always
the moon sheds light, sustain me.
I lost myself the very day
my heart conceived its love for you.
    If you are the ocean, I am your wave. If I am a tree, you are my root.
    How can a promise come between us, when I am the scent and you the flower?'

130. The lotus bud then opened her mouth
and spoke in sweet and gentle tones.
'The sin of giving pain to one's parents,
the sin of causing a forest fire,
and all the other sins I cannot now recount,
of all these will I bear the consequences
if I do not keep faith with your love to its limit.'
They swore the oath before the Creator,
with Rudra, Brahma and Hari bearing witness.*
    One should love with a love that will endure, from its beginning to its end;
    that it will survive both now and hereafter, who can have any doubt?

*Lovers' Play**

131. When the oath was sworn their souls united.
They spoke together of passionate love,
the love in whose colour the universe is saturated.
They were steeped in love from a former birth
so readily did they reach love's full intoxication.
As a sign the Prince gave the Princess
a ring, studded with jewels and diamonds.
He placed on his own finger, tender as a leaf,
the ring the Princess wore on her hand.
    Their hearts were full of love as they enjoyed the delights and sports of passion.
    Sometimes their souls exulted in their love, sometimes they lost all consciousness.

132. As one they followed the path of love;
fear of being two their hearts would not allow.
Sometimes she gave delight with an embrace,
then stole his heart with sidelong glances.
Now arrows from her eyes wounded his soul,
now she murmured words sweet as nectar.
Sometimes she laid her head upon his feet,
sometimes she gave herself completely in abandon.
When her eyes robbed him of his life,
she gave him precious nectar from her lips.
There was poison in the blessed maiden's eyes, but fragrant nectar on her lips.
She'd slay him with her sidelong glance, then smile and bring him back to life.

133. Sometimes her flowing locks spread waves of poison,
sometimes her eyes cast spells to kill.
Now they would lose themselves in love's essence,
now they embraced in each other's arms.
Sometimes she loved with ever-growing passion,
at times her love was quite spontaneous.
Sometimes their glances met and *rasa* was born,
sometimes they raised love to ecstasy.
Sometimes the ocean of their love flowed over,
at other times each entreated the other.
At times, although drunk with love, she was too proud to look at him.
And sometimes so deeply did she feel her love she called herself her darling's slave.

134. She made him fall and faint with love,
then sprinkled nectar to revive him.
Sometimes they exulted in love's ecstasies,
sometimes they feared the pain of separation.
At times, their eyes became gardens of beauty,
and sometimes they gave up their youth, their lives.
Now they tasted the supreme bliss of love,
now they dedicated their souls to one another.
They felt ashamed when thinking of their families,

but turned again to pleasure and delight.
When she held back the love within her soul, the Prince could scarcely bear it,
but when they united without restraint, their lives left their bodies for love.

The Nymphs Return

135. As they exchanged tender words of love,
sleep came to their enraptured eyes.
The whole night they had been awake,
hungry for each other's love,
but, as dawn broke, their eyes closed in sleep.
The celestial beings then returned
to where they had left the Prince asleep.
When they came in they were astonished to see
that both their brows shone with love's radiance.
When they saw them, they knew the signs of love-making:
beds in disarray, flowers crushed and withered.
The Prince lay sleeping on the maiden's couch and the maiden lay on his bed.
Exhausted they seemed from passion spent, sleeping with beds exchanged.

136. They had exchanged their rings
and wore each other's on their hands.
Some of the maiden's bangles lay broken on the bed.
Her bodice's fastening was ripped open at the bosom.
Her clothes had been torn from her limbs.
On her breasts, nail-scratches showed clearly.
The necklace and garlands at her breast were broken,
her parting was gone, her plaits undone.
The bed was in total disarray,
the beauty spot on her forehead wiped off.
Marks of collyrium could be seen, manifest on the Prince's lips,
and the red betel* juice looked lovely against the black in her kohl-lined eyes.

137. When the nymphs saw these signs
they thought the two had tasted passion's delight.
'Why should we part these two,' they said,
'and sin by causing them separation's agony?
The pain of death lasts only for a moment,
but to be separated in love is to die
a hundred deaths in every moment.'
They thought some more, and then resolved
that this was against their rightful duty.
'They've had their hour of sweet love here.
Without him, his father and mother, his retainers, his subjects and his family,
all would break their hearts and die; we would be responsible for their deaths.'

138. When they finally agreed amongst themselves,
they lifted the Prince up with her bed.
They carried him and set him down
in the place from where they had taken him.
Then they went off happily to play,
while grief was born in the lovers' hearts.
The Princess, half-asleep, stretched out lazily
as if she had thrilled to a lover's passion.
Her handmaidens saw she had been making love,
for all the signs of passion were visible.
They were terrified by what they saw. 'What awful thing has happened?
If the king were to hear of this, he would burn us alive in a furnace!'

Madhumālatī is Awakened

139. The maidservants awakened the Princess and said:
'Who has come here and destroyed you?
Wake up and look at the state you're in!
You did not arise last night, and yet
you have set fire to your own head.
Why did you knowingly swallow poison?

For what did you squander your precious capital?
Why did you harm yourself, swayed by lust?
Why did you bind burning coals in your waist-band?
Why have you disgraced yourself,
why did you shame your family?
You have destroyed yourself, Princess, for the pleasures of a moment.
In piling sins upon your head you have exposed your family to abuse.'

140. The Princess was now wide awake and said:
'My friends, why do you abuse me thus?
Only a fool could act this way,
one who had no regard for family or virtue.
Do not deprive me of my good name unjustly.
Think well—you can make me touch hot iron,
an ordeal to prove my chastity,
but first judge the gravity of the sin,
then give me whatever punishment you like.
Dear friends, you have accused me of many things.
It does not befit me to keep secrets from you.
There are no differences between us. Sit down, and I'll tell you carefully about it.
I do not know if it was reality or a dream, nor do I know who dealt me this blow.

141. 'In a dream I saw a Prince,
but, though a dream, he seemed real enough.
The Creator had fashioned him
to be the image of the God of Love.
He was not Yama,* yet he took my life.
When Yama deals death it hurts only for an instant,
but the pain of love-in-separation
is a death that is died at every moment.
Dear friend, how can I escape this pain?
Without my soul, how can I live in this world?
I cannot stay an hour away from him.
Without any warning, lightning has struck me.

I doubt, sweet friend, whether my body can survive an instant without my soul,
though doubtless this cruel and heartless soul can manage without my body.

142. 'Everyone in this world loves life, O friend,
but for me it is better to die in separation.
Everyone has to die, but only once,
whereas I, dear friend, die every day.
He brought me love and then deserted me.
He cast a spell and stole my soul.
I had never in my life heard of sorrow
and suddenly I meet it face to face in battle.
Love's burning pain and my family's honour,
both have come to entangle my heart.
The pain of love is hard, dear friends, harder than I can ever describe.
Help me, if you can, by giving me poison so that I may die.'

143. Her handmaïdens then replied:
'Listen, O maiden, bear this sorrow
for a few days yet; this too will pass.
The fruits of joy grow from sorrow's blossoms.
Without grief, no one can ever find happiness.
O best of maidens, only if the soul knows grief
can one enjoy the blessing of a lover.
Only by staying awake through darkest night
can one experience the radiant dawn.
In this world, no flower grows without a thorn.
Who has ever found nectar without a snake?'*
Manjhan says, in this Kali age, no one can find joy without suffering.
Trees must first shed their autumn leaves before new greenery can be born.

144. 'Just as you are distraught away from him,
so must he worry and suffer for you.
Separation does not just wound one person,
dear friend, it is a double-edged sword!

The Creator who gave this pain to you
will grant its remedy; be patient in your heart.
That which the Lord has decreed for tomorrow
can never be won today, not even by force.
First cross the snake-infested thicket of thorns!
Then you can enjoy the fruits and flowers.'
Here the Princess suffered night and day the fierce flames of love-in-separation,
but now let me tell you what happened there when Prince Manohar awoke.

The Prince Awakes

145. When the Prince woke up and looked around,
from that instant his body burned,
consumed by the flames of separation.
That palace was no more, nor the night of love,
nor the passionate Princess who was steeped in love.
Feeling faint he looked around.
At every moment he wept, sighing deeply.
The more he remembered his darling,
the more he lost control of his senses.
As he recalled Madhumālatī's words,
separation's fire permeated all his limbs.
Sometimes his mind was conscious, and sometimes it could not be contained.
He beat his head against the ground, and cried as he recalled her beauty and virtues.

146. Sahajā* was the Prince's nurse.
She ran to him, crying, 'My son! My son!
Tell me, my boy, what's the matter?
I am as much your mother as Kamalā.
My son, what grief has been born in you,
which makes the tears fall from your eyes?
Your face has withered away like a flower,
what sorrow has afflicted you thus?
Tell me what you suffer, my son,
so that I may find a remedy.'

He opened his eyes and looked at her face. Sighing deeply, he addressed her,
'There is no hope of a remedy, nurse, for the pain that has been born in my heart.

147. 'Nurse, the disease that afflicts my heart
has no medicine or cure.
My soul has gone away to dwell
in a place where intelligence is lame.
And my mind and my heart have gone,
to where the mind's eye is afraid to enter.
What I have seen cannot be described,
for I went to a place where all awareness fled.
My soul was stolen away, O nurse,
for only an empty frame has returned!
My soul remained with my darling, and my body lies here lifeless.
Was it a dream or was it reality? I do not know who robbed me of my soul.

148. 'Was it reality? Was it a dream?
I wish I could say, but I cannot.
How can I call it a dream,
when all that I found was so real?
I see before my eyes an ornamented bed,
and a maiden with a ring on her finger.
On her lips are marks of kohl,
and red betel stains on her eyes.
On her breast I see her necklace.
All these are clear before my eyes.
O nurse, the flames of separation have taken hold within my body.
Only death can extinguish them, or union with Madhumālatī!

149. 'Listen, nurse, to the tale of my sorrow.
I'll tell you everything, frankly and openly.
Life has departed, leaving this body,
and my soulless body is on the point of death.
I cannot speak further of my grief—

if my soul were here, I could talk again.
Since my life's love has stolen my soul
my body has become lifeless, dead.
Madhumālatī holds my life in her hands.
Nurse, my body doesn't contain a soul.
    Listen, nurse, no one in this world should be parted from his love.
    It is better to lose your life, far better than to lose your beloved.

150. 'Why did my eyes ever look at that girl,
for whom I was flung into separation's fire?
How can a man enjoy pleasure and happiness,
once love comes into his heart?
The soul in my body was a moth,
consumed utterly in the blaze of love.
Love's trade has cunningly fooled the world,
for in it there's no profit, only loss of capital.
The world knows the truth of the saying:
the man who's mad for profit loses money.
    Happiness, joy, pleasure, and self-respect—all have left me, dear nurse!
    All that remains in my heart is the sorrow of parting from Madhumālatī.

151. 'When the fire of love is kindled in the heart,
it consumes everything except the beloved.
Love's agony is the hardest of all sorrows,
a thousand deaths every moment, every day.
My life's breath is gone, leaving my body—
why did God make the grievous pain of love?
My royal pride, my precious youth have gone,
since my soul came under separation's sway.
Now I climb the hard, dangerous path of love—
either I lose my life, or I find that maiden again!
    Nurse, watch me run to plunge myself into the ocean of love!
    I will either bring out the pearl, or give up my life in the attempt.

152. 'No one knows how hard parting is,
only my body knows this pain, and God knows!
I renounce all royal pleasures as poison,
and cling to separation's sorrow as nectar.
Now I have set my soul on this path,
may love take me to its very limit.
Either I shall lose my life on the path,
or God will unite me with my darling again!
Nurse, how little of my suffering you have heard,
for the tale is long, and life is short.
I cannot recount this matter of love, O nurse, with only my own mouth.
Even if I had a thousand tongues and all four aeons, still I could not reach its end.'

Manohar's Illness

153. The sun rose and the world became radiant.
But the Prince woke up ablaze with separation.
His senses gone, his soul maddened—
separation took command of his body's fort.
The drum of separation resounded everywhere.
His soul was a subject, and separation king.
He had climbed up on the path of love,
and could not turn his body from it.
He ripped up his clothes and tore out his hair.
The sorrow of separation was too hard to bear.
He stood up and knocked himself down again.
Hearing the uproar in the palace, his family and subjects all came running.
His mother Kamalāvatī ran to him, restless, tearing her sari in agitation.

154. Through town and country the rumour spread,
that a tumult raged in the royal palace.
Physicians, exorcists, wise men came,
mother and father and relatives ran to him.
The King said, 'I gave up my life, my wealth for him.

May his life increase by my remaining years!
Spend whatever wealth you need,
but make the Prince live again somehow.
Help me, bring my son back to me.
Take my life if you need, but revive him!'
    The physicians came and felt his pulse, began to search out his illness.
    But the channels of sun and moon were clean, and his body perfectly sound.

155. Again and again they took his pulse.
But how could they diagnose his trouble, separation?
They used all the methods of medicine,
but could not find the Prince's disease.
Then one of the doctors spoke,
'This seems to be the pain of separation.
The Prince has been struck by the arrows of love.
This disease is none of our business,
for his body has no defect in it.
Let us go and inform the King.'
    The pandits, exorcists, and doctors rose, very disappointed with their findings.
    For the Prince was suffering from love's agony, for which no cure is known.

A Mehtā with a Cure

156. In the kingdom there was a Mehtā,
a village headman renowned to be clever.
No one could match him in any way,
the world called him a treasury of wisdom.
His skill was famous in all quarters.
Justly was he called the Sahadeva* of the age,
for his virtues were known throughout the world.
He was very learned in the fourteen sciences,
and understood the problems of the heart.
He knew the uses of gems and incantations.
For one herb, he could quote a thousand applications.

Hearing that the Prince was stricken, he came to
investigate his affliction.
He took the Prince's pulse with his hand, and declared
his body free from illness.

157. He examined the Prince in many ways,
and found his humours—wind, phlegm, and bile—
to be perfectly balanced and normal.
He said to himself, 'His disease
is not hidden in his veins at all.
All eight limbs are healthy and sound.
At every moment, his eyes shut and open.
The channels of sun and moon are clear,
but why does he heave such deep sighs?
Why does he never close his eyes in sleep?
This is nothing but the pain of separation.
Tears drip down from both his eyes, his senses are
beyond his control.
For the one who is wounded by the sword of love, there
can be no cure at all.'

158. Then he addressed the Prince face to face:
'O Prince, to whom have you pledged your heart?
Who has robbed you of intelligence?
Where did you taste the nectar of love?
If you tell me everything, I'll see to it
that you meet the one you love.
Even if she is a heavenly nymph,
I'll bring you together through a magic spell.
O Prince, do not let your soul lose hope,
for I will traverse the three worlds
to fulfil your heart's desire.
Tell me truly, privately, just where and to whom did you
lose your soul?
For with my skills and magic, I can unite the *cakora*
bird with the moon.*

159. 'If she exists in heaven, earth, or hell,
I will bring her here to meet you.

I can climb up to heaven and draw
nectar from the moon, and bring down
a heavenly nymph with my magic spells.
Ask me the mysteries of the worlds
of gods, men, or serpents, and I'll tell all.
I can bring back the ones who have gone,
and raise the dead with my incantations.
Through magic I can invoke Śeṣa* or Indra.
If you want, I can move the mountain, Sumeru.*
Tell me then, do not hide anything, the person for whom your heart is in pain.
Did this agony arise spontaneously, or did someone give you this pain?'

160. The Mehtā's words were full of *rasa*,
and the Prince was deeply moved.
Since he found him sympathetic to his grief,
he told him all about his dream.
'O Prince,' said the headman,
'Life is most precious in this world.
Do not throw it away for a woman.
A woman is never faithful to anyone,
nor does anyone benefit from loving her.
The man who loves a woman in his heart
is disappointed like the parrot on the silk-cotton tree.*
No one who makes a woman his own knows anything in this world.
Can you make the bitter *nīm* tree* sweet by sprinkling it with nectar?

161. 'If woman's behaviour had been good,
would she be called "snake" in the Turkish tongue?*
No one can control a woman in this world.
Woman is only medicine for those sick for beauty.
She is a demon incarnate in the world.
No one should fall for her outer adornments.
If she loves you she'll burn you with separation.
If she's weary of you she'll kill you instantly.
She appears as pure as the full moon,

but within she is black as the darkest night.
  Woman is the thorn on the *ketakī* blossom*—O wandering bee, keep well away!
  As you look at her beautiful form, never forget that it brings grief in the end.

162. 'The moment you see her, she robs your senses.
When she touches you, she destroys all wisdom.
It's well known: when you make love to a woman,
she devours the vital spirit in your body.
Don't think that woman is a blessing to the world.
Man is a bee, woman the *ketakī* bud.
As long as she slakes her own desire,
she will love more passionately than a man.
She will love a man warmly, forcibly,
but only for satisfying her own purpose.
  Understand well in your mind that women have never been faithful in all four ages.
  Do not lose your self in vain, O Prince, for the sake of this love for a woman.

163. 'O Prince, do not take on sorrow
by giving away your soul in vain.
In this world it is futile to love a woman.
If a man associates with a woman,
both are struck by a thousand thunderbolts.
Give up entanglement with women, O Prince!
Has a woman ever kept faith in this world?
Woman was born from the left side,
always know her to be inauspicious, O Prince.
Even the scriptures call her "Vāmā",* of the left.
Only a madman would consider her right, auspicious.
  In woman are concentrated all signs of ill omen, excepting one auspicious virtue:
  from women—that's all they're good for—are born all the great men of the world.'

The Prince Rejects the Mehtā's Approach

164. The Prince, when he heard these unpleasant words,
was astonished and couldn't contain himself.
'Headman,' he retorted, 'You are the Sahadeva
of the Kali age, but if someone else had just said that,
I would have told him off. Only a man
whose heart has never known love's agony
could say such foolish, mad things.
How can such talk come out of your mouth,
when you know the nature of the three worlds?
I have lost my selfhood, but if my soul
were in my body I might heed your advice.
  Listen, O Mehtā, I have lost my soul and embarked on the road of love.
  Were my soul still in this bodily frame, I might have heard your preaching.

165. 'Love has never blossomed in your heart,
so how could you know another's pain?
You're skilful and clever, certainly no fool,
so why do you knowingly give such advice?
Borax transforms gold in separation's fire,*
but neither fire nor smoke touches your body.
My body has become ashes and flown away,
who can listen to your tales and teachings?
The snake has gone, why beat at its hole?
Why do you knowingly make a fool of me?
  Rise, O Mehtā! I touch your feet, for I had hopes of you both now and in the hereafter.
  But why do you, a man of understanding, try uselessly to tie up the wind in a net?

166. 'Separation's anguish is difficult to bear.
No one knows the agony of the sufferer.
People come and speak pleasant words,
but fire blazes up in his breast as he listens.
Once love has entered one's heart,
it only leaves with the life's breath departing.

How can intelligence overcome love?
Separation's wind blows out the lamp of reason.
Only madmen do not know this:
where there is love, no reason prevails.'
    The Prince's ailment was incurable. No herb, no mantra* in this world could heal him.
    Those who try to obscure the sun of love in clouds of dust are fools.

The Prince and his Parents

167. Then the Mehtā came to the conclusion
that this illness was beyond his powers.
He tried everything—words, medicines,
all his skills as a healer—but all proved useless.
When his heart lost all hope of a cure,
he became dejected and left the Prince.
He went to the King and cried out,
'Go quickly to the royal apartments!
Go now and protect your son!'
The King heard these words and panicked.
Too shocked to utter a word, he ran.
    The King cried out loud in his grief, and the whole palace was in an uproar.
    Hearing the tumult in the royal house, the city was overwhelmed with sorrow.

168. The King flung his turban on the ground,
and all the ladies of the palace wept.
Kamalā came and fell at her son's feet:
'Son, what disaster has happened to you?
Don't make me lose hope, my son!
You are my hope in this world and the next.
Tell us your pain, your mother implores you.
What defect has made you a beggar?
What is this fire, that burns the triple world?
What power has taken away my life?'
    When he saw his dear parents' faces, compassion was born in the Prince's heart.

Opening his eyes, he told them of the sorrow given
him by Madhumālatī.

169. With tears in his eyes, the Prince said,
'Father, I have lost my soul.
If you grant me your royal permission,
I will seek my soul and bring it back.
I do not know where in the two worlds
the city of Mahāras is, where my soul was lost.
If you command me I will go
to unite my body and my soul,
to make matters well again.
Maybe the same destiny will be kind,
which brought me love in a dream before.
With your permission I will seek my soul, for my
worldly life is finished.
Perhaps fortune will favour me, for then I'll find my life
and soul again.'

170. His mother and father were overcome
with emotion when they heard the Prince.
Both of them touched his feet.
'Be sure of this, our son,' they said,
'You are the life of our two bodies.
Better that you kill us now, son,
than to abandon us in old age.
The realm will crumble into dust without you,
and we will die with broken hearts.
The sunlight of our lives grows dim,
and Yama, lord of death, surrounds us.
You are our Śravaṇa,* our sorrow's support.
O son, our dire old age terrifies us—we beg you, do not
desert us now!
You are our ferry across life's ocean. Without you, who
would take us across?

171. 'Do not count on us any longer, for our lives
are lamps flickering out in the light of dawn.
Do not rob your parents of hope,

for once we part we may never meet again.
When we leave this Kali age,
only through you will our name live on!
Like Daśaratha* pining away for his son,
we will die without you, Manohar.
First kill us both and take our lives,
then go to foreign lands, dear son!
    Do not abandon us alive, for we have no one else to call our own.
    Weeping, we will remember your virtues, and break our hearts and die.'

The Prince Assumes a Yogi's Guise

172. The Prince did not hear a word
of whatever his weeping parents said.
Whoever loses his senses on the path of love,
can comprehend nothing in the two worlds.
So acute was the pain of separation
he could not control himself.
He asked for a begging bowl*
and a yogi's staff and crutch.*
He marked his forehead with a circle,*
smeared his body with ashes,*
and hung shining earrings in both his ears.*
He took his drinking cup firmly in hand,
and tightened the strings of his ascetic's viol.*
    Letting down his matted locks,* he donned the patched cloak and the girdle of rope.*
    With loincloth tied around his waist, the Prince took the guise of a Gorakh yogi.*

173. The yogi forged within his trident
suffering, indifference, and renunciation.
His rosary was a basil-bead necklace.*
Around his neck hung the horn whistle.*
his shoulder was the crutch for meditation.
his staff and the thread of Gorakh,

he controlled his mind and his breath.
He put on his feet the sandals of love,
and arranged on himself the deerskin of renunciation.
He assumed this guise for a vision of Madhumālatī.
For her sake he assayed wretchedness.
He sat in meditation, thinking, reflecting, and his eyes and ears were steeped in love.
He took on this guise for a vision of his beloved, but it seemed as if Gorakh had awakened.

174. This ascetic appeared a perfected soul
as he set out for a vision of Madhumālatī.
If he gained perfection on the path of yoga,
he might yet meet his beloved again.
Through a vision of the Guru love is born,
and the viol sounds the mystic note of absorption.
Through the beauty of Madhumālatī
his consciousness had been sunk in ecstasy.
He had made constant the breath in his body.
Mind and body were consumed in separation's blaze.
He had cleansed his limbs with the water of his breath.
The Guru's beauty had entered his eyes, his voice resounded in the ascetic's ears.
Sitting in silent absorption, the yogi contemplated the vision of Madhumālatī.

Manohar's Departure

175. His father and mother then returned,
saw him and sighed deeply in their hearts.
When she saw his face smeared with ash,
Kamalā washed it with tears from her lotus eyes.
'O son,' they said, 'You are our only hope.
Why abandon the kingdom to become a beggar?
All our wealth and treasure is yours,
we acquired and saved it for you.
If it is of no use to you today,
then what use can it ever be to us?

We will take all our wealth and treasure, and make our
relatives and retainers accompany us.
If we ever meet Madhumālatī, we will ask for her hand
in marriage.'

176. In the morning the King assembled a company,
and accompanied the Prince for forty miles.
There were elephants, horses, and much treasure.
Who could count the army that followed them?
The King sent off all the companions and men
who had come with them to accompany the Prince.
Off they went, questing for Mahāras,
where Vikram Rāi was lord of men.
They came to the shore of an ocean,
impassable, deep and fathomless.
With elephants, horses, companions and servants, and
much treasure and store,
the Prince embarked on a ship. How can one erase
what's written in one's fate?

The Shipwreck

177. They boarded ship and set sail on the ocean,
but no one can know the writings of fate.
For four months they sailed on the water.
After this evil times drew near.
The sea was in swell, darkness everywhere,
and the helmsman lost his bearings.
He could not decide which way to go,
and the ship fell into a mighty whirlpool.
Suddenly it crashed into seven hundred pieces,
and the waves battered it from every side.
All sank into the water—his friends and companions,
the treasure and store,
every sign of royalty, all the beasts and horses—and
vanished without a trace.

178. The Prince gave up every hope of life,
and began to invoke the name of God.

'You are the Protector of the triple world.
O Lord, whom could I call on except you?
You are the giver of life to the world,
stretch out your hand and save me as I drown.
The one who remembers the Creator
in times of danger, finds that fire
has turned into a bed of flowers.'*
At that moment God showed mercy
and the Prince found a support in his drowning.
Through the grace of God a wooden plank floated in front of the Prince.
The Prince caught hold of it as he was sinking, just as life was leaving his body.

179. That wooden plank became his support
when huge waves rose again around him.
When again he was drawn under the waves,
the Prince abandoned all hope of life.
Then he lost all knowledge of where he was,
and of where the current carried him.
The surging waves took him and put him down
where moon and sun did not shine.
The surf left the Prince unconscious on that shore,
and subsided back into the treasure-filled ocean.
When the Prince came to his senses again, he lay half-stunned on the shore.
Around him there was nothing and no one, save his pain and the mercy of God.

The Prince Finds a Maiden

180. All the trappings of royalty were lost, and only
his sorrow for Madhumālatī remained with him.
He looked around but there was no one there.
Except for his shadow, he had no companion.
In a dark wood where no mortal had been,
the Prince had been set down by God.
He got up and started towards the wood's interior,

goes out to wilderness
himself - like

no birds even flapped their wings.
...ing an impassable path, grief his only companion,
...n forward one moment, sat and cried the next.
   Blood rushed from his head to his feet, and back from
      his feet to his head.
   He would stop to sit a thousand times, before he could
      traverse a mile.

181. He wandered on alone in the dark forest,
   on a difficult path, hard and insurmountable.
   Lions and tigers roared, and elephants trumpeted,
   but the Prince was alone, without any friends.
   He walked on without resting for an instant,
   his tongue repeating the name of Madhumālatī.
   Then he came to a grove of plantain trees.*
   Evening fell and the light retreated.
   Since it was impossible to see anything,
   the Prince settled down there for the night.
      He sat in meditation, concentrating on the Guru, and
         remained there deeply absorbed.
      The night of separation passes like an age, in which the
         knower awakens to love!

182. The dawn came, the Prince began on his way,
   on the path of love he gave his head, then set foot.*
   The pain of separation had seized his body.
   He cried, 'Madhumālatī! Madhumālatī!'
   Recalling her, he struck his head and mouth
   violently, as if he were performing *zikr.**
   Having lost his love, he could not recognize himself.*
   His senses had fled, all his knowledge had gone.
   'I will not fall back,' he resolved,
   'from giving my life on the path of love.
   If I had a hundred lives, I'd sacrifice them all.'
      Walking onwards through the forest, the Prince saw a
         four-cornered pavilion.
      When he realized what he was seeing, his mind began to
         speculate about it.

183. Wondering in his mind for a moment,
the Prince set foot inside the pavilion.
He saw a marvellously coloured new bed,
on which slept a Princess, drunken with sleep.
Sweet fragrances had been sprinkled on the bed.
Bees hovered, intoxicated, not leaving her side.
The Prince advanced towards the bed,
and fears and doubts sprang up in his mind.
Her face was like the moon, her beauty youthful,
and she lay there unconscious. The Creator
had shaped her form without blemish.
She was virtuous and clever, and could enchant men's minds in the world.
Blessed was the Maker who made her, and blessed too was the sleeping maiden.

184. Who could describe her sleeping on her bed?
It was as if the lotus had captured the honey-bee.
Did her eyes reflect nectar or poison?
Who had fashioned her two lovely eyes?
Her forehead could not be described at all.
One moment it seemed the full moon,
the next the moon of the second night.*
Her face, like the moon, cherished her doe-eyes.
These does drew along the chariot of her moon-face.
The mole on her cheek was matchless,
a single spot equal to a thousand adornments.
The Princess, adorned in all sixteen ways, lay fearlessly on her bed in the bliss of sleep.
Her two eyes were like *cakora* birds gazing longingly at the face of the moon.

185. Poison flowed from her serpentine curls.
The man who saw them lost life and youth.
Her firm breasts, full of nectar untasted,
were inverted like two golden bowls.
The soles of her feet were red with dye.*
Every pore of her body exulted in youth.
Her black braid cannot be described,

it seemed like the serpent Śeṣa
were crawling up the mountain, Sumeru.
Seeing her beautiful lips took one's life.
The sages of the triple world
could not contain themselves at the sight.
From head to foot her form was etched out like a painting soaked in natural colour.
Even a moment's vision of her would trouble one's heart for a lifetime.

186. She seemed like the moon resting through the day,
having risen in the heavens at night.
The Prince thought, 'Maybe she is
a heavenly nymph banished to earth
by the curse of Indra.* Or perhaps she is
Jupiter descended from the sky
to rest here a while. Maybe
she is a witch of the forest,
and has assumed this form by magic.
How could a mortal live here
where there is no one for a hundred *yojanas*?*
Is she the goddess of the woods here in disguise, or is my mind deceiving me?
Has someone enchanted me? Is a spirit from the cremation ground bewitching me?'

The Maiden Awakes

187. Soundly that lovely maiden slept,
bursting with youth, lovely and lovable.
When he saw her his mind was enchanted,
so he went to the bed and sat down.
Sometimes his mind was full of fear and doubt,
and sometimes he grew fearless with love's savour.
The maiden turned over in her bed, stretching
involuntarily with a languid yawn.
As she stretched out her lovely arms,
both sun and moon began to shine.*

Her eyes opened and grew alert, and she drew bac
bows of her eyebrows.
Indra in heaven, all men on earth, and even the hooded
Śeṣa below grew alarmed.

188. The maiden awoke and opened her eyes,
like two clever deer suddenly alerted.
When her gaze fell on the Prince
she was confused and feared him in her heart.
Then that lovely maiden, matchless in form,
began to speak naturally, in words full of *rasa*.
She asked, 'Who are you?
Where have you come from?
Who has driven you to such madness?
Your form, so like the God of Love, is mortal.
What is your name? Why don't you speak?
Tell me truly who you are, whether you are a ghost or a
vampire.
You seem human, like a royal prince, so why have you
left your palace and home?

189. 'For whom do you suffer separation's pain,
that you should leave your palace, your home?
Speak the truth, truth is precious in the world.
No one can be a match for the man
whose heart's companion is truth.
The truthful man never tells a lie,
for truth is the essence of this world.*
Tell me truly, who is it that you love?
What is her name? Who has intoxicated you?
Truth is the helmsman of the ship at sea.
Without truth, no one can cross this ocean.
I speak the truth, and you must believe that truth is
your friend in the world's nine regions.
If a mortal lives a life of truth, he ascends to Brahma's
cosmos* in his own body.

190. 'Either you have reached the supreme state,
or someone has robbed you of your mind.

Are you mad? Have you lost your senses?
Or perhaps your mind knows enlightenment.
Has someone stolen all your money?
Did an enemy give you kite's flesh to eat,
casting an evil spell on your heart?
Are you inflamed with passion's wine
and cannot control yourself at all?
Perhaps it is pride that prevents you from speaking.
Are you frightened looking at this place?
Only through speaking the truth, O adept,
does one attain perfect enlightenment.
  O yogi, do not be afraid! Rid your heart of all doubts and misgivings.'
  All this the pure and moon-faced girl asked him with natural friendliness.

191. 'Has something spontaneously affected your heart?
Or have you been reading the scripture of love?
Did your mother curse you to exile?
Or did someone practise magic on you?
Has the marrow in your brain been excited?
Or did the Creator make you mad?
Have you found out the secret of God,
has someone's beauty made you forget yourself?
Is your soul soaked in the colour of *sahaja*,
or are you intoxicated with the wine of love?
  Have you lost your life's capital, or is there some sorrow in your family?
  Or were you forsaken by a lovely maiden, for whom your heart suffers in separation?'

Manohar's Reply

192. Then the Prince rose to answer her,
'Alluring maiden, most worthy of love,
I a traveller from a foreign land.
ind, my head, and my foot
on the path of renunciation.

I want to ask the truth about you.
Tell me only the honest truth.
I have come wandering over
the earth's four quarters, and did not find
a mortal for a hundred *yojana*s.
Where are there traces of humans here?
So perhaps you are the witch of this place.
You are a witch who has assumed a beautiful form, for I see the signs clearly.
Otherwise no human being could ever live in such a desolate forest.

193. 'How could a human being survive
in a forest where no birds fly?
As I wandered through this forest of fear,
it seemed to rush in to devour me.
How could a mortal ever be here?
No mortal ever existed in such a form,
so you are some ghastly creature in disguise.
Tell me your name—who are you?
Why do you live in this jungle?
You have no friends or companions here,
so how do you live in this dark wood alone?
Your eyes are does, your voice the cuckoo's, your face is the moon, your waist has a lion's grace!
You do not seem frightened alone, but live in this forest grove without fear.

194. 'To whom do you tell your joy or sorrow?
Have you dedicated your life to someone,
that you stay here night and day?
I cannot see anyone around.
You seem like a renunciant
and your heart is very sad.
I sense in you the fragrance of love.
I do not know what secret you'll disclose.
My eyes cannot comprehend you at all,
but your words speak to me of mysteries.
Are you the wife of a celestial musician,

or the darling daughter of a king?
Tell me carefully, so I may be able to understand the mysteries of love through you.*
Who is your dear beloved? O beautiful one, who is the king whose darling you are?'

The Mango Grove

195. Then the lovely maiden spoke,
'I am a king's daughter, his precious darling.
My father is Citrasena and Pemā* is my name.
My home is the city of Ease-of-Mind.*
Fortune was fickle and evil days came,
separating me from family and loved ones.
I was young and innocent, and had not tasted love.
In my father's kingdom I knew only youth.
I spent the days in frolic and play,
and wasted the nights in sleep without care.
I did not know the sorrow of separation, nor the pain and burning of love.
Fun and games, happiness and clamour—these were my daily occupations.

196. 'Citbisarāun, Ease-of-Mind, was a beautiful city,
and all around it was my father's mango grove.
Cool was its shade and dense the mango trees,
as if Paradise itself had come down to earth.
The trees were well cared for and bore luscious fruit,
canals of cool water ran around their roots.
Beautiful birds roosted on the trees,
playing happily and cooing in sweet voices.
In that mango grove it was eternal springtime,
and the breeze blew its scents in all directions.
Mangoes like sweet nectar hung always on the blossoming trees.
Celestials, sages, and wise men came there to enjoy repose.

197. 'A pleasant pavilion stood there, full of pictures,
and there we would go for fun and frolic.

One day, all my girlfriends came to me, saying,
"Let's go to the mango grove and play!"
I said, "If my mother agrees I'll come
and play with you in the mango grove."
Then I rose and went to my mother.
She kissed me and made me sit on her lap.
"Mother, if you would allow me,
I'd go to the garden with my girlfriends."
She said, "My darling, play here at home today—do not go there!
My heart is uneasy, and I am afraid to let you go out."

198. 'When my mother said these words,
a childish whim made me cry and fuss.
She wiped my tears and consoled me gently,
telling me I was grown up, no longer a child.
Then she said, "You are a virgin girl,
the prop and support of your parents' life.
I will not let you out of my sight,
you must stop going daily to the mango grove."
But then she relented and told me,
"Hurry up and go, and don't be late,
play for a little bit, then come straight home."
I heard this and my heart was joyful, all sorrow left me for happiness.
All my girlfriends were thrilled, happy that I had permission to play.

199. 'Then my mother called all my friends to her.
She adorned them first with beautiful flowers.
Then she put fragrant sandal on their golden bodies,
which appeared to be made of the nectar of the moon.
All were clever and spontaneously lovely,
with bodies formed from molten gold.
Sometimes their youth would peep out shyly,
sometimes they seemed like simple children.
Their youth was perplexing. One did not know
whether they were mature, or simply children.

Youth and childhood debated over them, each staking its claim,
blessed was our sweet youth and those days, blessed our innocent pleasure.

200. 'Let me think and describe their beauty:
blessed God embodied them in this Kali age.
They had not yet tasted the delights of love,
nor yet had passion's lord aroused their bodies.
The fury of desire had not inflamed their limbs,
nor yet had the golden bowls of their breasts risen.
Youth's bud had not yet opened in bloom,
still steeped they were in innocent love.
They had not yet embraced a lover in passion,
nor had they known love's sulks or sweet cajolings.
Childhood had not yet left their beautiful bodies, and they had
not yet sampled, even by mistake, the taste of the wine of love.

201. 'They had not yet learnt to put on the bodice,
they were innocent of the savour of love.
Nectar did not yet drip from their lips.
Their eyes had not learnt the wiles of seduction.
They had not yet slept in passion's embrace.
Love's intoxication had not awakened in them.
They had not yet voiced the joy of love,
dressed in the garments of consummation.
Not a suspicion of desire existed in their hearts.
They had not yet rested on a lover's arm.
All of them were thrilled and happy, going to the mango grove.
Why did I not use my intelligence? I lost my freedom by going there.

202. 'Fortune went against me that day.
I set off happily, excited and childlike,
with my doe-eyed friends, who walked
swaying gracefully like *haṃsa* birds.*

Their lips were filled with sweet nectar.
They cooed like cuckoos, singing delightfully,
lovely as creepers swinging on the bough.
Their waists made one fear that at a touch,
God had made them so fine they would snap.
Their navels were like pools of nectar,
with black braids on guard like vicious serpents.
Clever and intelligent, all these girls were wise and skilled in the arts.
Their eyebrow-bows and eyelash-arrows slaughtered all by looking at them.

203. 'Playing I came to that delightful grove,
where the army of the love-god was in full array.
The birds' sweet singing delighted the sense.
Partridges cooed wistfully for their mates.
Here black bees clustered close to the flower,
there cuckoos sang in the fifth note of the scale.*
Here tender blossoms opened from the bud,
there, peacocks and cuckoos made their home.
Everywhere there were flowers, colourful and fragrant,
and all through the garden, love's tumultuous ecstasy.
Even bodies which had never known passion would have been swayed by the sight.
That lovely garden with its army of love would have aroused desire in the dead.

204. 'My friends rejoiced when they saw the mango grove.
They sported and played as young girls do.
Some counted cuckoos and made them fly,
others ran to see the peacocks dance.
They all played, joy in their hearts.
Some plucked blossoms, clasping them to their breasts,
others adorned their hair with the flowers.
Some made garlands and posies of buds.
Whoever found a sweet-smelling, colourful blossom,
ran to show it to me excitedly.
Happily they explored the enchanting forest, plucking the fragrant flowers,

with eyes like does and faces like lotuses, they were buds
the bees would not leave.

205. 'The maidens played happily in the grove,
lotus-faced, with sweet virginal bodies,
and fragrant perfume on their limbs.
The black bees clustered close around them,
abandoning the scents of the flowers.
They swarmed around a maiden's head,
or tried to settle on another's breasts.
Some caught the scent of unopened lotuses
on their lips, and clustered to drink honey.
The black bees wanted to sample by force
the savours of love which were yet untasted.
When the bees stung the lips of all of them, the girls
grew very restless.
The bees clung close in front, and attacked their
serpent-like braids like peacocks.

206. 'The virginal girls were like lotuses in bloom,
with black bees humming cruelly around them.
They were so disturbed they could not speak.
When they drew breath the bees rested on their lips.
They were all very upset, their make-up ruined,
their bodices were torn and necklaces broken.
All were agitated, their partings were wiped clean,
the marks on their brows destroyed.
The sixteen adornments they had put on at home
had now been ruined in the mango grove.
The lovely maidens ran, hiding their faces in their
hands.
Entering the picture-pavilion,* they shut its doors
behind them.

207. 'In this state of restless agitation,
the lovely maidens ran into the pavilion.
Many had broken the bangles on their hands,
others had ruined their necklaces.
Some felt their lips and breasts,
some wept seeing the stings on their bosoms.

Some were laughing, others crying,
and many were afraid to face their parents.
Some had tresses flowing in disarray,
others had the collyrium in their eyes wiped out.
    All their adornments were quite destroyed, and some cried while others laughed.
    So frightened were they by the bees, they could not go homewards again.

208. 'Then they discussed the situation, saying,
"Let's go home and leave the pavilion."
Many said, "How can we go home?
If our mothers question us, what shall we say?"
Some were afraid of their mothers at home,
but most feared the black bees at large.
Four of them, who were sensible
and less afraid, said, "Let us go.
We will lead the way, you follow."
    Then they opened the doors wide and went out, apprehensively, all in a group.
    They could not open their mouths out of fear, but spoke through gestures and signs.*

209. 'They all came out of the picture-pavilion.
Their fear had not left them yet.
Scared, they huddled together in one place.
Suddenly, a horrible demon appeared.
My girlfriends nearly died of fright.
Seeing him, I was petrified,
and ran to hide under the trees.
But the demon came straight
to where I was hiding and seized me.
    Out of sixty girls, he singled me out and snatched me up.
    Within the twinkling of an eye, he brought me to this wild forest.

210. 'It has been a long year in this place.
Even in my dreams I don't hear a human name.
Seeing your human form today

I have come alive for an instant.
I am a body without life in this place,
and how long can a lifeless body live?
Parted from my family, I burn night and day,
while my cruel life will not leave me.
Grief has overwhelmed my heart
and taken away all my joy.
Still I am forced to keep on living.
    How long can I continue to live in this world suffering such pain?
    Like cracks appear in a drying-up pond, my body will crack and die in agony.

211. 'I left my soul there and came here.
I cannot live any longer without it.
One day I shall die from this sorrow,
for how long can I remain alive like this?
My body is numb and life flutters on my lips,
I have left my body and the hope of life.
O Prince, just look at this pitiable wretch,
a lifeless woman speaks these words to you.
The day the demon abducted me
I abandoned joy, love, and happiness.
    Without life my body lives on, and I burn in the fire of separation.*
    How can one call it living when one's days are spent in separation?

212. 'Twelve long months have I wept blood.
Better to die than to suffer separation.
My heart breaks when I remember past joys.
The sorrow of parting, like a set of shears,
has cut away all the flesh from my body.
My heart breaks with agonizing pain
when I see this lonely, dark forest.
Grief is my companion and separation my friend.
In a previous life, God assigned me this ill fate.
The tree of my life bears sorrow as its fruit.
Maybe I caused someone to suffer

and now he takes his revenge on me.
    Quietly by night and day, separation drains my life's blood away,
    one day it will finish with the blood, and eat the empty shell.

213. 'I have told you all my story.
Grief is my only companion here.
When I was in my mother's lap,
I never harmed even a bird.
I cannot tell what sin I did
that brought me to this horrible fate.
In these woods and dark forests
there is no one to share my sorrow.
Apart from grief and burning,
I do not feel anything at all.
Nothing diverts me even for a moment.
This woman wishes to leave her life,
for the world is a heavy burden for her.
    There is pain and grief in my heart, and my body is consumed with fire.
    O God, how long can I live on in this agony of separation?

214. 'I have told you my joys and sorrows,
all there is to know about me.
Tell me now of your own grief.
What has brought you here?
I do not think sorrow was with you at your birth,
for your face proclaims you to be a prince.
Fortune has favoured you, for it seems
that a jewel shines from your forehead,
like the full moon with all its lustre.
Apart from your own shadow, however,
you have no friend, no brother, no loved one with you.
    I am astonished that all alone you crossed the ocean and came here.
    How was it that the fearsome ghouls and demons spared you?

215. 'The moon and sun in heaven
do not shed their light here.
How did you, a human, come here?
I ask you, tell me about yourself.
What city are you from,
and what is your father's name?
Tell me from what land you come.
Is your clan a high-born one, or base?
Is your family royal or beggarly?
Your body is emaciated, as though
you were about to die.
I see neither flesh nor blood on your frame.
From beginning to end, I have told you my story.
Sit by me for a moment and tell me of your own sorrows.'

The Prince's Fear

216. Thus Pemā finished her entire story.
The Prince listened to everything she said.
When he heard about the demon,
his mind was fearful, and he thought:
'I must go away from this place.
If the demon comes here now,
he will slaughter me in an instant.
Where can I go to escape from him?
If I die now, I would regret it forever,
because a great task lies ahead of me
for which I left home and renounced my kingdom.'
Holding this resolve firm in his mind, the Prince stood up to leave.
But Pemā ran to fall at his feet, her eyes glistening with tears.

217. The Prince raised the maiden up.
When he saw her face, his heart
felt pity over her pain. Affection
was born in his mind, he was captured.
The ocean of love billowed over.

His heart burnt for Pemā's sorrow,
as if ghee* had been poured on the fire
which already burnt within him.
As he saw her the Prince's heart
was deeply moved, and compassion
stirred. He was unable to go.
As he saw her face, his heart was moved,
and boiled over to flow as blood in his veins.
   Only those who have felt pain within can understand the pain of the afflicted.
   Without this grief, how can you know the pain, the burning sorrow of another?

*Pemā's Sorrow**

218. Pemā wept such tears of blood,
that whoever heard her grieved deeply
in his heart. She was overcome
with emotion, her heart was convulsed.
Waves of blood welled up in the ocean
of her eyes. Grief overwhelmed her,
she could not utter a word.
She sighed, unable to speak at all.
Tears brimmed over in her eyes
like pearls pouring from their broken shells.
She opened her heart to the waves of sorrow.
Every pore of her being wept piteously.
   The sun, the moon, and the stars, Vāsuki,* Indra, and Kubera,*
   earth, heaven, and Mount Sumeru—all wept with Pemā's sorrow.

219. The red blood which Pemā wept in her grief
was the colour in which the parrot had washed his beak.
The crow and the cuckoo were burnt black
through her sorrow's flames,
and the trees went through a fall of leaf.
Lotuses and the colour of spring festivals

gained their redness from her tears.
All the flowers burst forth from their clothes.
The heart of the pomegranate cracked
into pieces when it saw her. On the branch
the lemon and the citron turned pale yellow.
The orange drank a sip of her blood
and turned blood-red. The date
broke its heart, stricken at her sorrow.
The mango blossomed, maddened by sorrow, and the *mahuā** lost all its leaves.
On hearing of Pema's pain, the sugar cane split into sections with grief.

220. The bee and the serpent were scorched
in this forest fire, and the caper bush*
abandoned all its leaves for sorrow.
From a sip of that blood, the henna*
was steeped in the colour of redness.
From grief, the jasmine flower* grew small.
The flame-of-the-forest* covered its head
with that fire, and the buds closed,
as if embracing the sorrow of Pemā.
Boughs laden with fruit bent with sadness.
Lilies and lotuses sank into the water.
The rose apple* turned black on the branch
from grief, and the green jack-fruit
wrapped itself in a thorny sari.*
The *ghunghuci* berry,* red with a black dot, reddened itself by crying tears of blood.
The whole world knows it went to the forest ashamed, face blackened by this sin.

221. The *baḍahal* fruit turned yellow*
in the flames of Pemā's sorrow,
and everyone knows this is why
the tamarind grew twisted.*
Out of grief the trees bit the earth,
gripping it firmly with their teeth.
The wishing-tree left this world altogether.*

The green pigeon,* weighed down with sadness,
came down to the earth, and the black bat
hung itself upside-down out of sorrow.
The kite, terrified by Pemā's grieving,
became sometimes male, sometimes female.
The vine was terrified, and clung
fearfully, timidly to the tree.
The drongo lost its own voice and began to warble in many tongues.*
Then it burnt itself black as coal, out of grief for Pemā's affliction.

222. Then Pemā sighed deeply and spoke
sweet words: 'Listen, O Prince!
Don't fear the demon in your mind.
Be not afraid, and stay here confident.
The demon has gone away somewhere,
and he left not a moment ago.
He wanders about the whole day,
and comes here at night to guard me.
O lord of men, tell me what you suffer,
the grief which made you assume this guise.
Until you tell me everything that has happened to you, O Prince!
You may be sure that I shall not allow you to go from here.'

Manohar Explains

223. The Prince replied, 'Hear me, O Princess,
O royal darling! I became a beggar
suffering in separation from Madhumālatī.
How can I describe the indescribable?
If I were to speak and to write
for aeons, still it would not be finished.
Were I to speak of it, my mouth
would not be able to tell the tale,
for the story of separation can never end.
Listen now to the origin of my agony,

for there is no end to it in the four aeons.
Let me tell you how love and grief
and separation came about, although
no one has found its end in this world.
  If the seven seas became ink, and the seven heavens were paper, O Pemā!
  Even if I were to write through the ages, the sadness of separation would not lessen.

224. 'Since you have asked me, Pemā,
listen and I will tell you my grief.
Kanaigiri, the city of gold, is a pleasant place,
paradise itself come down to earth.
The whole world knows my father's name.
He is the illustrious Sūrajbhānu.
Ten thousand *kosas** his kingdom stretches—
horses, elephants, limitless wealth and armies.
Only one child was born to him,
who fell into the grip of separation's sorrow.
  Grief for Madhumālatī has entered my soul, how can I describe this pain?
  It feels like suffering has no place in the world, except for my afflicted soul.

225. 'Listen now to the beginning,
the origin of my sorrowful story,
how grief became my soul's companion.
It is a tale which cannot be told.
I'll tell a little, explaining its true meanings.*
One day sleep had come to my eyes.
When I awoke, sorrow awoke.
I saw a dream that was real.
What I saw, I cannot describe.
If I call it a dream, it seems real.
If I call it real, it was not so.
  I do not know what it was I saw—was it real, or was it a dream?
  It was too real for a dream, but it was not reality that I saw before me.

226. 'I saw a maiden's curling black tresses
like poisonous serpents writhing about her head.
When my glance fell on her mole,
it captured my soul with every passing moment.
For one drop of nectar from her lips,
a thousand drops of my heart's blood thirsted.
How can I describe her lively eyes,
like a pair of wagtails on the wing?*
A sidelong glance took my life in an instant.
Wherever my gaze fell on her body,
it was transfixed and could not move.
The pointed breasts of that maiden pierced my eyes so painfully,
I cannot now dislodge them, they stick in my eyes again and again.'

227. The Prince then recounted all that had passed:
how he was enamoured of Madhumālatī,
of their first meeting on that night,
and how their beds were interchanged.
And he described their mutual vows,
and how they had exchanged their rings
as testimony to their true oaths.
He told her how he had left
his father's palace in the guise of a yogi,
how all his wealth had sunk in the ocean,
and the mounting wave had washed him shorewards.
The Prince wept as he described to Pemā all the sorrows he had gone through:
'No one can know what fate writes for the future, and what will happen next.

228. 'Pemā, my soul is no longer in my body.
I am speaking these words without a soul.
I can understand neither love nor separation,
for I have eaten a thief's drugged sweets.*
Capital and profit, loss and gain—
I had all these when my soul was with me.
Suddenly the spark of separation fell on my heart,

and all was consumed in the blaze—
capital and profit, loss and gain.
When my eyes have drunk sweet nectar,
how can my heart be content with just her name?
    Night and day these eyes have drunk the nectar of the
        beloved's beauty.
    What solace can it offer my heart to recall her name
        again and again?

229. 'When Madhumālatī's beauty entered my eyes,
I knew for certain within my heart
that the beauty which let me drink of love's delight
would set me wandering from land to land.
The blood which I drank in separation from her
flows out of my eyes as tears of blood.
Tears rain in sorrow from my eyes.
I place great hope in this rain.
Perhaps that first lightning flash of my fate
will flash again when it sees this downpour.
    Hope does not desert my heart when I see this rainy
        season of my eyes.
    Love's lightning, my destiny, may flash again, since it
        shone here before.

230. 'I have lived in this hope for many days,
and God has brought me to you today.
I shall cool my heart with your words of nectar.
In you, I catch the scent of Madhumālatī's love.
When a man falls into the fathomless ocean,
his foot may suddenly chance on a shallow.
O excellent maiden, when I saw your face,
it saved me from drowning in an ocean of grief.
I have set my soul on the path of love,
and cannot find it on searching my body.
    I abandoned the pleasures of kingship, and lost my
        precious youth and my soul.
    emā, I have set out on the path of love, and who
        knows what may happen next?

231. 'O Pemā, I have told you, one by one,
all the sorrows of my heart.
I am alone here in this terrible place,
and separation's pain overwhelms my heart.
No one even mentions the name of Mahāras.
Pemā, I am blind, I don't know where to go!
Now there is no one left with me,
and grief is my only companion.
In you I sense the fragrance of love.
I feel that God will send me good news.
O Pemā, the scent of Madhumālatī's love comes to me from you.
With tears in my eyes, I have told you all the tale of my sorrows!'

Pemā Consoles the Prince

232. When the Prince had finished the story
of his suffering, Pemā's heart
was filled with sympathy. She said,
'O Prince, you are tired of grief,
so you make separation's long sorrow short.
Blessed is the life of the man
who sacrifices his all for separation's agony.
Not every drop in the ocean makes a pearl,
nor is every heart radiant with separation's light.
One among millions in this world
knows the pain of separation in his body.
Are jewels found in every ocean? Or elephant-gems in every elephant?*
Does sandal grow in every forest? Can separation be known by every heart?

233. 'The man in whose heart God puts pain
is the king of all the three worlds.
He who climbs on the path of love
loses his soul. Love is a road
to travel with one's soul or one's beloved—

not both. The flames of separation
flare up in all the directions
and the one who is not touched by them
is the most unfortunate wretch.
No one should call separation pain.
In this world, separation is a joy.
The man to whom God shows separation
can see in all sorrows only happiness.
Manjhan says that love-in-separation is the herb of immortality in this life.
Whoever finds it becomes immortal in all ages; death cannot come near him.

234. 'Whoever longs for love's nectar-sweet fruit
loses his selfhood spontaneously, naturally.
The man who chooses this path,
and does not welcome death,*
can never taste love's immortal fruit.
First, take your head in your hands,
then set foot on the road of love!
Whoever takes separation to his heart
can illuminate his spiritual eye—
to him, all three worlds are clear.*
May the Creator never give life to a man
who is never drunk with the wine of love.
The agony of separation is a fathomless ocean, as the world knows.
The man who can dive in and bring up a pearl is the true diver.*

235. 'The man whose heart is not consumed
by the flames of separation's fire,
might just as well have not been born.
He who has not devoted his heart
to the practice of love, has not attained
the reward of being born in the mortal world.
Only the man whose soul burns in separation
can truly benefit from life in this world.
How can one call that grief a sorrow

from which one gets the treasure of the beloved?
The man whose heart and soul are on fire
spontaneously gives up his own selfhood.
  In the ocean of love, when waves rise and crash in the waters of sorrow,
  poor wretched lovers fall in, abandoning all hope of continuing life.

236. 'Only the man who loses life and youth
knows the essence of love-in-separation.
Love is a gamble in which only he wins
who stakes his life on a throw of the dice.
The ocean of love is deep and fathomless.
Only one in a million can swim in it.
Does separation come into the world in vain?
Separation's form is creation itself.
The man who applies the kohl of separation
to his eyes, can see that the world
is just a manifestation of separation.
  Manjhan says that the mortal creature who did not delight in separation's agony
  is like a guest in an empty house, coming into this world and leaving it as he came.

237. 'Whoever does not turn head over heels
cannot traverse this path correctly.*
Whoever opens his eyes to all forms of beauty
dies and gains life beyond comparison.
Whoever gives one soul on this path
gets in return a hundred souls.
Through silence, he speaks of everything.
His ears hear all of the story
which cannot be told in this world.
His vision embraces all existence
and his form becomes immortal.
  The man in whose body desire is born, from the manifold feelings of separation,
  is the bridegroom of the triple world, for the Lord has given him this pain.

238. 'Only he gains the fruit of worldly life
who sacrifices his soul on this path.
If you lose yourself in love for someone,
they become the guide and show the way.
When knowledge is born spontaneously in the heart,
how can anyone lose their way in love?
The five elements* become as one,
and the body is transmuted into the soul.
Spontaneously all things reveal the state of *sahaja*
and the soul appears manifest in bodily form.
Separation's pain is a treasure of happiness, do not fret under this suffering!
The Lord creates some to keep faith in love, and they rule both now and hereafter.

239. 'No one should be distressed by grief
for the end of grief is happiness.
Joy is the clear rainwater in the black clouds,
that streams down between sorrows in the world.
When trees lose their leaves in Phāgun,*
they soon sprout new leaves and buds.
Henna is crushed between two stones
before it can come into its true red colour!
Only the pearl pierced in many ways
can be placed at the breast of a lotus-like lady.
Know that happiness in this world comes between two periods of sorrow.
Though the night is at its darkest, there is the brilliance of the dawn to come.

240. 'O Prince, since you have suffered great sorrow,
now God has granted you a lucky meeting.
If the line of fate is on your forehead,
then your night of grief will end in daybreak.
If the compassionate Lord has mercy on you,
in a few days you will meet that girl.
You have fallen into the deep ocean of sadness,
but I can ferry you across with happy news.
Hear then from me news of the one

for whose sake you are fettered by sorrow.
    You embarked on the ocean and plunged into it, and put on the garments of grief.
    But now good days are drawing near—listen and I will give you good counsel!

Pemā and Madhumālatī

241. 'Listen as I tell you about the one,
for whom your soul is consumed with passion.
She is the princess of the city of Mahāras.
Out of love for her, you became a beggar.
She and I played together as children.
Madhumālatī was my childhood friend.
She and I were always together,
and enjoyed the delights of girlhood as one.
Now, O Prince, I do not know how she is,
since the Creator put me in this dark wood.
    Always together as girls, we two would play and dance the *dhamār*.*
    But now it is a year since we parted, when God cast me into this forest.'

242. When the Prince heard her sweet words,
he was overjoyed and fainted with delight.
Love returned and went to his head,
like borax making gold shine in the flame.
Love made his soul revive afresh,
flaring up like ghee cast into burning fire.
His soul went out to Madhumālatī.
He fell without breath to the ground.
In a little while, consciousness returned.
Opening his eyes, he was aware, percipient.
    His body trembled with separation's pain, and his legs were weak and unsteady.
    Tears filled his eyes as he began to utter what he had to say to Pemā.

243. 'Listen, O Pemā,' said the Prince.

'From the time my heart was overwhelmed
with passion for Madhumālatī,
I have neither seen nor heard of anyone
who knows where her country lies.
Since the time she appeared in my dream,
I have heard no news of her.
Now she has banished sleep from my eyes,
and I cannot see her even in a dream.
Only he can dream, O Pemā,
whose eyes can rest happily in sleep.
    Since she revealed herself in a dream and left, sleep has disappeared from my eyes.
    Please help me now, for God's sake, so that my life's breath can return to my body.

244. 'Tell me now the sweet tale I ask for,
for its *rasa* would revive this dying man.
Where is she who is as dear to me
as life itself? How do you know her?
Today, O Pemā, is an auspicious day,
for today I shall hear news of Madhumālatī.
Advise me how I can meet that girl,
whose virtues are my daily rosary.
O God, when will that day come
when I shall see that matchless moon-face?
    As Lakṣmaṇa was struck by the mighty lance, so I am filled with separation's pain.
    O Pemā, you must be my Hanumān, and find for me the life-restoring herb!'*

245. As he spoke, he began to faint,
but then he remembered where he was
and his strength returned of its own accord.
One moment he was aware,
and the next, restless and unaware.
What victim of love can restrain himself?
He put his head on her feet and wept,
and the water from his eyes
washed that moon-faced maiden's feet.

'O Lord,' she said, 'giver of life
to the triple world, why do you not
let him meet the one whom he loves?
Since you have brought such a Prince
into the world, O Master, do not
give him the agony of separation!
Let them suffer all other sorrows as they occur in the world around,
only, O God, do not give these young lovers the pain of separation!'

246. That excellent maiden, full of virtue and beauty,
began then to recount a tale sweet as nectar.
'O Prince,' she said, 'Become conscious now
and listen carefully to this nectar-sweet tale.
Vikram Rāi is the King of Mahāras.
His power extends ten thousand leagues.
In his house is a maiden daughter,
the matchless light of the three worlds.
The sun and moon do not rival her beauty.
I do not have wit enough, O Prince,
to describe even the reflection of her beauty.
Her auspicious beauty is like an ocean whose limits cannot be conceived.
How can my poor and helpless tongue hope to traverse this sea?

247. 'Listen to another pleasing thing:
Madhumālatī is like a sister to me.
We have known each other from the time
when we were children in our mothers' laps.
One day her mother was standing
with a girl-child held in her arms,
and ten handmaidens stood around them.
My mother's glance fell on them.
She saw a group of several women
and apprehension grew within her heart.
One of them was foremost in beauty and virtue; on her brow shone the line of fortune.

She held in her embrace a girl who was like the
incarnation of a heavenly nymph.

248. 'My mother gathered up her courage to greet her
and bowed her head low to the ground.
Then my mother entreated softly,
"Come and sit down by me, O best of women!
I feel extreme shyness and cannot speak,
but sit down by me and I shall serve you."
When she saw my mother's good nature,
she knelt down on one foot and then sat down.
Sitting there the two embraced closely
and swore to be as sisters to each other.
My mother anointed her with *catursama* paste,* and
dressed her in a new sari.
Glad songs were sung throughout the city, and kettle-
drums beaten in every house.

249. 'Then my mother asked her thus:
"My sister, swear to God to tell the truth.
I see on you all the signs of royalty,
and my mind is confused and amazed.
Tell me your name and where you are from.
Of which royal family are you the Queen?
Are you a *gandharva*,* goddess, or nymph?
Or have you been created in mortal form?
Enlighten me about the skill by which
you are able to fly, now here, now there.
Since you have come here, and we have recognized our
mutual love and affection,
I shall preserve this love between us, O beautiful one,
even to the end of my life!"

250. 'That excellent maiden spoke then,
in slow words, sweet and tender.
She said, "My city is Mahāras, its king,
Vikram Rāi, protector of the earth!
He is a great king of the *gandharvas*,
endowed with virtue, power, and might.
I am his wife, Rūpamañjarī,

blessed by fortune with beauty and goodness.
The child that you see in my embrace
is the greatest fruit of my life.
Now that such love has been born in my heart for you, I shall come
on the second day of every month, to meet you and to renew our affection."

251. 'Until now she has fulfilled her promise,
and she comes to our house
each month on the second day.
In one year, that excellent lady
comes twelve times to our house.
And the Princess Madhumālatī
always accompanies her mother.
O Prince, if you go to Citbisarāuṉ,
go to our house and mention me.
My brother and sister, father and mother,
all will serve you and love you devotedly.
If they hear news of me, they will listen compassionately to your tale of grief.
They will arrange for you to meet Madhumālatī, think of this as my own word to you!

252. 'All my girlfriends and companions
will be most attentive to your need.
All my family and relations
will help you as much as they can.
The love between you is long established
and you have made promises to each other.
Just as you suffer the pangs of separation,
so too will she be suffering in her body.
Nobody will know anything, not even a whisper,
and you will spontaneously win
Madhu, the object of your deepest love.
Since the love between you is old and true, here is my advice for you:
go from here to my homeland, and there you will find your soul-mate.'

The Prince's Resolve

253. When the Prince heard this story
of love, full of the sweetest nectar,
his body turned pale yellow.
He paled at the mention of his beloved,
but his soul remained with him.
His sad face, full of despair,
blossomed like a lotus as he listened.
As he understood more and more,
he rejoiced gladly in his heart.
For sheer happiness, his heart
could not be contained in his body.
He had been unhappy with separation's pain,
but now he thrilled to hear his darling's name.
    As the lotus and the lily blossom in the light of the sun and the moon,
    just so the Prince's heart exulted with love, when he heard this nectar-sweet tale.

254. His heart exulted, his mind rejoiced,
like the lotus and the water-lily open
to the sun's radiance and the moonlight.
'Listen, O Princess,' said the Prince,
'From now, I vow to regard you as a sister.
You have given me good counsel
and sustained me, now I will be kind to you.
I was without hope, my existence was lifeless,
and you sprinkled nectar and revived me.
How can I go and leave you like this?
How can I abandon you to save myself?
    I know that your family would hurry out to welcome me with all homage,
    but merely to tell them your message would be a stain on my family's honour.'

255. Hearing the Prince's words, Pemā was moved,
and her lotus eyes filled with tears.
She laid her head on the ground and cried.

Such was her grief that she wished to die.
Heaving a deep sigh, she said,
'O Prince, abandon hope for me.
Do not destroy yourself for my sake,
but do as I have advised you.
Whatever happiness I have granted you,
take it and go forward on your path.
Do not throw away your life in vain!
    There is no hope of salvation for me while I live, O Prince!
    Do not destroy yourself in vain, for the sake of saving my life.

256. 'Do not be anxious about me, O Prince,
but go and taste your own promised fruit.
I am dying through my own luck,
do not, O Prince, die for my sake!
I am a maiden in a demon's clutches.
Who else but God could rescue me?
Even if we were to go a thousand *kosa*s,
and hide ourselves inside the earth,
in the twinkling of an eye he would come
and wipe all trace of us from the world.
    For one, my heart was always grieving before this at my own distress.
    Now that I have heard your sorrow, my grief has doubled all the more.'

257. Hear now the brave words which the Prince
happily spoke to the beautiful maiden.
'If God grant me victory,
I shall kill this demon and rescue you.
Banish fear from your heart, O maiden,
for I am a demon-slayer of the line of Raghu.
Pemā, if I do not protect women and cows,
my mother's family will be dishonoured.
If I leave you and run away now,
even death will not be able to wash away
the shameful stain on my family's honour.

If I run away and abandon you for fear of this demon,
O Pemā!
I shall earn disgrace for the rest of my life, and stain my
family name.

258. 'Why do you frighten me with this demon?
Why scatter ashes to make me afraid of fire?
What can the demon dare to do to me?
He is like a worm who will die easily
when he comes into the light.
Just you see how I take his life,
and destroy him in an instant!
I shall raise fire with the brilliant edge
of my sword, and blow away the demon
in clouds of wind and smoke.
If a warrior flees at the moment of danger,
he brings disgrace to his family
and his mother is ashamed of him.
Except for the truth, O Pemā, nothing is immortal in
this Kali age!
If I abandoned you and fled, I would shame my family's
name.

259. 'You have taken Madhumālatī's name,
so how can I leave you and go?
O excellent maiden, just you see what I can do
when I recall my love for Madhumālatī.
O best of women, through faith in my beloved
I can do things I never could accomplish.
In one blow I shall fell him to the ground,
and cut him up into many pieces.
See how I let flow a river of blood,
and satisfy the jackals and vultures with his flesh!
If God gives me victory over the demon, then there will
be celebrations.
If not, then I shall take Madhumālatī's name, and care
not whether I live or die!'

260. When the Prince had spoken these brave words,
Pemā's heart was set at ease.

The two, absorbed in pleasant talk, forgot
that the time for the demon's return drew near.
Then Pemā said, 'Listen, O Prince,
be alert now, for this is the time
when the demon returns every day.'
Hearing this he became very frightened and said,
'I have no weapons, how can I slay the foe?'
Pemā responded, 'Have no fear!
Take courage, for I will give you weapons.'
　When he heard about the arms, the Prince rejoiced in his heart and asked,
　'Where did you get these weapons? Tell me everything about them!'

261. Pemā responded, 'I'll tell you all
about the weapons, since you ask!
These weapons which I have here
belonged to the men whom the demon ate.'
She brought before him all the arms,
and the Prince selected those he liked.
He made ready the weapons he needed:
swords and spears, lances and daggers.
He was fearless because separation's essence
had entered his soul, and because he had on
the guise of a Gorakhnāthī ascetic.
　Smearing himself with separation's ashes, the Prince looked like Death embodied.
　Now he could destroy all the three worlds, not just this wretch of a demon!

The Demon

262. When the Prince looked in all directions,
he saw signs of the demon towards the south.
He came flying between heaven and earth,
and stopped over Pemā's pavilion.
His form was fearsome, his nature grotesque.
Both his feet were on the earth, and yet
his head reached all the way to the heavens.

The demon's form appeared like dark clouds
lowering in the sky in the rainy month of Sāvan.*
Five heads he had, and ten mighty arms,
and his ten eyes shone like stars in the sky.
The lines of his teeth looked like white gourd-melons* put together and set in place.
His colour was black and frightening, and on seeing him, the soul was afraid.

263. When the demon saw the Prince standing there,
he blazed with anger from head to foot.
He laughed and said, 'Who are you?
What is your name? Has Death
already seized you, that you come here?
Death is here, and hovers over your head.
Your bad luck has brought you to this pavilion.
Are you so annoyed with your life?
Or has Death come to plunder your house?
Has your life's span reached its end?
Have you received a summons from Yama's mouth?
O mortal, you are edible, a meal which the Creator has provided for me.
Your death draws nearer to you—I have found my favoured food!'

264. Pemā prostrated herself in the pavilion.
With joined hands, she entreated Hari.
The maiden prayed, her head on the ground,
'O merciful Lord, grant victory to the Prince!
You give joy to the three worlds, O God.
Whom could I beseech except for you?
Do not snatch my hopes from me.
The Prince has only your protection, Lord!
I can only be courageous and do my duty,
but ultimate success is in your hands alone!
O Lord, you alone grant salvation and freedom, you are the hope of those in despair.
The earth, the heavens, and the nether world—all of Creation prays to you.'

265. When the Prince heard the demon's words,
his whole body burned with fury.
He said, 'Stop bragging, demon!
It is your death that draws near now.
I shall kill you and take Pemā from here.
Then I shall be truly called a member
of the illustrious dynasty of Raghu.
Now is my manliness aroused.
Do not take deluded pride
in the size of your huge body!
I will wrench out all your ten arms,
and hack off your five heads
and throw them into the dust.
    I am a spark from the fire of Raghu's line, and you are a mound of cotton.
    In an instant I shall burn you to ashes, if the Creator so desires.'

The Battle

266. When the demon heard these venomous words,
his ten eyes blazed red with rage.
The more he heard, the more he burned
with anger, and when he shouted out loud
it seemed the heavens were thundering.
The demon pounced on the Prince, saying,
'I shall tear you up, living as you are,
and scatter the pieces in all ten directions.'
But as he jumped, the Prince drew his sword
and cut off a head and two of his arms.
The demon bowed down, picked up arms and head,
and flew up in the sky roaring with laughter.
    In an instant, he had affixed his head and arms on his body,
    and came down and stood ready to face the Prince in battle.

267. The Prince heard the demon coming.
He became alert and took up his bow.

When he looked carefully at the demon,
he saw that his heads and arms were intact.
The demon saw the bow and arrows
and did not approach the Prince.
From a distance he displayed his magic power.
Putting on a magical form the demon drew near,
saying, 'Now I am going to eat you alive!'
He opened his maw, terrifying to behold,
and ran forward towards the Prince.
The Prince set arrow to bow and fired.
    Just as the demon reached the Prince, the arrow struck him in his heart.
    When the arrow hit, the demon became invisible, and fled roaring into the sky.

268. So the day passed and night fell.
The Prince had neither won the battle,
nor had the demon been slain.
Then the demon grew restless with hunger,
and said, 'You and I will fight tomorrow.'
As night fell the demon left in search of food.
Pemā came then to the Prince and spoke:
'O Prince, there was something I forgot to say.
Hear now how the demon can be killed.
I was not able to tell you before,
but I know how to slay the demon.
    Though the three worlds should combine, still they would not be able to kill him.
    Were they to hack him into a thousand pieces, still he would come alive again.'

269. Then Pemā explained to the Prince:
'Listen, here is how you can kill the enemy.
In the garden you see towards the south,
is a tree heavy with immortal ambrosial fruit.
It is dense, shady, and laden with fruit,
and in it lives the demon's soul.*
Until that tree is destroyed,
there is no way to slay the demon.

To uproot the tree is to kill the demon,
otherwise he will never be slain.
Let us go now, you and I, to the garden to destroy the tree with its fruit of immortality.
When you wound the demon, his heart will break, and he will die easily enough.'

270. When he heard about the fruit
that granted immortality, the Prince
rose up and looked towards the south.
Now he knew in his mind with certainty
how the demon lived on after being killed.
'Pemā,' he said, 'Come with me,
and show me this immortal, ambrosial fruit.'
The two of them set off together,
just as the demon came by
with fire blazing from all his heads.
But Pemā led the Prince onwards
on to the tree with the fruit of immortality.
When he saw the tree, his heart rejoiced and his soul was overcome with joy.
He became certain that now God would grace him with the pennant of victory.

The Tree of Immortality

271. The Prince examined the tree carefully.
He saw that it was dense of leaf,
a *karṇikāra* tree* laden with fruit.
When he saw it his heart filled with pity,
for a fruit-bearing tree should not be cut down.
Then that excellent maiden asked the Prince:
'Why do you delay over an enemy's life?
If one can overcome one's enemy,
tell me, O Prince, why should one delay?
Take careful heed of what I say.
No fire is too small—do not underestimate
even a glimmering, a flicker of fire!
Hurry up and delay no more, if you are thirsty for your enemy's blood.

If you find him in your power, do not even let him draw breath!'

272. When Pemā had explained this to the Prince,
his consciousness became aware again.
He stood up and approached the tree.
Flexing his arms, he made firm his resolve.
He grasped the tree with both hands.
Calling on the name of Hari, he pulled up
the tree of immortality by its roots.
Then he took all its leaves, branches, and fruits,
and burnt them up in a fire he made.
The Prince then took the heavy wood
of pain, and cast it into the bonfire.
Having uprooted the tree of immortality and burnt it down to ashes,
happily the Prince and Princess returned to their four-cornered pavilion.

Manohar's Victory

273. Night passed and the sun spread its rays,
and the demon came roaring to the door.
Black was his form and fearsome to behold,
and he had a discus in either hand.
When the Prince heard him coming,
he took his bow in his hand,
and strapped on his sword, thirsty for blood.
He gathered up a spear and an axe,
and smeared ashes on his face and body.
He took staff, discus, and trident,
and prayed to the Lord for protection.
Recollecting Hari in his heart, he came out looking like Death incarnate.
The demon saw him and grew angry, and let loose a discus to kill him.

274. The demon hurled his discus in wrath,
but the Prince shielded himself successfully.

The demon then threw his second discus,
but Manohar warded it off with his shield.
When the discus hit the shield,
the sparks of fire reached the heavens.
Then Manohar took his chance and pounced.
He wounded the demon in his head.
The demon's fifth head, endowed with special power,
fell to the ground, gashed by the sword.
When he was wounded thus fatally, the demon picked up his head.
He flew towards where the garden was, in the direction of the south.

275. The Prince then ran towards the garden,
to find out about what would happen
with the demon and the tree of immortality.
He saw the demon staggering about,
fatally wounded in a vital place.
The demon came and threw down his head
in the place where the tree had been.
When he did not find the tree,
he despaired and knew his end was near.
Fire was ravaging the house of his life,
his spirit was about to leave his body.
Just as a tree whose roots have been hacked up suddenly falls to the ground,
so the demon dropped to the earth when the spirit departed from his frame.

276. Seeing the demon had given up his life,
Pemā rejoiced in her heart.
She ran towards the Prince,
waved her sari's border over him,
and pressed it to her heart thankfully.
She said, 'What can I sacrifice to you?
Had I but a thousand lives in my body,
I would dedicate them all to you.
Blessed is the father who begot you,
blessed the mother who suckled you with her milk.

Let us quickly leave this place,
so that God may grant us salvation.
    My heart is filled with fear, and my soul trembles with apprehension,
    lest this demon who has fallen dead should spring to life again.'

277. The Prince said to that alluring maiden,
'Your heart's cause for fear is gone.
Drive out all sorrow from your mind,
for God has taken away grief
and given you joy in its place.
Suffer grief no more. It is my worry,
even if we meet a hundred thousand sorrows!'
They both arose and set out on their way.
For four months they travelled through thick woods,
until at last they came to an inhabited land
and saw the fairest beauty of the age of Kali.
    Finally they approached Pemā's home, the pleasant city ruled by Citrasena,
    a town unparalleled in beauty, with dense mango groves around it in all four directions.

Pemā's Homecoming

278. When Pemā saw the city of Citrasena,
her heart and mind were full of joy.
When she saw the tall and graceful palaces,
she was overcome with excitement.
Approaching the Prince she said,
'Be happy now, let your heart celebrate,
for this is Ease-of-Mind, my father's city,
Citbisarāuṉ, about which I told you.
O royal Prince, take off your yogi's garb,
be aware that your courage has borne fruit.
    Cast sorrow from your consciousness, celebrate with joy,
    for in this very city, you and Madhumālatī will meet again.'

279. When the Prince heard the name
of that alluring maiden, he trembled,
and his body burnt with separation.
At the mention of meeting Madhumālatī,
he revived like a corpse coming back to life.
It was as if a thirsty man had found water,
or as though night had ended for the *cakī* bird.*
It was as if the honey-bee had caught
the sweet scent of the jasmine flower,
or the lotus had blossomed with the sun's rays.*
He became like the *papīhā* who caught
the raindrops of the constellation of Svātī,*
or the lily overwhelmed with love for the moon.
When two lovers of old meet again, after being parted for an age,
the rejoicing in their hearts cannot be equalled by a palace's festivities.

280. Then that excellent maiden, Pemā,
approached the Prince and explained,
'Listen, O Prince, to what I have to say.
I am the daughter of this city's royal house.
How can we enter the palace dressed like this?
Why should we amuse the mean-minded?
My mother and father, and all their retainers,
will rush to see us, whether they're related or not.
Let us stay at a caravanserai today,
and send a letter to my mother and father.'
Thus the Prince and that lovely maiden stayed in a village that day,
from where the city of Citbisarāu̱n was but a *kosa* and a half.

281. The King was sitting enthroned in court,
when suddenly his heart leapt for joy.
'Today,' he said, 'the omens are good,
for my heart fills spontaneously with joy.
My right eye and arm are quivering today
as though a loved one were coming to my embrace.

These auspicious omens foretell
that I shall meet someone as dear as life to me.
Fair signs such as these do not deceive,
an absent loved one will come to me today.'
His mind was happy, his heart rejoiced, and affection arose spontaneously in his being.
To his house would come a long separated one: thus did the signs foretell.

282. Pemā sat down and wrote a letter
in which she told of all her sufferings.
Hearing it would cause the stoniest heart
to crack open as if struck by lightning.
When the tale of her grief arose within her
it became ink and flowed out onto the paper.
As she wrote of her sorrows in the forest,
it seemed that the sufferings would not end.
After her grief she wrote her salaams
to her mother and father, and to the family.
She sent her love and affectionate hugs
to all her girlfriends and companions.
Sisters and brothers, close relatives, and the members of her family—
all of them she remembered, and to every one sent her salaams.

283. When she had finished writing her sad tale,
she sent for a messenger to deliver it.
Pemā fell at his feet and said,
'Please move quickly, without any delay.'
The envoy took the letter and ran.
He went rejoicing, so that his feet
scarcely seemed to touch the ground.
The envoy sped more swiftly than the wind,
faster than the eye could follow.
Within moments he had arrived
and stood at the door of the royal palace.
The envoy summoned the watchman and said, 'Go and tell the King

that a messenger is at the door, with a message from his daughter Pemā.'

284. The watchman heard this and ran,
and broke the news in the royal palace,
'An envoy has come to the palace gates,
speaking sweet words most wonderful to hear.
He said something about a message
from your darling daughter Pemā.
When I heard the name of Pemā, I ran.
My mind was so overwhelmed with joy,
I did not wait to hear anything further.'
The King and Queen ran when they heard,
like fish out of water rushing back to the river.
Her mother and father, relatives and retainers, and all her girlfriends and companions,
rushed to the palace door, when they heard the name of that excellent maiden!

285. All ran when they heard Pemā's name,
and reached the door of the royal palace.
The King ran, unable to help himself.
The Queen could not control hands and feet.
The envoy advanced and saluted them,
and told them that Pemā was safe and well.
Then he gave them her letter,
which Citrasena clasped to his heart.
The Queen grew restless and asked,
'How far is my dear one from here?'
The envoy responded, 'A *kosa* and a half from here lies a village.
Our Princess has stopped there herself; it was she who sent me to you.'

286. When he heard, the King mounted his horse.
All his family and retainers accompanied him.
A palanquin was prepared for the Queen,
and sounds of happy celebration rang out.
Behind the Queen came all the girlfriends
who had played with Pemā since childhood.

All the thirty-six working castes of the city,
ran when they heard the name of Pemā.
Horses were harnessed and saddle-cloths fastened,
and the messenger went on ahead of the King.
  I'd sacrifice myself on that day, that blessed hour, and on the moment of meeting.
  I'd sacrifice body, mind, and soul, and give up wealth, the world, and all.

287. Her family came to meet Pemā,
and made propitious offerings as thanks.
She touched her parents' feet,
and greeted all the others with embraces.
Then came all her girlfriends to meet her,
those who had played with her in childhood.
Then all her serving maids came,
singing as they touched her feet in greeting.
The women of the thirty-six castes came next,
with sandal paste on their bodies,
vermilion colouring the partings on their heads.
  The city rang with celebrations throughout, and her family was overwhelmed with joy.
  Auspicious songs were sung in every house, and everywhere there was a happy tumult.

288. Then Citrasena asked the girl,
'Who rescued you and set you free?
Who released you from the demon's power?
How did you reach safety and freedom?
Tell me how it has happened
that the Lord was so kind to you.
Who was this second incarnation of Rāma,
who killed Rāvana and set Sītā free?*
Say who is this companion of yours,
who has made our dark world light again?
  For without you the whole world remained pitch dark for our eyes.
  Tell us through whose courageous deeds our world has become radiant again?'

289. Pemā began to tell her father,
'There is with me a Prince,
courageous, nobly born, and wise,
who is in love with Madhumālatī.'
She told her parents then of all the sorrows
suffered by the brave Prince.
The maiden then described how he had
challenged and killed the demon.
Indeed she recounted to her father,
all the brave acts which he had performed.
'The Lord', she said, 'brought the Prince to the forest
where I was imprisoned.
I told him all my grief, and heard from him the true
essence of his sufferings.'

290. 'I told him truly how the demon
had brought me to the forest.
And then the Prince described to me
how he fell passionately in love
with Madhumālatī. When I was sure
in my heart that he had abandoned himself
completely to Madhumālatī's beauty,
then I told him all that I knew
about that lovely maiden, Madhumālatī:
how we were bosom friends and close,
and had known each other since we were little.
I also informed him of the promise Madhumālatī's
mother had made,
how she always comes here faithfully on the second day
of every month.

291. 'When the Prince heard about her,
he thrilled and his body turned pale.
He fell at my feet and said,
"I dedicate my life to you!
I have not yet found my true love,
but you, O Princess, have given me new life.
If I leave you here in the forest,
it would shame my mother

and stain with dishonour my entire family.
You are a friend of Madhumālatī's,
so how can I abandon you in the forest?"
He killed the demon and rescued me, all with his own strength and confidence.
Treat him with all respect and honour, for he is my adopted brother.'

Manohar is Welcomed

292. Citrasena heard this and sent his minister,
who brought the Prince in with all honour.
The King stood up and embraced him,
and offered him the seat next to his own.
He said, 'How can I praise you enough?
How can I overcome even a little
of the embarrassment I feel in my heart?
O Prince, it is through your brave deeds,
that the soul which had left my body,
has returned once again to its frame.
Regard this kingdom and throne as your own,
without hesitating at all in your heart.
Stay here with us as you would stay in your father's royal palace.
Leave aside your grief, your ascetic's garb, play and enjoy yourself.

293. 'And whatever your heart desires,
the Creator will surely bring about.
My beloved daughter Pemā
will serve you devotedly all the time.
Treat all my servants, my retainers,
as if they belonged entirely to you.'
The King had a palace prepared near by,
and there the Prince was taken to stay.
Everyone served him all together,
that he might tarry there and not go elsewhere.
The Prince, however, remained an ascetic out of love for Madhumālatī.

His body remained there, but his soul had gone to the
one whom he loved.

The Prince is Sorrowful

294. For several days the Prince remained thus,
but the fires of separation burnt away in his heart.
'Hear me, O girl,' he said to Pemā,
'Love's fire blazes up in my body.
If you give me permission, I would go
in search of my darling love.
Perhaps my sleeping fate will awake,
and I may meet in manifest form
what lies hidden in my heart already.
Love's flames will not be quenched for an instant.
My body is ablaze with separation's undying fire.
It is a difficult fire, this separation, for it consumes my
body moment by moment.
Pemā, it is a pain which is so intense that another
cannot even bear to listen to it.'

295. When the Princess heard Manohar's account
she became very sad and said,
'Why are you so distressed now?
I have told you the entire secret,
but it seems your mind has forgotten it.
Tomorrow is the second day of the month,
which is the occasion for her visit,
and that girl will come here with her mother.
At dawn you should go and sit down
in the picture-pavilion in the garden.*
As soon as she and I meet,
we'll come to the pavilion on the pretext of play.
If she remembers her past love, and the two of you
recognize each other,
spontaneously you will come together in love, you and
that alluring Princess.'

296. Joy overwhelmed the Prince's heart
when he heard the time of union was near.
He remembered everything again,
and fell down at Pemā's feet.
She raised his head from her feet and said,
'Tomorrow morning, I will unite you.'
His mind was satisfied on hearing of the reunion.
He happily arose and came to the pavilion.
The night passed like an age for the Prince.
For love's sake, he stayed awake all night.
Only one kept awake by separation,
can know how long is the night of pain.
The night passed and day dawned, with the sun spreading its radiance.
Madhumālatī came with her mother to the kingdom of Citrasena.

Madhumālatī's Arrival

297. When Madhumālatī recognized Pemā
they rushed to embrace each other.
Both friends were clever and youthful,
full of love's newly blossoming savour.
Madhumālatī asked, 'Listen, dear friend,
who rescued you from the demon?
Tell me your story, O friend.
Who reunited you with your family?
Tell me everything and in detail:
how did you attain safety and salvation?
Did the demon release you himself, or did someone bring you back by force?
Swear that you will tell me all, the truth about what happened to you.'

298. Since Madhumālatī had asked her
to promise to tell the truth,
Pemā began to recount her rescue.
'One day I wept as I remembered my family,
and went to sleep alone in my sorrow.

My heart was immersed in grief
when, in a dream, I saw your face.
You took my arm and raised me up,
and said, "Come, let's go and play!"
I sat up, awake, but there was no one there.
I wept desperately and cried aloud for help.
　But then it seemed to me that the good Lord had become happy with me,
　for the dark night of grief was relieved in just an instant.

299. 'Suddenly it was a happy time again.
The waters of joy quenched sorrow's fire.
A Prince, smitten with love for you,
was sent by God to where I was.
I made him swear to tell the truth,
and asked him all about himself.
In tears, he told me how he fell in love.
He described his sorrow for you so movingly,
that my heart's calm was lost as I listened.
His sorrow made my heart sore with grief,
water flowed from my eyes, drenching my blouse.
　Driven almost senseless, wounded by love, and crying, the Prince told me all—
　the affair of that love of old between you, and the events you shared together.

300. 'I dedicate myself to your feet,
you who have snapped my fetters of grief.
What sacrifice can I offer you,
through whose grace I have been redeemed?
I was drowning in the sea of grief,
when you became my boatman.
Were I to sacrifice my life for you,
I could never repay my debt to you.
Had the Prince not been enamoured of you,
how could I have escaped from captivity?
　I would sacrifice a thousand of my lives for you, and willingly too.

Through your grace God has granted me liberty and salvation!

301. 'I tell you, Madhumālatī, the Prince
asked me many times about our relationship.
So I told him openly of my sorrow,
putting aside my shyness in front of the Prince.
Then I spoke of our close friendship,
telling him plainly how it was between us.
When he heard your name he fell down senseless,
and writhed about as if stung by a snake.
When his consciousness returned to him,
he answered all my questions clearly.
In separation from you he smeared ashes on his body and became an ascetic.
He killed the demon and brought me here. Blessed is the mother who gave him birth!'

Madhumālatī's Astonishment

302. Madhumālatī was astonished when she heard.
She said, 'How could he know me?
Who is this Prince? How could I know him?
How is it he is enamoured of my beauty?
Where could he have seen me?
Who could have told him my name?
I am the Princess of my father's house,
so how would I know a strange man?
If my mother and father were to hear of it,
they would bury me alive as I stand here.
O Pemā, why do you disgrace me through this public accusation?
My gain is your gain, dear friend, and my loss is your loss.

303. 'You are wise, clever, and understanding.
Aren't you ashamed to talk like this?
I urge you, as forcefully as I can,
to speak at least a semblance of the truth.
I am from a noble family,

and the daughter of a royal house—
aren't you ashamed to say this about me?
It is only because of our childhood friendship
that I suffer your abuse so lightly.
The moon is in the sky, the white lotus
in a pond below the earth—
how could there be love between the two?*
My eyes have not seen his form, nor have my ears heard his name.
How could you disgrace me so for one whose name or home I know not?

304. 'Wise friend, please think before speaking.
Such talk can sink a woman's honour.
Your words have stung me like poison.
Can anyone weave such fantasies
like thread spun from mere dust?
I am still a girl in my mother's lap.
How could I have a friendship with a man?
I don't know whether he is dark or fair.
What kind of love? For what man?
How could anyone insult me like this?
One can only draw a picture
when one has found a proper surface.
What you have said, dear friend, is impossible; no one would say such things.
The class of women is a heap of ill-fame, and destroyed only through talk.'

The Token of Identity

305. When she heard Madhumālatī's answer,
Pemā looked at her lovely face and said laughing,
'Look me in the eyes as you speak, girl,
so I can see what nonsense you are talking.
Your eyes are learning new tricks now,
to deceive me with lies and falsehoods.
Do not expect to use cunning

to hide your pregnancy from a midwife!
It may be all right to deceive others,
but one should not lie to a friend.
I know everything about you, from the beginning to the end.
Mad girl, can love ever be hidden? Tell me everything openly and frankly.

306. 'Tell me truthfully what's happened
and stop your boasting to the skies.
Your face is pale, your body wasted—
love's anguish in you is clearly apparent.
Tell me all—how far can you dissemble?
Mad one, love cannot remain hidden.
You are my friend, dear as life to me.
Why then do you not speak openly?
If you do not trust me yet,
ask me and I will give you your token.'
Pemā borrowed the ring from the Prince and gave it to the lovely maiden.
She said, 'Where did you leave this? Take it if you recognize it as your own.'

Madhumālatī Distraught

307. When Madhumālatī saw the ring,
both her eyes brimmed over with tears.
She tried very hard to hide it,
but tears flowed uncontrollably from her eyes.
Love and musk cannot be concealed—
the one has a beautiful scent,
and the other yields separation's agony.
Love can never be hidden from others—
one's eyes well up and all the world knows.
Separation from one's beloved
is always apparent, can never be covered up.
Remembering her love of old, says Manjhan, a restless yearning awoke in her heart.

Unable to control herself, she flung her arms around
Pemā's neck and cried aloud.

308. Pemā forcibly freed her neck,
cheered her up and consoled her.
But Madhumālatī, distraught with separation,
her mind confused and bemused,
spoke in anguished tones and asked,
'Where is that Prince, dear friend,
who assailed me with love's agony
in my dream and then left me?
When I awoke from the dream
I found the bed was his, not mine.
And the signet ring in your hand,
he took away with him, giving me his ring.
Till now I have kept separation's fire contained, fearful
of my family's honour.
Out of shame I never told anyone, but secretly bore this
agony in my heart.

309. 'Separation is hard, and great my heart's pain.
My life is utterly shameless
for it will not depart this body.
What blessed hour was it
when we fell in love for the first time?
I do not burn in this fire all alone.
Is there anyone in the world
whose heart is not ablaze?
Until now this fire has burnt me in secret,
but now it blazes openly in all ten directions.
How long can this fever burn secretly,
now that the bonfire flares up everywhere?
I do not know what sort of magic beauty God came
down to show me.
I saw it but for an instant, yet I shall suffer throughout
my lifetime.

310. 'The pain of separation set fire to my heart,
a conflagration which blazes higher daily.

Why did my mother nurse me with milk?
Why did she not feed me poison instead?
Why did the midwife who cut my cord at birth
not put it as a noose around my neck?
Without him I cannot live for a moment,
nor could I ever renounce him.
Dear friend, death is not in my control,
so how can I attain salvation and die?
I cannot endure the pain of love-in-separation, nor can I die by wishing it.
I cannot live, nor can I die, and my heart's fire will not be quenched!'

Pemā Explains

311. Madhumālatī then recounted for Pemā
all the things that had happened earlier.
When she heard the lovely maiden's words,
Pemā's eyes brimmed over with tears.
'Whatever you suffer for the sake of your love,'
she said, 'later you will reap a tenfold happiness.
For a single joy you must suffer a thousand griefs,
yet a single grief can yield a thousand joys.
For a single flower, dear friend,
you must gather daily a thousand thorns.
Once having embarked on the ocean of love, no one should ever turn back.
Either you will obtain the jewel of your beloved, or lose your life in longing.

312. 'Today', she said, 'is auspicious for you,
and your mind's desire will be fulfilled.
Dear friend, Saturn is in your sixth house,
so you will gain the treasure you have lost.
Jupiter is in the ninth house, so you are sure
to meet the one from whom you are apart.
In the third house, Mars is strong—
your beloved will come to your bed himself.

The sun is shining in the tenth house,
taking away sorrow and bringing joy.
    The Twins are in your eleventh house; the Moon, Venus
        and Mercury in the house of your birth.
    According to all my calculations, all seven planets are
        favourable to you.

313. 'O maiden, Rāhu* is in your eighth house,
so you will surely meet your darling.
I know the Prince is heavily burdened with suffering,
and you are tormented just like him.
Today you will meet your dear beloved,
for whom you have endured such distress.
Contemplating you in his mind, O maiden,
he has forgotten the entire world.
From the moment he saw your brilliant face,
his eyes have found the whole world dark.
    Come and see the condition of the Prince for whom
        there can be no one but you.
    He has lost everything for your sake—his body, his
        mind, his life, and his youth.

314. 'His body has been burnt to ashes
in the flames of separation—
seeing him, one feels compassion.
Not a *ratti** of his body's flesh remains,
and separation cuts away at his bones.
If you have stolen someone's soul,
at least grant him pity in return.
Princess, show yourself to him just a little,
then you may give him heavy grief again.
Dear friend, be fearful of the ways of God,
one pays for the deeds one commits.
    Can love ever fail to bear fruit in this world? Listen to
        what I say.
    May you never have to endure the sufferings of the
        Prince.'

315. Then Pemā raised her up by her arm
and went with her towards the garden.

ome, let's go to meet the one
ue in the two worlds.
shyness, put away heartlessness,
e kind, see him for a little while.
How could you turn away from one
who is ready to give his life on the path?
In this world one shares happiness
only with those whose grief one shares.'
Pemā then sent a handmaiden to go to the Prince and to tell him
that she and Madhumālatī were standing at the door of the pavilion.

Manohar and Madhumālatī

316. When the maid announced the sweet name Madhu,
the essence of truth showed its signs on his body.
He trembled and was unable to speak.
Consciousness left him and his eyes closed.
Just as pewter grows pallid in the fire,
his body turned pale in all its eight parts.
Pemā took water and sprinkled it on his face,
saying, 'Awake, for the hour of success has come!
Speak if you have anything to say, for who knows
when the Creator will bring such a day again.
Today the fates are smiling on you, take hold of your consciousness.
Your reward is courageous perfection,* it now stands at your head.'

317. When the Prince heard Pemā mention
courageous perfection, he awoke again.
He said the words seemed sweet as nectar to him.
He said, 'What a glorious day this is!
Now I have got the scent of my beloved.
The garden of love is blossoming
and the whole world is full of its smell.
Whose fragrance is borne on the breeze
which intoxicates me without wine?

O my precious, most matchless beloved,
come and see love's blisters on my heart!
For your sake I have abandoned all that I possessed in the universe.
Only my suffering for you did I keep, for it's the essence of my life in the world.

318. 'The line of love you engraved on my heart
has not been erased, but deepens day by day.
The sun of happiness has gone down, O maiden,
but dawn has not yet come to this night of grief.
Perhaps now the night of suffering has passed
and the rains of Svātī can fall on the *cātaka* bird.
There is nothing I have not already lost,
on the gaming board of your love's sorrow.
Meet me today, put your arms around my neck,
for who knows if tomorrow will be like today?
If you have something to do today, why do you not do it this instant?
For nobody knows what may happen tomorrow in this dark Kali age!

319. 'My eyes have been beholders of your beauty
from the moment it first became manifest.
On the day that the first forms of your beauty
became apparent, I was enamoured of it.
The more your beauty illuminated the world,
the more my soul was caught in separation's spell.
Your beauty and my pain, O maiden,
have become a legend in every land.
Since your beauty increases day by day,
how can I become free of the pain of love?
Whoever has unveiled your face and looked at your beauty openly is blessed.
I have rushed to kiss those fortunate eyes, in which your radiant beauty dwells.

320. 'Your crooked eyes invite me with sidelong glances.
Your gaze, poised between your lashes, thirsts for blood.

The fire of love-in-separation has consumed me,
more than the whole world put together.
My heart can no longer bear this agony for you,
since it is not made of stone like yours.
As my soul burns in separation's fire,
I remember you more and more.
Why did God inflict the pain of love on me,
if he did not also make you merciful?
    Having suffered this grief alone, my heart knows one thing for certain:
    either my arms will enfold your neck, or my severed head will be in your hands.

321. 'I do not burn in this fire alone.
Who in the world does not desire you?
No one would know the story of our love,
if my two eyes had not told it crying.
Whoever finds his soul in your body
would surely take it back from you.
My soul was lost, and I could not find it.
Whoever I asked pointed to you.
Since I joined my soul to yours,
it abandoned me and became yours.
    What kind of bargain was this? Did I go there to trade at a loss?
    In all of this I've lost my capital, so what hope can there be of gain?'

322. When Madhumālatī, the lotus bud,
heard his words, she blossomed.
Opening her lips, her store of nectar,
she spoke, 'I feel shame before my friend,
yet modesty does not remain
when love awakens in the heart.'
Pemā said, 'Do not be shy,
but think that you and I are one.'
Then she who was consumed with grief
abandoned her modesty and said,
'My lord, I am half my former self,

consumed with sorrow for you.
Out of modesty, I have not told anyone
of my pain, but burnt secretly in my body.
    On one side there was my family's honour, on the other
        the pain of love.
    Both sides were very difficult for me—harm my family or
        suffer in my heart.

323. 'You say you suffered grief for me,
but how could you endure the terrible blaze
of love-in-separation? From shame
I kept my love concealed, spoke to no one.
All my friends and companions
knew nothing of my secret pain.
On the one hand stood Death,
on the other, my suffering for you.
When Death saw my sorrow for you,
he drew back his hand in defeat.
Death is content to kill only once, but separation
slays a person from moment to moment.
    You were capricious and heartlessly cruel. You played
        with the world and then left.
    How could a helpless woman like me survive, struggling
        every moment to keep alive?'

324. When the Prince heard her words,
he cried and said, 'My sorrow is not hidden
from you—you know every detail
of what you have done to my heart.
Why do you ask about the grief
of one who lives within your heart?
Why do you ask me about my sorrow?
Ask yourself what you have done to me,
for I live always within your soul.
Why enquire from me about grief?
    Your abode, O maiden, is forever within my innermost
        heart.
    Why then, knowing its every secret, do you ask me
        about my sorrow?

325. 'How could you hide your face from me
if your locks did not act as a veil?
Your flowing locks and my soul
become enamoured on seeing your face.
Just as at noon on a harsh day
one cannot look at the sun directly;
there is nothing between the sun and the eye,
but the sun's brilliance acts as its own veil,
so perhaps it is with your radiant face.*
How could my feeble hands reach out
to draw the locks away from your face?
Gather up your locks, O maiden, and let the bright radiant sun come out,
so that my eyes, burnt by separation, may be satisfied by my darling's beauty.'

326. 'If someone seeks to look at my beauty,'
said Madhumālatī, 'then he must hear
something very special I have to say.
He should hesitate to open my eyes,
but should first borrow vision from them,
then come forward. My beauty requires
no ordinary sight, but that special vision.*
When you gain that sight from my eyes
and have a vision of my beauty,
then nothing else will satisfy you.
I tell you, O Prince, it is certain
that you cannot see me with your eyes.
Renounce your life, your youth, your body and mind, your eyes and ears.
Only then will your real eyes open, through which you will understand everything.'

327. 'You live always within my heart,'
replied the Prince, 'and my tongue
i... antly repeating your name.
... ace is in my eyes,
... need have I to borrow vision?

Your vision is within my eyes
which are blind without your light.
What could my sightless eyes hope to see,
unless you are within them?
The places your radiant beauty does not light
are shrouded in darkness, though the sun shines.
O maiden, where the lustrous moon of your face does not rise,
there, though a thousand suns should shine, only darkness remains.

328. 'You remember all the things we said,
and the vows we took with God between us?
Your face is the full moon that illumines the world.
How can it remain hidden, O maiden?
You dwell forever in my heart—
why do you hide your face from me?
Satisfy me, give me the nectar of your lips,
that my departing soul may tarry in my body!
Quickly reveal your beauty, girl,
or do you seek to destroy my life?
Have I committed a sin, do I have a fault, that you hide your face from me?
My only fault is this, that I have raised you above the totality of Creation.'

The Promise of True Love

329. Hearing his words the lotus bud blossomed,
and accepted the love in the Prince's sweet words.
'I am very much afraid of my family,' she said,
'Who would sin and destroy everything they had?
I would be ruined, my family would suffer abuse,
and my parents and relations would be disgraced.
If you swear an oath, my darling,
I will come and sacrifice myself to you.
Give me your solemn word of honour, my lord,
and I will come to embrace you close.

he burning blaze of love I feel in my heart, not the
e of fear,
et not the black stain of sin blemish the cloth of my
tue!

330. 'I tell you truly, O Prince, once honour is lost
it can never be regained. If you boil water
and let it cool, it loses its flavour.
A withered flower does not lose its scent,
nor does its beauty fade forever,
but it can never regain its splendour
or be treated with the same respect.
Just so, if a woman loses her honour,
she ruins her life for herself completely.
As long as my father does not offer me to you in the
sacrament of marriage,
there can never be carnal love between us, but you may
take any other pleasure in me.'

331. The Prince replied, 'Listen, dear love,
we swore an oath to each other at the beginning.
We called on Rudra, Brahma, and Hari,
to witness the promise we made together.
That promise still holds true between us.
No one should set foot on the path of sin.
Now again I swear a binding oath.
I am not making this up at all,
but this is my solemn promise:
As long as the tree of righteousness
does not bear lawful fruit for me,
I shall not eat forbidden fruit, though it be sweet.
Until we are legally joined in matrimony, O most
alluring of maidens,
sin shall not enter between us, for this is the ordinance
of God.'

332. When she heard the vow, the Princess
let down her veil of shy modesty.
When he saw the radiance of her face,

the Prince grew restless with love.
When she saw him thus, the maiden ran
and raised him up as he lay there helpless.
She said, 'Do not think I was proud, my lord!
I have left all pride and embrace you in my arms.'
They both stood up and embraced each other,
burst into flames, like gold and borax in the fire.
On the day when two parted lovers unite and their hopes are fulfilled,
all three worlds are happy—heaven, earth, and hell celebrate their joy.

The Lovers United

333. No one can know the secret mystery
of the things that passed between their hearts.
It was like a thirsty man falling into the Ganges,
or a dead man coming back to life again.
Her two breasts entered his heart, and his lips
satisfied themselves with the juice of her lips.
How can the tongue describe the joy
that two lovers feel when united with one another?
Their two bodies joined with one another,
and one or two watches of the night passed thus.
Though drowning in water to their very noses, the lovers remained yet thirsty.
I have described their outer state, but who can know what happened within?

334. Then they sat down on the bed together,
splendid, like Ratī and fish-bannered Kāmadeva.*
Sometimes they spoke of their former sorrows,
and at times they remained in close embrace.
The sun set and the moon rose,
and the two rested on the same bed.
They say the true reward of earthly life
is when two parted lovers reunite.
In their joy they stayed awake all night,
but what is morning to eyes filled with sleep?

They slept happily together, lips joined to lips, breast to breast.
Seeing them together one could not tell whether they were two or one.

335. Pemā placed a silken curtain across the door,
and stayed on guard outside the pavilion.
She had sixty girlfriends with her,
and each of them had four serving maids.
All of them were pretty and youthful,
with matching ages and appearances.
Laughingly they all played there together.
Pemā was the moon, they were the stars.
All around the picture-pavilion and its doors
they set up barricades of silken cloths.
Here Pemā played games imbued with the essence of *sahaja* with her friends,
but there a creeper of doubt was spreading in the heart of Rūpamañjarī.

Queen Rūpamañjarī is Amazed

336. As Queen Rūpamañjarī was seated,
she suddenly became worried in her heart.
Upset and perplexed in her mind,
she stood up, apprehensive at heart.
She sent for Madhurā and said to her,
'My daughter has gone off and left me thus.
The two girls left here in the evening.
Now nobody knows what's happened to them.
For what reason could two royal Princesses,
leave home and spend the night in a pavilion?'
Madhurā replied, 'I will send a maidservant to them with a message,
and they will come back in a moment. Sit down and do t worry.'
jarī said, 'I'll just go for a moment
ere Pemā and Madhumālatī are.

Otherwise I shall be worried and anxious,
for I have a suspicion about that picture-pavilion.'
'Listen to me, O Queen,' replied Madhurā,
'you are clever, wise, and always practical.
The path is long and the night is dark.
Why go to the picture-pavilion at all?
You sit here and I will send for them,
or if you want, I shall fetch them myself.
The two are girlhood friends, enjoying themselves and playing games together.
What business have you and I to intrude among these young girls?'

338. Madhurā restrained her in many ways,
but the Queen remained restless in her heart.
'They are childhood friends playing together,
enjoying themselves in their father's house.
They have been separated for many days.
Let no one stop them playing together!'
But Rūpamañjarī would not be stopped
from going immediately to the pavilion,
though Madhurā was most embarrassed.
She took twenty maidservants with her,
and went with the Queen to the pavilion.
Even though Madhurā stopped her many times, the Queen would not listen.
She went herself to the picture-pavilion, and saw there all the signs of love.

339. One is ashamed to describe what she saw
when the Queen reached the picture-pavilion.
The sun's rays were hidden in the moon's orbit.
Seeing the sun, the moon had given up its brilliance.
The Queen saw this and became black as Rāhu.
She came to Pemā and abused her roundly,
'Shameless one, don't you care about my honour?
Why have you let this virgin cloth be stained?
I left her with you, trusting in your care.
Why have you brought disgrace on my family?

The saints have said so before, and their sayings have been proven true,
that one becomes evil oneself if one associates with evil people.'

340. Pemā said, 'Now listen to what I am saying.
You are a mother to me, so I suffer your words.
I am not upset at your insults or abuse,
since I regard you as I do my mother Madhurā.
But first you must establish that I have sinned,
then you may abuse me as you wish.
Don't let your heart deceive you, O Queen,
these two are as pure as Gaṅgā water.
I know everything about their former love,
and all that has happened between them.'
Pemā then told the story from the beginning, of how the two lovers had met,
how their beds were changed and their rings, and how their hearts were now at peace.

341. The Queen called Pemā to her side and asked,
'Give clear answers to these my questions.
Tell me why he behaves like this.
Is he an unhappy beggar or a lordly king?
Is he from a noble family or a base one?
Why is he dirty—is it from separation's sorrow?
Did he hear about Madhumālatī from someone,
or did he fall in love the moment he saw her?'
Then Pemā told her all there was to tell,
'Kanaigiri is a beautiful fort, and Sūrajbhānu is its king and protector.
He is the heir to that kingdom, and his mother Kamalā's life's support.

342. 'But listen, O mother, in these two lovers' minds,
there is nothing except seeing and touching the other.
I am not such a fool that I would mix
water and purest milk. Her pool of nectar*
is as full today as the day she was born.

Although they are absorbed in love,
they have not destroyed themselves with sin.
They are still thirsty for the water of the Ganges.
The lotus bud has not opened yet,
nor has the intoxicated bee entered into the flower.
The rains of Svāti are still thundering, massing in the sky for the oyster shell.*
The Lord has kept Madhumālatī as pure today as on the day she was born.'

The Lovers Separated

343. When the Queen heard Pemā's words,
she was relieved and her heart became calmer.
'Truly,' she said, 'she was always crying,
and concealed her tears from me out of shame.
Sometimes she seemed amazed and looked around
everywhere; at times she was still and silent, unseeing.
Sometimes she leaned her head against the bed-frame,
at times she would stand up and laugh aloud.
Sometimes she would talk to herself in the mirror.
At times her eyes brimmed with tears of blood.
Sometimes she would not eat for several days, at times wrap her face up and weep.
At other times she slept with her face covered, distraught with the pain of separation.*

344. 'What came over you, you wicked girl—
why did you throw ghee on a dying fire?
As it is she was indifferent and renouncing him,
so why did you strike her with this lightning?
She did not even remember her own self,
so why did you hurl this thunderbolt at her?
Someone brought into her bedroom
a golden bed, studded with precious gems,
and since then she has lived constantly
as if she were dying at every moment.
She does not eat food, nor drink sweet water.

lay I have learnt everything, so now I can
ınderstand this mystery.
ıy did you cut off a greening branch? And by what
*dharma** did you then act this way?'

345. So angry was the Queen that she became senseless.
She was weeping as she said to her maidservants,
'Separate these two lovers instantly,
like water slides off the feathers of a wing!'
The women turned the two lovers apart,
as if splitting one body in two pieces.
Their eyes were shut in such a charmed sleep,
that they did not awaken even when turned.
They cast the Prince down in Kanaigiri,
and took Madhumālatī to her palace.
The Queen then left the picture-pavilion, went to
Madhurā and said,
'If you will permit me, I should like to return home
tomorrow morning.'

346. When the Prince woke up in Kanaigiri,
he was perplexed and utterly bewildered.
He could not tell if it had been a dream or reality.
Astonished, he contemplated what had happened.
He beat his head repeatedly and cried,
washing his lotus-face with tears of blood,
throwing dust on his head as he wept.
Where was that heavenly pavilion?
Where was the nymph with whom he had been?
As night passed and morning broke,
the Prince set out to find his woman, thinking,
'How wonderful was that heavenly pavilion, and being
together with that nymph!
Who was it who destroyed my royal happiness,* all in
one quick instant?'

347. Smearing ashes on his head, he set off weeping,
no companion with him but the Creator, thinking,
'I will hold my beloved in my eyes and meditate on her.

What can appeal to me in worldly life now?'
Intoxicated with love, he had no companion.
Never did his love lessen, and never did he speak.
Night and day he travelled on alone,
accompanied only by the love of Madhumālatī.
With just the glowing radiance of his love,
dauntless, he crossed forest and ocean,
traversing everything that lay in his path.
He was following that very same path that had brought him success in the past.
But when Madhumālatī awoke, she wept, for she saw she had lost her treasure.

348. When Madhumālatī awoke, her body burned,
consumed by separation from head to toe.
She sighed deeply and her heart brimmed over.
Abandoning shame, she wept tears of blood.
When streams like the spring rains of Bharaṇi*
burst forth from her eyes, her bed seemed
as if it had been flooded with scarlet ladybirds.
When she opened her mouth to cry aloud,
her teeth flashed like lightning amidst roaring thunder.
Her flowing locks opened like the dark night
that obscures the full moon in the rainy month of Bhādoṉ.*
As the pain of love-in-separation assailed her body, Madhumālatī wept and wept,
and people, astonished, found a second rainy season sweeping through the world.

The Queen and Madhumālatī

349. When she had taken leave of Madhurā,
the Queen returned to her city of Mahāras.
She rushed to Madhumālatī's side,
and found her weeping and sighing deeply.
Her golden body now resembled the dust,
and her tears had drenched her moon-like face.
She was tearing her bodice into threads,

and her eyes were red and inflamed with weeping.
Remembering her beloved's likeness,
the maiden cried and covered her head with dust.
When first love had sprung up in her, she was still an innocent girl.
Now she was in her prime, so how could she be satisfied with just her darling's name?

350. When one is hopelessly, madly in love,
one does not listen to what anyone says.
When separation's pain rules the body,
awareness, wisdom, and shame remain no more.
The maiden could in no way be consoled,
but flung herself about on the ground weeping.
The Queen approached her saying,
'You have destroyed the honour of our family.'
With both hands she slapped Madhumālatī.
'You are the ruin of our family! What has come over you?
You have barely stopped drinking mother's milk, so how can you feel this separation?
Why do you not stay here peaceful and chaste, until the moment of destiny comes?

351. 'You have disgraced your mother and father.
O ruin of the family, why did you not die at birth?
Wicked girl, you have blackened our family name.
I am bitterly sorry you were ever born.
If, O destroyer of the family, you were dead,
we would not be the laughing stock of the land.
How can we remove this blackest of marks?
Any other stain would have washed off,
but not this one.' The Queen tried hard
to make Madhumālatī see reason in many ways.
But the girl, maddened by her love,
refused to listen to even one word.
Although the Queen made many attempts, her daughter could not understand her.
How can someone accept any instruction, if their life is not in their hands?

352. When the Queen failed to make her understand,
she tried first soft words, and then harsh ones.
The girl would not listen to her mother's screaming,
but recited only the name of the *siddha* yogi.*
When wisdom and advice had no effect,
the Queen was perplexed, as if she'd been robbed.
Only the intelligent can listen to wise counsel,
how can one give advice to the mad?
Then the Queen became afraid and said,
'What shall I do? I fear that no good will come
to my family as a result of their meeting.'
    Taking a handful of water, the Queen uttered a spell
      and sprinkled it over her face.
    The moment that it touched Madhumālatī, the girl
      became a bird and flew away.

*Madhumālatī Transformed**

353. Madhumālatī was in the form of a bird,
and no one knew where she had flown.
As it is, she was maddened by love;
with wings, she became even more deceptive.
She flew faster even than the wind.
Many pursued her, but no one could catch her.
The whole city rose up and ran after her,
but none found even a feather, let alone the bird.
Rūpamañjarī repented her deed in her heart and said,
'What have I done? Why was I so foolish?'
    Both father and mother wept themselves senseless over
      their daughter.
    Their tears washed the black pupils of their eyes until
      they were purest white.

354. Madhumālatī abandoned all her concerns,
except to repeat in her heart, 'Beloved, beloved.'
She left aside all worldly attachments,
and renounced her family and relations,
the girlfriends with whom she had played,

all desire for joy, happiness, and amusement.
The enjoyment of all worldly pleasures
she renounced, and the hope of life.
She gave up her parental house,
left all her wealth and worldly goods,
and all her friends, companions, and relatives.
She renounced her kingdom, the comfort of her bed,
sleep at night, and food in the day.
She abandoned all the desires and joys of her heart, and
made the trees her home.

355. Madhumālatī left all behind and flew off,
anxiously searching, seeking her love.
She was distraught and roamed restlessly,
as if maddened by a scorpion's sting.
She roamed over mountains, seas, and forests,
but she could not find the object of her search.
In her grief, she wandered the world,
over vast deserts and to great cities,
but her heart's desire was not fulfilled.
She sought him in every tree and house,
in countries far and near, and among all people,
ranging from kings to lowly beggars.
She visited all the places of pilgrimage—the Kadalī
forest* and the Godāvarī river,*
Mathurā,* Gayā,* and Prayāg,* and Jagannāth* and
Dvārkā,* seeking only her lord and lover.

356. Day and night she wandered restlessly,
maddened by love and quite intoxicated.
One day, as the maiden was flying along,
she saw someone who looked like a Prince.
Pausing for a moment on her way,
she saw he was a radiantly handsome Prince.
That Prince's name was Tārācand.*
He came from the Citadel of Winds, Pavaneri*
in the fair Fortress of Respect, Māngaṛh.*
He was handsome, well formed, and wise,
and wore the bright garb of a brave warrior.

He was complete in knowledge, of noble birth, and the image of the God of Love.
So very like was he to Manohar,* that Madhu saw him and felt drawn to him.

The Wondrous Bird

357. She flew down and perched on a tower,
looking extremely lovely and attractive.
Her feathers were green, her legs red.
Her beak was beautiful, and her eyes
were large and gleamed like a pair of pearls.
As she fixed her eyes on Manohar's likeness,
she found a refuge from the fire of separation.
When the Prince's gaze fell on the bird,
compassion and affection awoke in his heart.*
His eyes concentrated for a moment on her.
Beggars, noblemen, and courtiers observed her.
Everyone said, 'Such a rare bird never has been seen before in this Kali age.
Millions of years have passed in this world, but such a wonder has not been seen.'

358. Madhumālatī was overjoyed to see his likeness
to Manohar, and hoping that it was he,
flew down and perched on a rooftop.
She thought, 'Let me cool my burning eyes,
and quench the fires of separation by looking at him.
A drowning man rushes to clutch a straw—
even a straw supports those who are sinking fast.
Can one who wants mangoes be sated with sour berries?*
One whose heart is burning with separation's fire,
cannot be content by looking at a likeness.'
But when Madhumālatī gazed at his face, she became immersed in his beauty.
Prince Tārācand's heart also became restless, like a fish that is parted from water.

359. The Prince was entranced by the bird's beauty,
and signalled to an attendant with his eyebrows.
The attendant understood and sent servants running.
They returned bringing all the fowlers in the city.
He ordered them to spread their nets everywhere,
and to take grain and to scatter it there.
Love held the bird's heart captive,
and her two eyes remained gazing at the Prince.
She paid no attention to the snare and the net,
but kept on contemplating the Prince's face.
A moment passed and the bird became alert and wished in her mind to fly away.
But the Prince cried out, 'If that bird flies away, my heart goes with her!'

The Fowlers' Net

360. The net was spread out all around her,
and grain was scattered here and there.
Had she been a bird, no doubt her heart
would have been greedy for the grain,
but she had forgotten herself in love.
For a moment she cherished his likeness
to Manohar, then spread her wings to fly.
As she flapped her wings to fly away,
the Prince stood up wringing his hands
and said, 'If this bird flies away,
all my senses and intelligence will go with her!'
Said the Prince, 'She is flying away! Let me catch her in my hands!'
As he ran to catch her his crown jumped off, and all its pearls were scattered.

361. The pearls* fell and rolled through the net.
The bird, seeing this, turned to look properly.
Although she wished to fly away,
she paused for a moment, attracted to the pearls.
The Prince cried out, 'This bird lives on pearls.'
brought him many shining pearls,

and the Prince took them by the handful.
They brought many unpierced pearls,
and scattered them around everywhere
like the bright stars shining in the sky.
Then Madhumālatī decided in her mind to sacrifice her life on the path of love.
She came into the fowlers' net herself, that she might obtain her desire, Manohar.

362. When Madhumālatī knew for certain
that love for Manohar filled her heart,
she thought, 'I have been in this form
for a year, but have heard no news of him.
This face that so resembles him,
brought me hope so I forgot myself
and settled here for just a moment.
Now let me fall into his snare
and divine all of his secrets.
Then I can tell him my heart's secret.
Perhaps in doing so I shall find
some news about my darling.
Or if I die, I will obtain the reward
of travelling on the path of love.'
Resolving thus she dropped down quickly, like a moth into the lamp of love.
She enmeshed her feet in the net, so that she could not free herself.

363. When the bird was ensnared, the fowlers ran
and brought net and bird living to the Prince.
When the Prince saw her his mind exulted,
like a lotus blossoming at sunrise.
He brought a cage made all of gold,
and put the delightful bird in it.
His gaze did not leave her for an instant.
He scattered before her jewels and pearls,
and all the kinds of food that birds eat.
The Prince did not leave the cage for an instant, nor did he entrust it to anyone.

He kept the cage himself, holding it close to his heart
day and night.

The Wondrous Bird Speaks to Tārācand

364. Three days passed in this manner.
Neither bird nor Prince ate anything at all.
Then the maiden thought in her heart,
'Why is he killing himself for me?
He is a young and handsome Prince.
If he dies, on my head lies the guilt for it.'
Thinking thus the Princess said,
'Why, O Prince, are you full of sorrow?
What kind of love could there be between us?
How can a bird and a man be in love?
I am a bird—I have given up my life and youth to
obtain this sorrow.
You are a pleasure-loving Prince—why do you have to
endure this grief?'

365. The bird again opened its immortal mouth
and uttered delightful, matchless words,
'I am a bird and you are a Prince.
How can love flourish between us?
You are a Prince who enjoys every pleasure,
I, a bird who wanders stricken by separation.
What kind of love do you envisage between us,
that you have given up food and water for three days?
Had you seen my former beauty but once,
then everything you could do would be inadequate.
But the Creator robbed me of the kingdom of my
beauty and made me into a bird.
I simply do not know my future. What lines has fate
traced on my forehead?'*

366. The Prince thrilled to hear her speaking,
like a *cakora* gazing at the moon.
When the royal Prince heard her words,
he was amazed and became very thoughtful.

Then he made her swear a solemn oath,
and asked, 'Tell me the unbiased truth about yourself.
You are on oath, lest you not speak true.
Are you an animal, bird or human being?
How were you transformed into a bird?
You have sworn to speak only the truth.
  What is your name? Where are you from? In what country lies your home?
  What sin, what misdeed did you commit? How did you come to be a bird?'

367. When the bird heard the Prince's speech,
her eyes welled up with tears of blood.
She cried bitterly as she answered,
'Since you have asked me the truth on oath,
I will tell you all my heart's secrets.
There is a city called Mahāras,
and its king is Vikram Rāi.
He is my father, mighty and powerful,
ruler of the country of Bhārata
in Jambu, island of the rose-apple tree.*
Over his head is the parasol of royalty,
and he adorns both throne and kingdom.
I was born the daughter of his house,
but suddenly this strange condition befell me.
  My name is Madhumālatī, and I am a princess from a royal house.
  O Prince, who can erase the lines of fate God has inscribed on one's brow?'

368. Then Madhumālatī told the Prince everything,
all that had transpired with her in the past.
She told him truly of that first wondrous night
when they had been brought together in love.
She described in great detail, one by one,
all the sorrows she had suffered in separation.
She told him, too, of how they had met
a second time in Pemā's picture-pavilion,
how they had been separated as they slept,

and how, when they awoke once more,
they found themselves in different places.
She told how her mother had sprinkled water and cast a spell for her family's honour.
She related the whole story for the Prince, from beginning to end in every detail.

369. Then she related the tale of Prince Manohar,
from its beginnings to the present moment:
the first night when he recognized her,
and the sacred promise of love they took,
of how the Prince left his father's palace,
and how his ship sank with all his goods.
She told how he happened to meet Pemā,
and how he was comforted to hear news
of the beautiful Madhumālatī. The Prince,
she recounted, had killed the demon to save Pemā,
and brought her home with great honour and celebrations.
She spoke then of how the Creator allowed them to meet in Pemā's pavilion,
how their eyes had closed just for a moment—in that instant they were separated.

370. 'O Prince, no sin has passed between us.
I do not know why this calamity befell us.
Where have they taken the Prince and thrown him?
I know not whether my love lives or dies.
When my body grew wings I could not stay,
but crazed with love, I flew away.
I have searched all over the world,
from the sun's rising to its setting place,
but nowhere could I find my darling.
My first love has turned to painful sorrow.
I was innocent then but am a woman now.
I have looked all over creation in the form of a winged bird—
I found no one who could give me a message from my Prince Manohar.

371. 'O Prince, I have set shame aside
and told you all my heart's secrets.
When I did not find him in my search,
I found the strength to ensnare myself
in your net. I saw in your form
the likeness of my darling, and flew down
to your roof hoping that it was my Prince.
If now, O King, you will release me
I will again become a traveller on love's path.
Either I shall find my beloved in my search,
or I shall give up my life on that path.'
Manjhan says, 'Whoever climbs on the pyre of love
does not care for life.
The life that is lost for the beloved's sake brings glory
both now and hereafter.'

Tārācand's Resolve

372. As the Prince heard the bird's sad tale,
tears of compassion filled his eyes.
He said to her, 'Listen, O woman
who yearns to sacrifice her life,
your grief has set my heart on fire.
Do not worry in your heart any more.
I'll accomplish what is necessary to save you.
For you, O maiden, I would do the impossible,
that the fire in your heart may be quenched.
With my strength and your good fortune,
O maiden, the Creator will make you as one again.
I will renounce my kingdom and throne, and embrace
all sorrows for your sake.
Perhaps through courage I may attain success, and your
heart's fire be quenched.

373. 'As far as life and my nature permit, I'll strive
to reunite you with the one you love so much.
First, I shall go to the city of Mahāras,
then in quest to Citbisarāuṉ.

Maybe God will grant me fame
and you will meet the object of your love.
My heart will find no peace at all
until you meet your beloved again.
But you will be of no use to your Prince
till you assume your former beauty.
First I shall proceed to the city of Mahāras, to give you your previous form again.
Then I'll search for the Prince and reunite you, provided that God doesn't end my life.

374. 'There are few people in this Kali age
who suffer in their hearts the grief of others.
A thousand lives should be sacrificed to him
who destroys himself to make a home for another.
One should be like the generous tree
which showers fruit even on the man
who pelts it with clods of earth.
The oyster shell loves those
who trouble it with grains of sand,
and gives handfuls of pearls in return.
And the man who digs up a gold mine
is granted gold, pure in all twelve parts.
Look at the poor fire-cracker* who endures sorrow so that others may be happy:
blood in its heart and fire at its mouth, only to give pleasure to others.'

375. Speaking sweet words he consoled the bird,
and set off with it to foreign lands
putting his own life in danger.
His heart was pleased to accept grief
for the sake of another's happiness.*
Embracing suffering, he renounced comfort.
He abandoned his kingly desires and joys,
and shaded his royal head happily
with the parasol of sadness instead.
te myself at the feet of those
earts take on others' sorrows.

Everyone suffers for their own sake,
but the one who suffers for another is rare.
Prince Tārācand burdened himself with grief to bring another happiness.
Count those who suffer for others' joys as truly human in this world!

The Great Task

376. Then the Prince sent for his childhood friend.
When he heard the summons, his boon companion
came running in the middle of the night.
Tārācand said, 'I have a great task to perform.
I shall leave my homeland and wander abroad.
If you are still the friend of my childhood,
and still keep your old affection for me,
accompany me on this venture.
Help me to complete it for the sake of the love
we shared when we were children together.
No one in this world could call you worthy,
if you did not accompany me to this station.
You are my only childhood companion, and also a brother to me.
Help me this time, I beg you, for the sake of our childhood friendship.'

377. When the Prince's friend heard this,
his body trembled from head to foot.
He said, 'Had I a hundred lives,
I would sacrifice them all for you.
If I do not accompany you today,
what use would I be to you in the future?
If my life is not offered to you,
what use can it ever have for me?
If I do not go with you now
whatever would I do remaining here?
You are leaving your kingdom and your army and going to a foreign land.

Were I to abandon you now and stay here, who would
ever speak well of me?'

378. At midnight the Prince sent a summons
for Budhrāj of the royal guard.
He obeyed the Prince's command,
came before him and salaamed low.
Tārācand told him, 'Go and saddle
a hundred horses, but bring only those
which the farrier tells you are fit.
Equip and bring here only those steeds,
chosen from among thousands of horses,
who know the meaning of every command.'
Then about a hundred horses were fitted out
with golden armour on their backs
and brought before Prince Tārācand.
So swift were they that the wind was not equal to the
rising dust from their feet.
They became furious if they even saw their own
shadows near them as they ran.

379. He took ten wagons loaded with provisions.
Choosing an auspicious moment, he set off
on his journey. He renounced his people,
his family and his fellow countrymen.
The Prince became a traveller abroad
only to bring happiness to others.
All his friends and companions left with him,
and became detached from this world.
The Prince distributed mounts to the nobles.
So swift were the royal steeds
that the wind could not surpass them.
Nor could their feet be seen as they ran,
as if they kept up with the mind's pace.
They set off on Saturday the seventh, an auspicious day
in the bright half of the month.
The Prince took Madhumālatī's cage with him and rode
on until they made camp.

380. Tārācand went along asking for Mahāras,
thinking all the while in his mind
that when Madhumālatī had assumed her form,
he would go in search of her lover.
Clasping Madhumālatī's cage to his chest,
he rode on thinking of giving joy to others.
The more he heard news of Mahāras,
the more his heart leapt with excitement.
Finally, when he saw the fair city of Mahāras,
it was as if nectar had quenched his burning heart.
Prince Tārācand dismounted when he arrived at the garden of Jaunā the florist.
She took a branch full of blossoms as an offering and came forward to welcome him.

381. Tārācand asked Jaunā, 'Tell me
why the city seems so gloomy.
There is no one at all who looks happy.
Why does everyone appear so sad?'
Jaunā said, 'Listen, O lord of men,
let me tell you why the city grieves.
Vikram Rāi is the King of this city,
and the Queen's name is Rūpamañjarī.
Vikram's glory burns bright as a flame,
and he is of the solar dynasty,
come to redeem this Kali age.
As the dynasty was coming to an end, a daughter was born in this family.
Her name was Madhumālatī, and her beauty was radiant in all the three worlds.

382. 'Through the actions of the Creator
she became possessed by madness.
Her mother lost her through her powers.
She left her family in the form of a bird.
From that day the King and Queen
have not taken food or drink out of grief.
They ruined their eyesight by weeping
and searched all over the world,

but could not find her anywhere.
With this distress in the royal house,
no one in the city could be happy.
Madhumālatī was the soul in the body of everyone who lived in this city.
When that soul left this body and went away, the city came to a halt.'

383. Jaunā continued, 'Listen, O protector of men,
since the day that Madhumālatī left
great sadness descended on the city.
All joy and pleasure left every heart.
Her parents were very distraught.
They were like bodies without any souls.
Since then I have not threaded any flowers.
If I did put flower garlands together,
on whose head would I tie them?
For whom should I make garlands
of blossoms, since God has taken away
the one who would wear them?'
When the beautiful Madhumālatī heard these words from Jaunā, she said,
'O Prince, if you give me permission, I would make myself known to her.'

384. The Prince said, 'Do you know her?'
She replied, 'She is a childhood friend.'
Then Jaunā came near the Prince,
and he introduced her to Madhumālatī.
Jaunā embraced the golden cage,
and tears overflowed from her eyes.
Madhumālatī too wept tears of joy,
though she had lost her former beauty
and was parted from her family.
Streams of tears flowed from her eyes,
weeping she recounted her previous sorrows.
Then that royal Prince made them stop crying by saying, 'Why do you weep now?

The night of your sorrow has passed now; the radiant sun of happiness has risen.'

385. The Prince called Jaunā to him and said,
'Go to the King and bring him this news.
Go and give her parents the glad news,
and tell all the members of her family.'
When the florist received this order,
she went rejoicing to the royal door.
Jaunā went to where the King and Queen sat,
and told them the happy news.
Vikram Rāi and Rūpamañjarī were overjoyed
when they heard the florist's good news.
Their faces, which had been eclipsed by grief like the moon by the demon Rāhu,
shone brilliantly now like the full moon, as they heard news of Madhumālatī.

Prince Tārācand Comes to Mahāras

386. The Queen fell at the feet of the florist
when she heard the news, and said:
'O Lord, when will the hour come?
When, O God, will that day dawn
when this mother shall see her daughter's face?
Did you see her yourself before you came?'
she asked, 'Or did you run here
having only heard the news of her return?'
Jaunā replied, 'What news do you mean?
O Queen, I speak only of things
that I have seen with my own eyes.
She is in the form of a bird,
not an ounce of flesh on her body.
She recognized my voice, called me to her.
When she told me her own name, I ran to embrace her at once.
Not to mention our friends, even our enemies would feel pity if they saw her.

387. 'O Queen, the Princess Madhumālatī
is with a prince who is learned and wise.
He is fortunate and from a stainless family,
like the full moon of the dynasty of Soma.
He has many friends and retainers with him.
I cannot describe his wealth and riches.
This is their second day staying with me,
and today they have sent me to you.
They told me, "Go and tell her mother
that in this world even a witch
does not devour her children."
They commanded me so I came. Put aside your sorrow and come.
Come and see the condition of the girl who is wholly without sin!'

388. The Queen ran as soon as she heard
and arrived at Jaunā's house on foot.
After her was the King, Vikram Rāi,
running behind with both feet bare.
When Tārācand saw the King in front,
he came forward to greet him with respect.
Behind the King was Rūpamañjarī,
whose soul had left her body behind.
She seemed like a body without life,
a mere shadow of her former self.
When she wept the whole city wept, distraught in their hearts as they saw her.
Even the Prince's eyes filled with tears when he realized Rūpamañjarī's love.

389. He said, 'Mother, do not cry.
Listen to what I have to tell you.
I managed to catch a wondrous bird
that spoke marvellously pleasing words.
She remained silent and did not speak
for three whole days but then she told me
about all her sorrows openly.
She said that her name was Madhumālatī.

Her father was Vikram Rāi of Mahāras,
and her mother was Rūpamañjarī,
exceedingly cruel and hard of heart.
  Telling me all the sufferings she had undergone, she wept piteously before me.
  When I heard her tale of grief, I lost all my senses and my presence of mind.

390. 'When I heard of her sorrows,
my heart was filled with compassion.
I abandoned all my own people,
my family, my kingdom, and my wealth.
I said to her, "Do not worry any more,
for I shall do what I can to save you.
I have renounced my kingdom and throne
and all the comforts and pleasures I enjoy,
for the great path of *dharma** I have entered
out of my compassion for you.
I shall follow the path of righteousness
so that you may obtain liberation."
I gave her my solemn promise
and put her cage on my head.
Leaving my royal throne, I set off.'
  Then the Prince placed the cage directly in front of the Queen, who saw it
  and cried out aloud, as if her womb had been engulfed in a roaring fire.

Madhumālatī Restored

391. Rūpamañjarī rushed to embrace the cage.
When she saw her daughter's condition,
she could not help but weep piteously.
Every moment she looked at the maiden,
streams of tears flowed from her eyes, unabated.
Her maids said, 'O Queen, do not be sad.
Be happy your heart's desire is fulfilled.'
Then the Queen, who had been in despair

and burning with grief, blossomed
like a lotus with the rising sun.
When that grievous sorrow,
so like a fierce sun, passed out of her body,
the peacock of joy climbed aloft
and called out, signalling the happy rains.
Every house in the city celebrated, and every family was blissfully happy:
it was as if the Princess Madhumālatī had been born a second time.

392. Every house in the city heard the news
that Madhumālatī, who had gone away,
had been found again. The city was happy,
and everyone was filled with excitement,
whether they were related to her or not.
The city which had been distraught with grief
blossomed like a forest in the springtime.
The Queen bowed down before the Prince
and put the dust of his feet on her head.
She said, 'O Prince, through your great effort
my departing life has remained in my body.'
Then the Queen took the Prince and all his party away with her.
They left the garden of the florist and proceeded to the royal palace.

393. All her family and relatives were happy,
as if the girl had been born that very day.
Sandalwood was ground into a fine paste
and applied all over the royal palace,
and red silken drapes were hung up everywhere.
Marvellous beds were brought and spread out,
colourful, attractive, and scented with perfume.
The Prince was made to sit on a throne,
and the Queen herself stood by his head
and fanned him with a royal whisk.
Then the Queen brought Madhumālatī
and seated her before the Prince.

Rūpamañjarī uttered a magic spell and sprinkled water over Madhumālatī's face.
Then that alluring maiden regained her beauty and left behind the body of a bird.

394. When she was set free from being a bird,
she took a mirror and looked at her face.
When she saw that her form had been restored,
she joined her hands and bowed down to God.
Her maids took her quickly and bathed her,
and dressed her in the finest clothes.
They adorned her with fine ornaments
and brought her back to the assembly.
The Queen could not contain her joy
when she saw her. She took a lamp
and worshipped her with it in thanksgiving.
She then hugged her close from moment to moment.
Then the King and the Queen talked together and considered carefully
whether they should offer the Princess to Prince Tārācand in marriage.

395. Then the Queen summoned her family
and they all put their heads together
to discuss the matter. They all said,
'People say that when a girl matures
her father's house is not proper for her.
If a daughter is ready to be married,
she does not adorn her parents' house.
Many a family has been ruined
through the downfall of a daughter.
Either she should live in her husband's house,
or dwell in the halls of death.
Until she is eight, a daughter is a girl.
If she lives at her parents' when she's nine,
people begin to abuse her father.
The Prince is endowed with every virtue and is from an illustrious family.

Let her be betrothed to him at once, do not delay the
engagement.'

The Queen and Tārācand

396. Then the Queen approached the Prince
and told him what she had in mind.
She said, 'O Prince, my heart desires
to offer you Madhumālatī in marriage.'
When he heard this the Prince said,
'Listen, mother, we have given our word
to each other with God as our witness,
that your daughter is my sister.
You are a mother to me as well,
just as you are to my sister.
A good man's word follows his soul:
if it goes, his life goes with it,
and if it is kept, he remains alive.
My duty now is to abide by what I have promised your
daughter.
Only if she meets her Prince Manohar can my heart be
happy again.

397. 'Mother, you must arrange it
so that she meets him once more.
He is as dear to her as life itself.
I have seen her grievous sorrow
searching through harsh, difficult places,
wandering through the world,
intoxicated with love for him—
I shall only have peace of mind
when she meets her love again.
Call all the courtiers of the King.
Command them to go to find Manohar.
I have heard this saying from my elders:
wh[illegible] searches, finds his desire.
[illegible]her, do whatever you can, arrange it so she can be
[illegible]ned with her Prince.

Only when their burning hearts have been cooled will
my heart be at peace.'

398. When the Queen heard Tārācand's answer,
she told him everything from the beginning,
'On the day that the two met in the garden
at Citbisarāuṉ, surrounded on all sides
by countless serving maids, we knew
that these two should have to wander
in every direction for their heart's desire.
In the grip of anger I spoke to her,
my mind quite clouded by darkness.
I was quite out of my mind,
but now my reason has returned.
In my anger, I could not look at the girl.
I had him sent home and put her here.
She would stand all day long, staring into space, eyes lifted to the sky.
All night she would lie here in despair, weeping as she recalled his face.

399. 'Were I to speak of my sorrow, O Prince,
even a stone would shatter if it heard.
O Prince, I have suffered for my actions.
For suddenly a shock of grief beset my mind,
and I did something so cruel and heartless
that nobody in the Kali age could have done.
If you throw away the jewel in your hand,
how can you find it even when you search?
Let me send someone to Pemā now.
It may be possible to find him once more.'
When Tārācand heard this he said, 'Send someone as quickly as you can.
Maybe we can find the lover burning in separation and all will be accomplished.'

400. Then the Queen called messengers to her,
and picked a clever pair from among them.
She wrote down all the news on paper,

all the events that had happened:
how Madhumālatī had become a bird,
and wandered the earth in search of Manohar,
of how Tārācand had ensnared her in his net,
and how she came with the Prince to Mahāras,
adding that he was a kind-hearted Prince
who had caused her to find the Princess again.
  Everything that had happened she thought over and wrote down.
  Then she sent the messengers off, with her seal-ring as a token for Pemā.

The Seasons of Madhumālatī's Separation

401. Then Madhumālatī, unbeknownst to her mother,
entreated the messengers with folded hands,
to explain everything to Pemā thus:
'You kindled this fire in my heart.
O friend, I have wandered the earth for my love,
but the fire in my heart was never quenched.
Maybe, O Princess, you can find him.
If you do, reunite me with my match.'
She recounted all her past sufferings
that she had endured, parted from the Prince.
  'In the form of a bird, I wandered every day for a year to find my Prince.
  Everything I shall reveal to you in detail, so listen carefully, dear friend.*

402. 'In the month of Sāvan,* when massing clouds thundered,
my eyes recalled my loved one with tears.
No one could know my unfathomable sorrow.
The days would not pass in my grief.
My eyes were in flood like the Gaṅgā and Jamunā.
When my tears of blood fell to the earth,
they became the scarlet ladybirds of Sāvan.
She who enjoys in this difficult season
the delights of the couch and the excitement of love,

enjoys the blessings that life has to offer.
I wandered as a cuckoo through every garden,
eyes bloodshot, body burning in separation.
    Only a stubborn soul can stay in its body without a lover in the month of Sāvan,
    with its massing clouds and torrents of rain, its endless nights and flashing lightnings.

403. 'In the fearsome nights of the dark month of Bhādoṉ,*
only separation's fierce fire shared my bed.
In the rains, the constellations of Maghā* and the Lion
tossed my body to and fro in pain.
The water of love dripped from my two eyes.
All the eight physical signs of love
were aroused in my body, and the seven skies
bowed down low to touch the earth.
Thunder crashed frighteningly all around me.
I was sure my soul would leave me at last.
What hope of life can a woman have,
who does not sleep by her lover
in the dark nights of Bhādoṉ?
    I wandered alone through wood and forest, with the pain of separation in my heart.
    Yet such a sinner was my shameless soul that it did not leave my body.

404. 'The nine nights of the festival of Navarātra*
heralded the cruel month of Kuṃvār.*
The wind whistled of the winter to come.
In the crisp autumn nights, the moon
shone cool and bright in the sky.
Everyone was celebrating the festive season,
but I was alone, exiled to the forest.
Night after night, cranes screeched in the lakes.
The colourful wagtails returned to the world.
As the birds reappeared, the rains subsided,
and the wet earth became firm again.
The season of Kuṃvār was happy and festive,
and young women blossomed with joy.

But my heart suffers such agony in separation that my mouth cannot speak at all,
and my eyes rain torrents of tears: how can I write down my sorrow, O friend?

405. 'The full moon of Kārtik* tormented this girl.
Its rays of nectar streamed down like poison.
Maidens were blossoming like lotuses,
night lotuses in the radiance of the moon.
They delighted in the cool nights of autumn,
spent in their lovers' passionate embraces.
My body was consumed with the fire of separation.
In the cool autumn moonlight,
I made my bed on burning embers.
Only she can enjoy those precious days,
who shares her bed with a sweet-talking lover.
The autumn nights are pleasant only for her, who lies in her lover's embrace.
Everyone celebrated the festival of lights, and I was alone in the forest.

406. 'Through the month of Aghan,*
the cold weather was at its prime,
bodies trembled with cold, warm fire felt good.
The days and my joys drew shorter together,
at every moment, nights and sorrows grew longer.
Each dark night passed like an age,
as I wandered from branch to branch in the forest.
Only she knows this harrowing agony,
who has suffered separation while in love.
My gravest fault, dear friend, was this:
I did not die when I parted from my love.
My sinning soul stained me with a terrible disgrace:
on the day we parted, why did it not leave my body lifeless?

407. 'The nights of Pūs* were intolerably difficult.
I, a weak woman, could barely endure them and survive.
How can a woman's nature bear a night
in which each watch passes like an age?

Everyone's heart held desire for their love,
and I wandered alone through the forest,
making my nest on the branches of trees.
Lovers take pleasure in the season of Pūs,
for youth is fleeting as the afternoon sun.
The steed of youth gallops on furiously,
and will not turn back despite your regrets.
Fortune turned away from me, O friend, when my lover turned his face away.
How could my lover abandon me blossoming in the prime of youth?

408. 'Listen, dear friend, how hard the month of Māgh:*
my love was in a foreign land,
and I had no friend but separation.
How could I bear the harsh cold winter,
without a lover in my bed, and I a young girl?
Suffering the agony of parting,
I perched on wintry branches all night,
hail and snow beating down on me.
How did Madhumālatī endure difficult Māgh,
her days of separation growing longer each moment?
Happiness went along with my love, and sorrow stayed to keep me company.
And separation's shears hacked at me, cutting away at bone and flesh.

409. 'And in the month of Phāgun,* my friend,
a disaster befell my suffering body:
I was burnt on the pyre like Holikā.
Not a single leaf remained on the trees,
the forest-fire of separation destroyed them.
Forests suffered a fall of leaf,
and all the gardens turned to dry thorns.
All the birds renounced the woods
when they saw red blossoms
light up the flame-of-the-forest.
Not a tree remained in the world,
to which I did not cling weeping in despair.

Dear friend, I had not yet found my love—I was sobbing myself to death.
My body, bursting with new youth, wasted away into dry thorn bushes.

410. 'Tender new leaves came out in Caita,*
and nature put on a fresh green sari.
Black honey-bees hummed everywhere,
and leaves and flowers adorned the branches.
Blossoms raised their heads from the bough,
and trees grew fresh flowering limbs.
The trees which shed all their leaves in Phāgun
grew green and fresh with leaf once more.
Without my lord, my own fall of leaf
has not, dear friend, grown green again.
My love gave me sorrow and abandoned me, my mother cast me into exile.
The sun beat down its harsh rays on me, as it entered the eighth mansion.

411. 'Sorely I suffered, dear friend, in Baisākh,*
when the forest was green but my body was burning.
Only if she shares her bed of joy with a lover
can a woman enjoy the bliss of spring in Baisākh.
Forests and gardens clothed themselves with flowers.
For me, spring was barren without my love.
How was Madhumālatī to survive Baisākh,
when the fire of separation consumed her every moment?
Petals and leaves of every colour,
clothed the trees yellow, green, and red.
Without my dear lord, O companion of my childhood, my youth bore no fruit,
its blossoms withered and fell to the ground, jasmine in the wood.

412. 'My heart cried out, "My love! My love!"
in the cruel summer month of Jeṭh.*
The sun shone a thousand times more fiercely.
The flames of separation raged inside my heart,

and the sun rained fire for all to see.
Secretly, separation burnt me up,
and openly, the sun's fire consumed me:
how could a woman survive between two fires?
Night and day, Jeṭh kept me burning.
Where could I find my lord* to cool me in bed?
Wherever this girl rested for a moment,
a forest-fire of separation leapt up around her.
First, I was separated, second, in exile, third, without friend or companion,
fourth, I was without form or beauty: when I sought to die, death would not come.

413. 'Dear friend, lightning flashed in the heavens
to herald the unbearable month of Asāḍh.*
Dark clouds like elephants turned to look back,
at the lightning which goaded them on.
Crickets and grasshoppers clamoured in tumult.
The scorched grass grew back,
mango trees blossomed once more.
The earth sprouted with life again,
but love never sprouted in my love's heart.
People built up pavilions and shelters,
and birds made their nests in trees.
Asāḍh passed in torment for me, dear friend, and all twelve months.
Now please, for the sake of the Creator, help me so I may be redeemed.

414. 'If the Prince come in search of you,
tell him every detail of my sufferings
entreating him with tears in your eyes.
Tell my lord I gave up my life for him,
wandering round the earth's nine regions.
Nowhere did I find a trace of you,
but my shameless soul did not leave my body.
Just as love is passionately attached to beauty,
my soul is intoxicated with love-in-separation.
Although my body could not reach you,

my soul was with you, my lord, night and day!
From the moment I was separated from you, I have been weeping myself to death.
Even though my body is far away from you, my soul is always at your feet.

415. 'When love for you awoke in my heart,
I gave up all my other friendships.
Just as my soul is with you, my lord,
give me your soul in exchange!
Or else, take out from my breast
the pain of love which afflicts my heart.
Listen, I am sinking in the ocean of love,
and without you I have no support at all.
You brought me love in secret, my lord,
but openly, you took my soul away by force.
In the body of a cuckoo, weeping tears of blood, my tongue repeated my lover's name.
I merged with the beauty of my beloved, roaming the world with my life* in my hands.

416. 'From the moment you came into my eyes,
I have been weeping night and day.
I am amazed, for although I wept incessantly,
I could not wash you from my eyes.
All the worries that were in my mind
were forgotten in my worry for my master.
Every concern fled from my mind
the moment I became anxious for you.*
May my beloved make me the dust
on whichever path he sets his foot!
I wish I could worship him with the lamp of my life at every step,
but the Creator has only given me one life to sacrifice for his sake.

417. 'For your sake, my darling,
I have become the dust on your path
that I may touch your feet somehow.

Though my life were to leave my body,
my grief for you will not desert this frame.
My lord, do to me whatever you please,
but do not inflict on me the pain of separation!
If you were to kill me with your own hand,
my love, I'd give up not one but a hundred lives.
But if I could find peace by sacrificing my life,
why did I not die sooner for your sake?
Do not think that an everlasting love will lessen upon separation.
Rather, love grows ever stronger as the days of parting lengthen!'

418. She wrote down all she had suffered,
adding much more in words to be told.
Madhumālatī fell at the feet of the couriers,
and entreating them, gave them the order to start.
Her messenger travelled for four days
until he reached Pemā's gateway.
The doorkeeper took the news to Pemā,
that a courier from Madhumālatī had arrived.
When the Princess heard Madhumālatī's name,
she came to the doorway to meet the messenger.
The courier advanced to face Pemā and saluted her in royal fashion.
He gave her the letter, then told her by word of mouth all the news from there.

A Message is Delivered

419. Pemā wept so much as she read the letter
she washed her dark eyes white with tears.
Then she said to the messenger,
'From the day they bore the Prince away,
I have found not a trace of him.
I do not know whether he lives or is dead.
Madhumālatī's own mother felt no pity
when she banished her child to the forest.

If she did not even pity her daughter,
what pity could she feel over killing others?
    If on that day his life was saved and Prince Manohar still lives,
    he will certainly come back—if he did not fall into the river of Death.

420. 'Why does her mother send to ask me,
when she should ask herself where she flung him?
But if the Prince still lives in this world,
he cannot continue without coming to see me.'
The Princess wept as though her soul
were being drawn out of her body
as she stood speaking to the messenger.
Just then a serving girl ran up to her
and said, 'Princess, your brother has come.
A yogi who looks like the Prince has arrived.
Come to the door that you may recognize him.
    When I saw his resemblance to the prince, I came running straight to you.
    I'm sure it must be Prince Manohar, in the guise of a wandering ascetic.'

421. The moment that she heard the Prince's name,
Pemā began to run. Filled with affection,
she came rushing to the doorway.
Then, when her gaze fell on the Prince,
a fire set the heart in her breast ablaze.
She ran and embraced the Prince,
her heart burning with pity and love.
Anyone would have felt pity for him,
for he was just a shadow without a body.
Not a *ratti* of flesh remained on his body—
separation's knife had pared him to the bone.
    Seized by sorrow, burnt by separation, only the hope of reunion kept him alive.
    y God grant that no one born into the world should ffer separation in love!

422. When that royal Prince's name was heard,
celebrations rang out throughout Citbisarāuṉ.
Then Pemā took the Prince with her,
and led him to the royal palace.
She said, 'O brave warrior,
take off your patchwork cloak!*
You have attained success on Gorakh's path.*
Advance now and embrace joy with honour.
Sprinkle a handful of water on your grief!
The dark night of sorrows has passed,
and brilliant happiness will put an end to grief.
If one crosses the unfathomable ocean of love,
swimming with one's life at stake,
and reaches safely the farther shore, courageous
perfection will attend one's efforts.

423. Then Pemā told the Prince all the news,
and read out aloud to him the message
that Madhumālatī had written and dispatched.
Then the maiden sent for ink and paper
and began to write an appropriate reply.
She started with the name of the Creator,
then told her of the Prince's welfare.
She said she was deliberately not writing
any other news, for her messengers
could report directly on what they saw.
She added to herself, 'How could I write of how the
Prince arrived at my house?
He had scarcely a scrap of flesh on him, nor a *ratti* of
blood in his body.'

The Reply

424. Pemā then wrote a letter to the Queen,
'I thought you had killed him that day
and had his body thrown away
on some mountain side or in the sea.
I had given up all hope for the Prince

when all of a sudden he came to me.
When I saw him alive, it was as if
I had found a great treasure.
At that moment your letter arrived.
It was as if rain had begun to fall
on the head of a poor creature
burning up in a raging fire.
The Prince heard your letter with such joy,
I feared his heart might burst from happiness.
  If you are sure and determined in your mind to carry out this wedding
  then come here and alight nearby, bringing all the trappings of ceremony.

425. 'If we are certain about your intentions,
then we can begin to make arrangements here.
If you are sure about the wedding,
the King should come to us forthwith.
In this age of Kali, true wisdom lies
in doing today the tasks of tomorrow.'
Pemā thus wrote her letter in reply.
She gave it to the messenger
with a token of recognition for Madhumālatī.
The Prince then wrote the tale of his sorrows
and gave it to be delivered to Madhumālatī.
  The Prince, hands folded in entreaty and touching the courier's feet, told him,
  'Give this letter of my sorrows in secret to the Princess Madhumālatī.'

426. 'First I call upon the Lord
who pervades all parts of the universe.
Second, I call on the name of Muḥammad
whose ship will take me to life's farther shore.
Now listen to my entreaty.
You took in the palm of your hand
th[illegible] that was in my body.
[illegible] me that I could see you
[illegible]ready to sacrifice my life.

I am in the condition you required
so you must keep the promise you gave.
One's beloved should never leave one, though the
may leave the body.
A million deaths do not equal the pain of one moment
of separation.

427. 'All that is most beautiful in creation
I brought and showed my soul.
It rejected everything and devoted itself to you,
finding you superior to all of creation.
My mind was fixed in meditation
on your beauty, and my breath
lost its way through my body.
My soul was so absorbed in you
I forgot even to recite your name.
How can your soul learn from you
the secrets of my heart's condition?
What does your soul know of others' sorrows—how
can it learn them from you?
Only they can know this terrible pain who have looked
upon your face.

428. 'All the immovable objects of the world,
are made of stone, O most alluring maiden!
Your heart is just like a stone, sweetheart,
else how could it constantly be without love?
You have no pity in your heart, nor compassion.
Princess, though your speech is sweet,
your heart is hard. You should cultivate love
like the coconut which is hard outside,
but has a tender and juicy heart.
Since grief for you became my companion,
I was able to bear this terrible suffering.
If I found that my soul was with you in a dream, when I
awoke
it would not return to me for it knew that your body
was its resting place.

9. 'O maiden, if you take a mirror and look into it,
you will begin to suffer grief for yourself.
When you see yourself in the mirror,
pain will pervade your body.
The fire of love will consume you utterly.
Your sickness will worsen with your own medicine.
The flames of love-in-separation
will blaze up and burn your own body.
Your own noose will fall around your neck.
When you see yourself, you will faint.
If you look at your own face, O maiden,
then you will know how others suffer.
Reveal your face and take a mirror and look carefully at yourself
so that you may see clearly how the whole world suffers for you.'

430. The messengers took back the written reply,
and happily announced the good news.
When they heard that Manohar was well,
the people of Mahāras celebrated joyfully.
The Queen sent for Prince Tārācand
and read the letter out to him.
When he heard the letter through,
the Prince said, 'God has brought about
that which was my heart's desire.
Let us swiftly prepare to leave.
We must not delay in matters of duty.'
The five musical instruments were loudly sounded and the whole family was invited.
King Vikram Rāi picked a good moment and they set off on the journey.

The Royal Procession

431. King Vikram Rāi assembled his party and set off
tle-drums resounding all around.
d of the drums caused such a tumult

that Śeṣa the serpent was frightened
and drew back his thousand hoods.
Prince Tārācand rode with the party.
The syces* led the horses from the front.
The Queens, for whom palanquins were readied,
set off happily, laughing and joking.
Madhumālatī sat calmly in her mother's lap
like the full moon of Caita sits
among the stars of the constellations
of Jarad: Viśākhā, Anurādhā, Jyeṣṭhā.*
The whole party left together, kinsmen, subjects, and retainers.
The sun was hidden by the dust of the army of elephants and horses.

432. They were travelling for ten days,
and then alighted by the shore of a sea.
Here they erected a mighty pavilion
and let the kettle-drums ring out loudly.
It would make this tale too long
if I were to praise the royal camp they built.
The King sent for all his ministers,
all the wise men and elders of state.
Tārācand was made to sit in their midst.
Once they were all together in assembly
they began their deliberations.
The ministers were all of one mind and, approaching the King,
they suggested that he send for both Pemā and King Citrasena.

433. The King was pleased to hear their opinion
and dispatched couriers to Citrasena.
Madhumālatī wrote a secret letter
with a great many entreaties for Pemā.
She then wrote openly the requests
made by Queen Rūpamañjarī,
'O Pemā, I want you to be here tomorrow.
Please come as quickly as possible

so that I may fulfil my purpose.'
The messengers took the letter
to where Pemā was staying,
the royal darling of her father's house.
  The doorkeeper went to Pemā and salaamed, bringing her the news
  that emissaries from King Vikram Rāi stood at the gate with a letter.

The Welcome

434. The Princess called in the messengers
and asked them everything in full detail.
They gave the letter into her hand
and told her the situation in words.
She called for Prince Manohar to come
and read the good news aloud to him.
Pemā then went to tell her father,
'Couriers from King Vikram Rāi have come.
The King has invited us to visit him,
and his camp is not very far from here.'
  As soon as Citrasena heard this, he set out in response to Vikram's invitation.
  Pemā herself, together with all her friends, was borne there by palanquin.

435. King Citrasena set out on his way
accompanied by a thousand nobles.
Ministers, lords, worthy kinsmen,
pandits and astrologers—all went with him.
Along with Pemā went her girlfriends,
many youthful buds with swelling breasts.
When Citrasena arrived at the entrance,
the guards went to inform the King.
When he heard, King Vikram rushed
and came all the way to the doorway.
The two kings embraced affectionately.
  Vikram Rāi offered King Citrasena the pavilion next to his own royal tent.

Pemā went in to the Queen's palace, where all the
women were staying.*

436. King Vikram Rāi then summoned
all his retinue, his priests and astrologers.
Men of divers skills assembled there.
Tārācand was also invited there
and given a seat of honour in the assembly.
Then Citrasena told Vikram Rāi
what he had heard from the pandits,
that if a task were undertaken
after thinking carefully about it,
then it would be certain of success.
Harigun the astrologer was sent for
and told, 'Calculate and compare the horoscopes.
Consider the auspicious and inauspicious
configurations, and determine a date and time
such that the couple will be able to maintain their love
and devotion forever.'

The Auspicious Moment

437. The astrologers drew up the horoscopes
and wrote in the twelve signs of the Zodiac
in their respective places. Then they filled in,
after due reckoning, the positions of the nine planets.
They considered the lovers' natal situations,
and also any adverse influences between them.
They settled, after careful consideration,
on the ninth day of the bright half
of the month of Jeṭh, in the sign of Aquarius.
The auspicious moment and day they fixed
was a Wednesday, the constellation, Anurādhā.*
Considering good fortune, prosperity and progeny, and
a long and happy life together,
thus the astrologers fixed on the right day for the
marriage of Madhumālatī.

438. The pandits had settled on the right configuration

after assessing all the planetary influences.
They had found it to be auspicious
and had chosen the hour for the ceremony.
Then King Vikram Rāi arose and went within
to tell the Queen what had transpired.
When the Queen heard, she arranged festivities.
The drum of joy was beaten at every door.
All the handmaidens who had come with Pemā
were dressed by the Queen in coloured silken robes.
Then the King requested Citrasena to go
to make all the arrangements on his side.
 The Queen affectionately embraced Pemā, clasping her to her breast.
 King Vikram Rāi sent Citrasena off with all due honour and respect.

439. The Queen explained to Pemā carefully
which day and moment had been chosen.
The maiden mounted her palanquin and left
with her father Citrasena, protector of the earth.
They entered the city to the sounds of music
and arranged the Prince's wedding celebration.
By the King's decree, all the markets were adorned.
The shops were hung with orange* silks.
A bracelet of thread was tied around Manohar's wrist
to ward off evil spirits and influences.
All the retinue was made ready for the ceremony.
 They anointed Prince Manohar's body with a fragrant unguent* mixed with saffron.
 Even though the wedding was seven days away, to the Prince it seemed an age.

The Wedding Procession

440. On Wednesday, the ninth day of the month,
King Citrasena's party set off at his order.
As they proceeded, the omens were good:
a deer and a crow were seen to the right,

a woman came towards them
with a child at her breast, and a brahmin appeared
anointed with twelve marks on his forehead.
On the right, there appeared a rabbit
and a donkey was seen on the left.
A milkmaid with curds on her head
was crying out her wares loudly.
Fish were seen leaping above the water.
Young women appeared before them
walking with pots filled with water.
The white kite* and the fox appeared, showing themselves as auguries.
With omens such as these, any enterprise will meet with sure success.

441. The wedding party moved on like an army,
with instruments playing and music resounding.
Many wondrous models were made of paper—
flowering trees, splendid houses and roads.
Boats were seen, draped with saffron cloth,
on which dancing puppets were shown performing.
Divers instruments made delightful music,
and there were other marvels beyond counting.
Many fruit trees had been planted at intervals
and camps and resting places set up along the way.
By Citrasena's order, all the thirty-six serving castes accompanied the Prince.
For seven leagues in all directions, torches lit up the world like blazing sunlight.

442. They brought fireworks with them—
Catherine wheels and countless Roman candles,
while the rockets, like arrows of fire,
dispelled the darkness of the night
and spread brilliance in the heavens.
It was impossible to tell day and night apart
to call one day and the other night.
Bards mounted on horseback went along,
calling out fair words, and the Prince,

wearing a garland of diamonds and pearls,
was borne along seated in a palanquin.
King Citrasena had assembled his retinue and led the
Prince's wedding party.
Blessed be the courage and success of Prince Manohar,
blessed his mother and father!

443. Madhurā had made all the arrangements
for the royal ladies in the women's quarters.
The Queen now went to wed Manohar.
How did Pemā travel with her handmaidens?
She had sixty companions, all of the same age.
Some were in palanquins and others on sedan-chairs.
Some were married, while the other girls
were still in the innocence of youth.
As they played delightfully in youth's enthusiasm,
they were like buds sprouting on forest creepers.
With lotus-like faces and full, youthful bodies
these girls could kill with their sidelong glances.
Some were in the full bloom of womanhood, while
others still had their innocence.
They were adorned in all the sixteen ways, and wore
priceless jewels on their breasts.

The Ceremony of Marriage

444. Evening drew on and, at the twilight hour,
the wedding party reached the King's gateway.
The party was welcomed and settled into quarters
prepared for them by King Vikram's orders.
By royal decree, a lofty pavilion had been built
within which was placed a golden pitcher.
The King had sent for diamonds and jewels,
and silken cloths to drape the pavilion.
Garlands of mango leaves and flowers
had been arranged on all four sides.
Two girls adorned from head to foot came in singing,
bearing on their heads the vessels for the offerings.

The Prince's mother-in-law-to-be gave her gifts,
together with the lamp for Āratī,*
which Pemā circled around the Prince's head, then
offered in all ten directions.

445. Ten girls then entered and, in melodious tones,
sang the traditional songs of abuse
about the Prince's mother. They pretended
that King Citrasena was the father,
and took happy delight in abusing him.
They teased Pemā through song and mimicry,
saying she was smitten with Tārācand.
Madhurā was not spared their abuse
for they made her the bridegroom's mother.
Again, they went after Pemā mercilessly,
called her Madhumālatī's serving-maid.
Prince Manohar gave them money as their reward,
whatever he thought best.
Then, with happiness and delight, they began to sing his
praises joyfully.

446. Then King Vikram sent two priests
to bring Manohar to the festal pavilion.
Bringing him in, they seated him
in the middle of the gathering.
Then they fetched Madhumālatī
to be at the Prince's left-hand side.
The learned priests chanted Vedic hymns
and offered oblations to the fire
full eighty-four times. Maidens sang
auspicious songs in Manohar's name.
The borders of the couple's robes
were knotted in the tie of marriage.
Madhumālatī then garlanded the Prince
and Manohar placed a garland
around the neck of Madhumālatī.
The couple circled the fire and Madhumālatī placed her
hand within the Prince's.

King Vikram gave his daughter in marriage, with the
gods and ancestors as witnesses.

447. Thus, the wedding ceremony took place
and the couple's hearts were calmed.
Blessed indeed is the Creator who,
out of disaster, had brought this to be.
After much grief and many obstacles,
the Creator had fulfilled their hopes.
In this world he is truly blessed who,
through the merits of a former birth,
meets his beloved unexpectedly.
They took the Prince to the chamber of joy
where the bed of pleasure was placed.
And, after much persuasion,
her hand-maidens took Madhumālatī
and seated her gently on the bed of love.
Fear stirred in Madhumālatī's heart, along with the
eagerness of the night of union.
Since this was their first time together, the maiden could
not look at the Prince.

The Wedding Night

448. Manohar took her arm and said,
'My sorrowing heart, which longed for you,
is now at peace. Give up your former cruelty,
abandon modesty and embrace me!'
All shyness gone, they spoke of love
and gazed directly into each other's eyes.
Those eyes which had thirsted in hope
now drank in love and beauty to the full.
Their grieving hearts were cooler now,
the fire subsiding as their hearts united.
Their eyes were joined in longing and their hearts
enmeshed in love.
As both their hearts became one, their souls began to
share in each other.

449. Their eyes drank in beauty till sated.
Somehow this sun and moon became one.
Still they could not turn face to face,
their hearts trembling before their first union.
The Prince sought to kiss her lips
but Madhumālatī averted her mouth
and turned her face away from him.
Mistaking them for lamps, she blew on jewels,
only to make their light even brighter.
She covered her face with both her hands.
When the Prince bit her lips she trembled in fear.
First, their hearts were madly in love; moreover, this was their very first time.
Thirdly, modesty overcame them, so the desire to make love was not aroused.

450. Then a handmaiden hidden there said,
'Why did you study the arts of love?'
Hearing what the maiden said,
Madhumālatī was truly astonished.
But she remained caught between shame
and her knowledge of what to do.
Should she display her arts, she would lose
her modesty; should she remain shy,
her skills in love-making would go to waste.
She recalled with amusement the story of the woman,
with a snake-charmer for a father-in-law,
who was bitten by a snake in her most private parts
but could not speak out for modesty.
The Prince scratched with the goad of his nails
her breasts, round like the swellings
on the forehead of an elephant.
Like a parrot he bit into her coral lips.
Looking at the depth of the waters of her youth, he could contain himself no longer.
Embracing her golden pitcher-breasts, he swam across the river of their shyness.

451. In the grip of love and passion they embraced,

and then her untouched jewel was pierced.
The bodice on her bosom was torn to pieces,
and the parting in her hair was all washed away.
The vermilion from her parting ran
into the spot on her forehead,
and the mascara on her eyes turned red
from the betel juice on his lips.
So heavily did he press upon her
that the garland round her neck broke,
and the sandal paste on her breasts rubbed off.
Her source of nectar broke forth then,
and the raging fire in their hearts
was quenched, the quest fulfilled.
Under the power of desire they spent the night, unable to turn from one another.
But their burning hearts were only cooled when the heavens opened and a stream flowed forth.

452. They spent the night in passion,
savouring the joy of the marriage bed.
In their hearts, separation's fire was quenched.
The Prince got up and came outside.
He took a bath and rubbed his body
with sandal paste. Combing his hair,
he dressed, then gave away some gifts
to acquire merit. Madhu's handmaidens
came into the bedroom and woke her up.
She awoke as if she had swum in a sea of bliss.
Her companions then adorned her
and put on her both clothes and ornaments.
They took sweet delight in asking her about the *rasa* of love. 'Tell us,' they said,
'How was your juicy night of love? Promise us you'll tell every passionate detail!'

*The Secret of Love**

453. Pemā took both her hands and asked,
'Tell me, how did you pass the night?'

Her other friends joined in, pleading,
'Tell us how your lover embraced you.
Don't be shy,' they insisted,
'How did the precious love-making go
between you and your darling?'
The Princess bowed her head
and kept on looking at the ground.
Hiding her face in shame, she said nothing.
The handmaidens persisted in their demand,
but she told them nothing about love's savour.
Then her friends continued to question her in every way.
They pleaded,
'If you won't reveal the secret of love to us, to whom
then will you tell it?'

454. Then the maiden opened her nectar-sweet mouth.
Hear what a priceless thing she said:
'Never reveal your mystery to anyone.
It is madness to exchange profit for loss.
You should keep love hidden in your heart.
Who would mount the gallows like Manṣūr*
for revealing his mystery to the world?
If I told you my secrets, what would I gain?
If you put water into a cracked pot
it drips out drop by drop and is lost.
Look at the pen carved of wood—what did it do when
it was a reed in the forest?
As long as its head was not cut open, it never revealed
its mystery to anyone.'

The Couple Depart

455. At dawn, Tārācand, the King and his nobles,
gathered up all the wedding gifts and dowry.
A hundred thousand horses were saddled up
with golden body armour on their backs.
Maddened elephants resembling dark clouds
were given in dowry, as the world knows.

Ornaments, all studded with jewels,
were arranged and put in a thousand boxes.
Loading up much gold and silver they set off.
The pearls and jewels were beyond counting.
    The names for all the different clothes were too much
        for even a poet to relate.
    They were loaded on to ten thousand bullocks and
        carried in front of the wedding party.

456. Setting out with the Princess Madhumālatī
were her thousand lovely maidservants.
Seeing them, even the moon hid its face in shame.
And with them were the sixty handmaidens
who had played with her since childhood.
All the guests from the groom's party
were given the finest stitched raiment.
The dishes Madhumālatī received
were all made of gold and silver.
Her garments were too many to describe.
The eight separate parts of her bed
were all studded with precious jewels
and covered in colourful silken sheets
with raised flowers woven into the fabric.
    Incense, camphor, deer's musk, and all the other
        fragrant substances,
    coconuts, raisins, almonds, and dates—all were loaded
        onto ten thousand bullocks.

457. When the dowry had all been loaded and sent off,
Prince Manohar came to Madhumālatī and asked,
'In which palace lives your brother Tāracand?
Take me with you and show me where.
I will go to him and dedicate my life to him.
I shall sweep the dust from his feet
with my eyelashes, lay my head at his feet,
and place his feet on my head in gratitude.
[illegible] endured great suffering for me.
[illegible] o and offer my life to him.

I have searched and searched, but found nothin
of dedicating to him.
As for my life, it is such a small offering that I a
ashamed to worship him with it.'

458. When she heard this Madhumālatī arose
and took the Prince to Tārācand.
When Tārācand saw the Prince,
he stood up. Manohar ran
and threw himself at his feet.
Each time Tārācand raised him up
he ran to fling himself at his feet again.
He said, 'Who has ever in this age of Kali
done what you have done for me?
For me you left your kingdom and your throne.
You have quenched the fire of separation
which was burning in my heart.
You abandoned your kingdom and brought back my very life to me.
If I cannot offer that life to you, what value does it have any more?

459. 'With hands joined I beseech you,
if you will fulfil my hopes, O Prince,
that until we are allowed to leave,
we shall stay here together
and pass our days in happiness.
As long as the Creator keeps us here,
we shall remain in this place together.
Here everyone is a native of this land;
you and I alone are strangers.
If you will permit me I shall go
and tell the King of our resolve.'
Tārācand was delighted with the idea and together the two young Princes,
exultant and full of excitement, went to pay court to King Vikram Rāi.

460. Hearing the Princes coming,
the King himself came to the door.

The Princes made their request.
The King said, 'Do as you wish.
The cities of Mahāras and Citbisarāuṉ
are both your own to live in.
The two of you may stay together
wherever your hearts desire.
You two here are the light in my eyes.
Similarly, there you will be the pearls
within the shells of their eyes.
  Wherever your minds wish to be, there you shall both
    stay together.
  My kingdom and throne are all yours, sport happily
    here with each other.'

461. When they got leave from the King,
the princes bowed their heads respectfully.
Madhumālatī meanwhile had met her parents
and mounted her palanquin to leave.
Her sixty companions, with her since birth,
followed after her making merry and playing.
And there were so many maidservants
that they were beyond the poet's counting.
They all came playing youthful games,
making music as they entered Citrasena's house.
  I cannot describe the heart-rending scenes as the
    princess was sent off from Mahāras.
  When they both go to their new homes, I shall only tell
    the tale after thinking hard.

462. The wedding party entered the city,
playing music on their instruments.
Women from the sixteen castes
brought out the lamps for Āratī.
In every house the city celebrated.
Songs were sung in the sweetest voices.
On the outside the city was adorned
with red silk, and who could describe
how lovely the interiors looked?
Madhumālatī was brought to the place

where the marriage bed had been made ready.
A palace was prepared as a pleasant lodging,
and Prince Tārācand was taken there.
Madhumālatī and Pemā enjoyed themselves happily inside the palace,
while outside Manohar and Tārācand pursued their royal sports together.

The Royal Hunt

463. Together the princes pursued their sports,
happily celebrating their new friendship
in pleasure and entertainment.
They spent their days eating, playing,
and laughing, and passed the nights
in sweet carefree sleep. Never for a moment
were they separated—the two friends
stayed together all the time.
At times they amused themselves by hunting.
Sometimes they competed on the polo-field.
Pemā and Madhumālatī remained in the palace
arranging the dance and music of the *dhamār*.*
They were always enjoying themselves, and never knew a moment's sorrow.
At an age between childhood and youth, they were still cared for by their fathers.

464. One day Prince Manohar summoned the hunters,
who ran when they heard his royal command.
The Prince asked the King's hunters,
'Is there any good hunting hereabouts?'
They told him that at a distance of five miles
many types of game roamed in abundance:
nilgai,* deer, buffalo, and wild boar,
and also stag, gazelle, and antelope in plenty.
'Send five stalkers,' he said, 'and let me know
when they have prepared an ambuscade.
Tomorrow for a watch or two we shall have some entertainment.

Go and tell the other hunters that no one should go
elsewhere.'

465. Early next morning the hunters came.
They announced that the ambuscade was ready
for hunting and that they should proceed.
The moment the hunting party heard
they quickly assembled and let loose
hounds, hunting leopards and cheetahs to run ahead.
Bearers loaded snares and nets onto their shoulders.
Archers set off, fitting arrows to their bows.
Gond beaters stopped the game from fleeing
while the archers drove them from the front.
Within the circle of encircling hunters
loud drums were beaten to direct the game,
and outside the circle nets and snares were laid.
Archers were stationed behind every tree and fires were
started in the forest
so that the panicking antelopes leapt over the bowmen
as they fled.

466. All of the archers had poisoned arrows
which they shot at the panicking game.
Here a rhinoceros charged madly about;
there, antelopes fell writhing in agony.
Wounded bears staggered round in circles.
Buffalo were lying on their backs,
kicking out with their hooves.
The cheetahs and leopards killed many deer.
The hounds overcame countless boar.
Many animals were caught still living,
but many died from the effects of the poison.
After hunting for about three hours, the entire group
returned home again.
The two princes, wanting some fun in the water, began
to swim in a river.

A Vision of Beauty

467. They said to themselves: 'The sun is very hot,
let us go home only when it's cooler.'
While the Princes were playing about in the water,
Pemā said to Madhumālatī: 'The two Princes
are not at home today, so let's go
to the picture-pavilion and swing there.
Today my mind wants to go to a place
where we can swing to our heart's content.
When shall we get such a chance again
to swing happily in our parents' home?'
Madhumālatī heard and got up happily, and they went
to the mango grove together.
The moment they heard the word 'swinging', all their
girlfriends ran to join them.

468. The lovely maidens took to the swings
and began swinging high and low,
singing songs in the sweetest of tones.
As they swung, one girl's hair came undone.
Another's garland broke on her chest.
Many girls' heads became uncovered.
The edges of many maidens' saris
began to flutter in the breeze.
They were swinging holding on
to the thin ropes of the swings,
so slender that their waists seemed
to join two separate bodies together.
As they swung they looked
like goddesses seated in flying chariots.
Their young breasts budded and blossomed, like
children coming into new maturity.
They tucked their saris into the sashes at their waists
and began to swing excitedly.

469. By evening it had become cooler,
and the heat of the sun had eased.
Grooms saddled and brought Arab horses,

and the two royal princes mounted.
So swiftly did they ride their stallions
that in a moment they were at the royal gate.
They asked where the Princesses were,
and were told they had gone to swing
with all their friends and companions.
Hearing they were not at home, they said,
'Why should we go into an empty palace?'
Together they set off for the painted picture-pavilion in the mango grove
where the daughter of Vikram Rāi was swinging with all her friends.

470. When the two arrived at the entrance,
they saw that the doors were open.
Manohar rode to the door and dismounted.
Seeing nobody about, he went into the pavilion.
As he entered he made no sound,
so nobody knew when he came in.
There they swung, mad with delight,
singing as sweetly as cuckoos.
Intoxicated with youth, they were swinging
with the borders of their saris fluttering,
making no attempt to cover their breasts.
They swung holding on to the swings' ropes, their jewelled earrings sparkling,
like goddesses who had flown down from heaven seated in their chariots.

471. Prince Tārācand was right behind him
and set both his feet within the threshold.
His gaze fell directly on Pemā,
who was swinging standing on her swing.
As she swung, her sari fell open at the breast.
Tārācand saw, and all knowledge left his mind.
Her ... swelling breasts were prominent
...d themselves into the Prince's sight.
...nt that he saw her breasts,
...d him of his life.

His body fell lifeless to the ground.
 His captive life came to live in his eyes, while his body
  lay senseless on the earth.
 He shook violently as if stung by a serpent, and he
  could not utter a word.

Prince Tārācand in Love

472. A maidservant who had gone to the door
saw the Prince lying senseless there.
She cried out to Madhumālatī,
'How can you swing? Come and help him!
Prince Tārācand is lying at the door.
He could be bewitched by a demon
or a voracious female witch.
Perhaps he has fainted from an excess of bile,
or maybe he has a fever or dizziness.
Maybe someone has put the evil eye on him
since he lies there with his arms on his neck.
 His eyelids will not close over his eyes and the blood in
  his body has dried up.
 He lies unconscious on the ground and nobody knows
  what he suffers from.'

473. The moment that she heard, Madhumālatī ran,
sobbing loudly, 'Brother, my dear brother.'
She lifted his head and put it on her lap,
praying to the Creator with folded hands.
She wept bitterly over the Prince.
With her hand she hit her forehead,
lamenting, 'What has happened to you,
O brother from a foreign land?
You who found my beloved for me
now sleep as though quite dead.
For my sake you abandoned your life,
but I have done nothing to serve you.
 Open your eyes and tell me of the pain in your heart,
  the weakness in your body.

If I could hear what is wrong then maybe I could devise
a remedy for it.

474. 'When I lost hope, you made my dream come true,
and I have done nothing to help you.
You abandoned your kingdom
and your throne to bring me here.
You united me with the one I could not find.
When my mother exiled me as a bird,
you made me human again.
When my mother cut the moorings
and cast me out on the vast ocean,
brave brother, you brought me to shore again.
On the limitless ocean of sorrow
I was floating without any support.
My bark was drifting without an anchor line or a
steersman to guide me—
you gave me anchor and support when I sank in the
middle of the ocean.'

475. Manohar was in the picture-pavilion.
Hearing the commotion he came running
to the door. Seeing Tārācand's condition,
he became very concerned, and sprinkled
cold water over the Prince's eyes.
After a long wait, Tārācand's soul
returned again to his body.
He sat up, breathing deeply from his chest.
Opening his eyes, he looked all around.
When Manohar thought he was steadier,
he had him taken to the palace in a litter.
The summons went out to all the different wise men to
be found in the city,
and hearing the royal command they all came to the
palace gates.

476. All the physicians and diviners
presented themselves at the palace
where Prince Tārācand was lying
bewitched by the enchantment of love.

They checked his pulse carefully
but could not discern any cause
for pain within his body, although
they noticed that his blood had dried up.
The psychic channels of sun and moon
were flowing normally in his body.*
But his eyelids would not close,
and he could not wake up from the spell.
Finally they pronounced that his soul
was infatuated with someone,
and he would only awaken when he saw her.
They said that he should be asked to tell whom he loved so passionately.
Therefore he must reveal the name of his beloved, since there was no other cure.

Beauty Revealed

477. Then Madhumālatī, that best of maidens,
approached Tārācand and spoke gently to him.
She came alone and sat near the Prince,
asking him, 'What pains you, dear brother?
If you have fallen in love with somebody,
I will bring her to be with you
and nobody will be any the wiser.
Apart from you, me, and the Creator,
no one else shall know a thing about it.'
Tārācand replied, 'I cannot speak,
so how can I tell you of my suffering?
I do not know the name of the beautiful one who has stolen my soul.
Moreover, I would feel ashamed to speak about such matters with you.'

478. 'Brother, how can you feel shame with me?
Forget this shame and tell me all about it.
If I knew her name I could bring her here
to be with you, even if she were a heavenly goddess.'
Tārācand replied: 'I saw her standing as she swung.

The moment my gaze fell on her my soul was lost.
Her two eyes shone as brightly as two stars
risen in daylight and shining on earth.
If you sit here and listen for a moment,
I shall tell you what I saw there.
My tongue can not recount what my eyes have seen.
Of her thousand qualities, hear but one as I describe her.'

479. 'Listen first while I tell of her parting,
like a naked sword set on her head.
I was slain by that sword
and cut in two the moment that I saw her.
It seemed like the flame of a lamp
burning in the darkness of her hair.
Her head was covered in red blood.
The cobras of her locks seized me
and devoured me whole. Where is the healer
who can remove the waves of this venom?
I was dazzled when I saw her forehead.
Even now my eyes see only darkness.
Just as one cannot look directly at the shining rays of the sun
so, when I saw her forehead, I was blinded and fell unconscious.

480. 'Her eyebrows were sharp pointed arrows,
murderous weapons that kill on sight.
Whoever she looks on, turning her glances,
his soul becomes her captive instantly.
Her eyelashes were like the finest arrows
which are only seen when they hit home.
Seeing her nose I was speechless.
How can I describe her lovely nose?
It is worth the whole of creation.
Her lips were *bimba* fruits* filled with nectar.
They were reddened from drinking the blood
vers suffering the pangs of separation.
Her lips, the colour of flame and full of nectar, caused only distress to me.

I do not know for whom they are nectar sweet, but to
me they were fiery sparks.

481. 'Seeing the brilliance of her teeth
I could not control myself—
I fell senseless as one struck by lightning.
Between them lives her priceless tongue.
When it spoke, a well of nectar opened.
And when my gaze fell on her mole—
let me tell you my true state—I felt as if
I had lost all power over my body.
Seeing the glow and beauty of her cheeks,
the mirror tries to clean itself every day
by rubbing its own face with ashes.
Earrings sparkled on both sides of her ears
as though lit up by a flash of lightning.
How beautiful were the lovely black lines of collyrium
around her eyes,
as if her eyes were reaching to her ears in order to make
friends with them!

482. 'Her neck was quite beyond compare,
as if the All-maker had fashioned it himself.
The three lines on the neck of that maiden
were snares for the innocent deer of my eyes.
Vermilion and saffron mixed together
filled her shining crystal throat.
Her two breasts had dark shades
over their tips. Spontaneously,
they came and pierced my eyes.
These two brave conquerors of souls
would have fought without the necklace
which acted as peacemaker between them.
Both her firm, cruel breasts were vessels filled with the
nectar of love.
I beheld the maiden's swelling breasts, like inverted
bowls of gold.

483. 'I can find nothing in the world
to compare to her lovely arms.

How can I praise them properly?
There is nothing which matches them.
Either I am too stupid to describe them,
or maybe the Creator Himself
made them uniquely beautiful.
Some might call them lotus stalks,
yet others, tender plantain stems.
I was enchanted on seeing her wrists,
their beauty enhanced by golden bracelets.
Her palms shone as pure as quartz
on which red minium had been rubbed.
    Holding the ropes with her leaf-like palms, she was swinging with her friends.
    The nails on her hands, when I saw them, were like the scarlet buds of the coral tree.

484. 'Through rubbing it with unguents
she had made her stomach flat.
No matter what I compared it to,
in the end it was still matchless.
Her navel was a deep, unfathomable pool.
Whoever fell in, wouldn't reach the bottom.
When she was swinging standing on the swing
her waist seemed to want to snap into two.
And when I saw her buxom buttocks
I could hardly contain myself—
a single mountain had split into two hills.
I don't know what happened when I saw her thighs,
they were like the golden trunks
of plantain trees, turned upside down.
    Her legs were murderous brigands who kicked at me with separation's pangs.
    If you looked at the soles of her feet openly, you'd see they were stained with blood.'

Madhumālatī Arranges Matters

485. The Prince finished telling his story.
When she heard, Madhumālatī was speechless.

She began thinking, puzzling in her mind
over whom the Prince had seen
and became very distressed.
'I do not have a companion like that,
though, of course, it might be Pemā.'
'My brother,' she said, 'be patient.
I will go and find the answer to your pain.'
Then Madhumālatī realized for sure
that it could be no one else but Pemā.
'I will call all my companions here and look into the matter at once.
Whether she be a maiden or a married woman I shall come and tell you.'

486. Madhumālatī rose and returned home,
where she explained everything to Manohar.
That beautiful one repeated to her beloved
all that she had told Prince Tārācand.
He was overjoyed when he heard,
and said, 'What is the worry?
When I killed the demon and took Pemā
back to her home, she was given to me.
I did not accept the offer then
because I had no deep love for her,
but now I shall take her
and marry her to Prince Tārācand.'
Saying this, the Prince and Princess both went to see King Citrasena.
He seated them all in a place of privacy and sent for Queen Madhurā.

487. Prince Manohar stood before the King
with hands joined in entreaty and said,
'Father, I have a humble request to make.
With your permission I shall ask you,
though I feel shame to say this to my father.'
The King granted his permission
and promised to take their words seriously.
They both then revealed the whole matter.

'Prince Tārācand belongs to a noble family.
He is the lord of great and powerful Māngaṛh.
He is learned, generous and truthful.
Your darling daughter Pemā is my adoptive sister. If you just say the word,
we can give her to Prince Tārācand and tie the marriage knot between them.'

488. The King heard, and looked at Manohar's face.
'Why', he said, 'do you ask me this?
From the day that you killed the demon
and snatched Pemā back, she was your servant.
Take her hand and give her in marriage
to whomsoever you please. Who am I in this?'
When the king delivered his promise thus,
they went back and set the house rejoicing.
The Prince immediately sent for astrologers
who worked out the stars and signs for the couple.
All the families, all the relatives and retainers, were sent invitations to the wedding.
Celebrations rang out in every house, and the whole city sang auspicious songs.

The Wedding Feast

489. News of the wedding spread abroad
and the work for the feast grew apace.
Monday, the thirteenth day of the month,
was the day fixed for the wedding.
Every house in the city celebrated.
The King invited every town and city.
When the thirteenth day arrived,
King Citrasena threw a grand banquet.
The finest couches were brought
and spread out. The King and court
all took their places. When they were seated,
the wedding feast was served.
Thousands of dishes were put before everyone.

The king and all the distinguished guests were given the 'five nectars'* to feast on.
Delicacies of every sort were placed before each person to savour.

490. When the wedding feast was over,
people began to return home
and all were given betel leaves.*
Then all the astrologers were sent for
and seated in the wedding pavilion.
Tārācand was put on a special stool,
and offerings were made in the sacred fire.
The beautiful bride, Princess Pemā,
was brought to stand on his left side.
She stood there looking as though
she had been carved out of the moon itself.
Mantras were uttered for Tārācand and Pemā.
The marriage knot was tied and the couple
circled the sacred fire seven times.*
Apprehensively, hesitantly, lovely Pemā placed a garland round the Prince's neck.
Then Tārācand took a necklace of flowers and garlanded the lovely maiden.

The Bridal Chamber

491. Sandal and saffron were crushed together,
mixed with perfume and the chamber anointed.
Inside and out and all around,
lengths of red silk were draped.
Then the wedding bed was brought in.
The Prince joyfully came in and sat down.
Then her handmaidens fetched Pemā,
who had been finely adorned,
and seated her on the bed of love.
The hair on her body became erect,
she perspired, trembled and sighed deeply.
Desire for first union awoke in both of them.

But the maiden would not abandon her pride, though her lover tried to persuade her.
Her veil guarded her like a proud fortress, so that no one could get near her.

492. Anger left, and passion stood proud;
her haughtiness vanished as love engulfed her.
That maiden who had been adamantine
melted in the heat of the rising sun.
The Prince took her hand and,
as he pressed on her fingers,
she trembled just as lightning appears
to quiver against the lowering clouds.
When his hands began to squeeze her breasts,
the maiden's hesitant breath began to quicken.
Their love was new, their bodies filled with youth.
They passed the night sunk in passion.
For Tārācand every single instant of that night passed in the bliss of love,
and Pemā, restless with desire, was crying out again and again for her hero.

493. They spent the night on the bed of joy.
Come the dawn, handmaidens brought in
water for washing. The Prince arose
and went out to the gateway
while Madhumālatī came in to visit Pemā.
'Tell me the truth, dear friend,' she said,
'how was your union with your lover?'
Pemā replied, 'When I asked you about this,
you did not tell me anything at all.
What went on between us during the night
I too can find no words to express.
When an adoring husband makes love to you, and two souls are in communion,
what happens then, dear friend, my tongue cannot describe out of shyness!'

[illegible] Princesses were very familiar,
[illegible]hed and joked together easily.

These two remained inseparably together,
their youthful bodies awake to desire.
Living in royal pleasure and budding with youth,
not for a moment were these sweethearts apart.
Likewise, the two Princes were as familiar
as if they had been bosom friends since childhood.
Words cannot describe their mutual love,
like that between the lovely lily and the moon.*
Madhumālatī and Pemā, and the two Princes who were close as brothers,
spent the rainy season in delight, while water and clouds engulfed the world.

495. They spent the rainy season in pleasure and delight,
until the star Canopus* began to shine
in the autumn nights of the month of Kuṃvār.
The heavens became radiant and clear.
The sun shone with a thousand rays
and the moon waxed full in all sixteen parts.
The clouds which covered the heavens lifted.
The ponds which were overflowing with water
could now be easily fathomed.
These two Princes sat down together
to discuss that the water had lessened
and the earth had become bright again.
Reflecting on this they went to the King,
and Citrasena called them into the palace.
Both the Princes folded their hands, and stood there entreating the King:
'If you will grant your permission, we will return to our own countries.'

*The Rite of Departure**

496. 'We would be happy to get your permission,
to seek an auspicious time and to set off.
If you grant it, we shall perform
the ceremony of the brides' departure

and set out for the lands of our birth.
Let us make all the preparations for the rite,
and then take Madhumālatī away with us.
We shall depart swiftly and not delay,
and perhaps we'll find our parents still alive.
Now is the time when we should serve them,
for the moon of their lives is positioned
in the twenty-seventh, the last station.
As the lamp dies down at dawn and the sun shines pale in the evening,
so are their lives nearing their end, maybe in months, maybe fortnights or days.'

497. Hearing of the rite of departure,
King Citrasena became silent.
Lowering his head, he gazed at the ground.
He was stunned, as if thunderstruck.
His eyes stared downward without blinking,
and his soul took flight from his body.
Awareness only returned after a long time.
They beseeched him, 'Go to King Vikram Rāi,
entreat him to allow the ceremony.
If King Vikram gives his permission,
we will perform the rite of departure
and leave for home with all our possessions.'
King Citrasena's heart was heavy with worry, but he thought to himself,
'Though a daughter may stay in her mother's house forever, in the end she is someone else's.'

498. With gentle words he sent the Princes back,
then went himself to Vikram Rāi.
He explained to the King that the Princes
had requested the rite of departure.
Hearing this King Vikram became silent
then said to King Citrasena,
'The very day God sends you a daughter,
she becomes the property of another.
It is no use keeping them here.

Go and prepare for the ceremony.'
  Dismayed at heart and amazed at the turn of events,
    Citrasena returned.
  He reported to the Princes all the things that Vikram
    Rāi had said.

499. Someone who had been listening outside
went and told Madhurā everything.
She was astonished to hear the news
and said: 'O God, what has happened?
I almost died crying when the demon took Pemā—
where has this thunderbolt fallen from now?
Now her departure will weigh heavy on me.
It would be better if she had never married,
but remained still an unwed virgin.'
Madhurā's eyes filled with tears,
and she burst into tears, saying,
'Parting is more painful than death!
  The first time the demon took her, the Creator brought
    her back and reunited us.
  Once she leaves now, we shall never meet again while I
    am alive on this earth.'

500. Hearing the bad news of the Princesses' departure,
both the royal palaces were deeply saddened.
The moment that Rūpamañjarī heard,
she swooned and fell unconscious on the ground.
King Vikram sat by her to console her.
He said, 'Can a girl remain forever
living in her mother's house?
It is only in her in-laws' house
that a girl has to spend her life.
There is no use for her in her mother's home.'
With tears in her eyes and a heavy heart,
the Queen then went to Madhumālatī.
  She explained things to Madhumālatī and told her what
    was to happen.
  'O Princess, you are going to that country from which
    nobody returns.'

Some Motherly Advice

501. Rūpamañjarī then sent for Pemā
and seated her with Madhumālatī.
With tears in her eyes, Madhurā
joined the Princesses and the Queen.
They began to explain things to the girls,
'Daughters, you are leaving your families
and going now to a foreign land.
Your husbands will carry you off to a place
from which no person ever returns.
Your lords will take you to an alien country
where you cannot even receive a message.
    Separated from you, however will we keep our souls in our bodies?
    Now, in just a few days' time, your lovers will take you away forever.'

502. 'You must serve your lords wholeheartedly.*
Do not let your minds wander from their service.
The male sex is extremely tyrannical.
You must divine their wishes day and night.
Serve them in the daytime as best you understand
and massage their feet all night long.
When your husband takes your arm
and bids you lie down with him,
lie with him on the bed and enjoy yourself.
Do not be too proud with your husband,
but use pride in the game of love.
    The wife who is very arrogant and sulks too much with her husband
    will force him, whether he will or no, to take another to wife.

503. 'If you see that your lord is very angry,
go and serve him, by force if necessary.
W[illegible] ur husband round through service.
[illegible]ng your lord like this
[illegible] be granted great happiness.

In the two worlds, both now and hereafter,
only she is the truly blessed wife
who has delighted her lord through service.
If you do not capture your husband's heart,
his mind and face will turn away from you.
Your lord's service will bring you happiness
in this life, and salvation in the next.
Even at the cost of your own life, you should serve your lord faithfully.
She whose life is at the service of her lord will be the Queen of both the worlds.

504. 'Protect the honour of your family.
Serve your husband above everything else.
Do not answer back to his mother,
and wash her feet yourself twice a day.
Suffer her insults with a smile,
and do not retort sharply to them.
Be obedient to her every word.
Never raise your voice to her in response.
Be friendly to your husband's other wives,
and live with them as if you were sisters.
Never raise your voice when you speak, and keep your anger under control.
Always maintain your honour so that no slight falls on your family's good name.'

The Handmaidens

505. When her friends heard Madhumālatī was leaving
the fire of affection was kindled in their hearts.
They ran to her just as they were
and took her weeping into their arms.
All her handmaidens were in tears
as they embraced her, recalling the times
they had played together happily.
'All the joy we had in childhood',
they cried, 'has returned to us now as grief.

How can we live with this sorrow,
after the sweet happiness we enjoyed together?
With you we enjoyed all the colourful pleasures of childhood together,
how are we to survive now you are leaving with your darling lover?

506. 'Had we known of this pain of separation,
would we have loved you in our childhood?
Now you are setting out for a foreign land,
how are we to keep our lives in our bodies?
If we had never known you, this great sorrow
would never have fallen on us.
Now your lord will take you off to a place
from where we shall not even hear about you.
As we remember again all our memories
of how we played together as children,
this pain of separation grows difficult,
no, even impossible to bear.
You are leaving for a foreign land, though we have to continue to survive here.
Our sinful souls put love to shame, since they cannot leave our bodies!

507. 'If youth were not blossoming in all our limbs,
our childhood friendship could continue forever.
It would have been better if the Creator
had kept us always as children,
but he forced this youthfulness upon us.
If youth had remained hidden in our bodies,
we would not be parted for the rest of our lives.
Dear friend, you leave as a married woman—
come tomorrow we also have to face that day.
Being young is good only if one finds a lover.
Otherwise youth and life are pointless.
If God would offer us childhood back again in return for being young,
a girl would exchange her youth a hundred times to have her childhood back.'

508. 'Dear friends, embrace me,' said Madhumālatī,
'the fire of love for you burns in my heart.
Tomorrow my love will take me by the arm.
My lord will deliver me to his own land.
I shall leave my family, my people
and go now to another's country.
Then, if the Creator makes it happen,
we shall meet again some day.
Put your arms around my neck and hug me.
Who knows if we will meet in this life again?'
Faced with parting from Madhumālatī,
her friends cried out aloud and wept.
Many of them fell at her feet crying piteously, others embraced her close.
Some lay on the ground in tears, burning with affection and love.

The Long Goodbye

509. When dawn came and the sun grew bright,
a disturbance was heard in the royal quarters.
Everyone raised their hands and asked
what the tumult was in the palace.
Those who knew explained to the others
that Madhumālatī was setting off
for her father-in-law's house.
Hearing there was upheaval in the palace,
everyone went there and crowded in.
Whether they were family or not,
they all came to the royal palace
when they heard the dreadful news.
Since Madhumālatī was leaving home, the city of Mahāras was in an uproar.
The Princess wept as she bade farewell to all the members of her family.

510. Madhumālatī said goodbye to her family
and retainers. She returned again and again

to take her leave of the doors to the main gates.
She bade farewell to her couch, bed and covers.
Clinging to the palace she said farewell.
She said goodbye to all her silken clothes
and her wardrobe. With tears in her eyes
she bade farewell to the gates and ramparts.
Falling down in the picture-pavilion,
she said goodbye to where she used to sleep.
Her spirits were low, her voice tired with speaking,
but she went and hugged her swing
and took her leave of it forever.
    Having said her farewells to her home, she said goodbye to her family.
    Then, as was customary, she took her leave of all the servants and retainers.

511. Madhumālatī was leaving her home,
her dear family and relatives forever.
She was leaving her baskets full of dolls
and all her constant companions.
She was leaving all her childhood friends,
with whom she had always played.
She had given up all illusory attachments,*
but still she hated to leave her home.
When she reflected on the truth in her heart,
then she was able to get up and leave her home.
    She was abandoning all her family, all her relatives and servants, everybody,
    as Vibhīṣaṇa left Laṅkā, fair city of illusion, untroubled by what might happen.*

512. The Queens beseeched the two Princes,
'When you go you take away our souls, our lives.
The fire of love in our wombs entreats you—
these two are your true soul-mates.
They have no other well-wishers but you,
so love them throughout your lives.
Mothers and fathers do not control destiny.
One must endure what fate has written

in the lines on one's forehead at birth.
Parents can only do so much:
bring up their sons and daughters
and arrange for their marriages.
After that, one suffers what God decrees for one's life, based on previous actions.
One must endure one's own good or evil, and answer for one's past behaviour.'

513. Madhumālatī ran to touch her mother's feet,
and the Queen raised her up and embraced her.
Love for the girl born from her womb flared up.
She could not endure this parting,
but beat her breast and wept copiously.
Madhumālatī, too, embraced her mother;
so tightly out of her love for her
that the Queen could not have escaped.
She would not let her mother go,
but hugged her tight again and again.
Realizing the extent of her daughter's love,
the Queen blessed her, saying,
'May you always be happily married
and may you be the Queen of the royal house!
As long as the Gaṅgā flows on the earth, and sun, moon and stars shine in the sky,
So long may the Creator keep your married happiness and your kingdom intact!'

514. Then the Princess touched her father's feet
and he lovingly embraced her.
Streams of tears flowed from his eyes,
and she asked, 'Why, O God?
Why did you send daughters into the world?
If no daughters were ever born,
no one would have to suffer such pain.'
The King replied, 'Do not despair,
for God has arranged a dwelling place
for my daughter in another land.
My people and retainers will always visit

and bring me news of how you are.'
    In no way could the royal Princess stop embracing her father closely.
    The more that people prised them apart, the closer they came together.

515. Seeing her saying goodbye to her family,
all the people of the town lamented.
Each of the city's thirty-six castes wept,
the young and the old cried for her
and the married women were all in tears.
It was as if she had taken out the city's heart
and made the city and kingdom lifeless.
While Madhumālatī was bidding farewell
to her own family, Pemā likewise
was saying goodbye to everyone.
Her entire family stood weeping,
but who could stop her husband
from taking her away forever?
    Her family, relatives, and retainers wept helplessly, all to no avail.
    For who can prevent a husband from taking his beloved wife with him?

516. Then the royal Princess, a married woman,
ran weeping to touch Madhurā's feet.
'Mother,' she said, 'hug me, say goodbye to me,
for today I become a foreigner
and belong to someone else.
Rūpamañjarī only gave me birth,
it is you who really brought me up.
I am leaving father, brother, home, and family,
today I depart for a foreign country.'
Madhurā wept, wrenched with grief,
as if she would wash away her sorrow with tears.
    The two Princesses bade farewell to their families and mounted their palanquins.
    They left behind all their loved ones, whom they were never to see again.

517. Meanwhile the two Princes went over
to where the Kings were standing
and fell down at their feet.
They embraced the two Princes and said,
'We are left here with only our sorrows.
We have entrusted to you the souls
which are the support of our lives.
We have few requests to make,
but you do know of the prestige of our lines.
We bow our heads at your feet.
Do now as you deem fit.
We have taken out the very souls of our families and sent them off with you.
Please protect our honour carefully, and do as destiny demands.'

518. When they heard this, the Princes
took hold of their ears humbly* and said:
'Fathers, how can you think like this?
Our mothers and fathers gave us birth,
but you brought us up as parents.
In your families the Queens are nurtured
whose pious offerings of water
bring salvation to our ancestors.
These shining moons add lustre to our clans.
They are the glittering jewels,
we the jewellers who accept them.
Just as gold leaves a shining line
when tested for purity on a touchstone,
they are the true adornment
on the brows of our respective houses.
So do not let your hearts be concerned on their account, your royal majesties;
just grant us your permission, lords, that we may set out for our native lands.'

The Couples Separate

519. The two maidens began their journey
accompanied by the two Princes.
All the dowry they had been given
was loaded up and sent off with them.
They travelled four stations together,
and then they were at their separate paths.
Tārācand, with tears in his eyes,
came to Manohar and Madhumālatī and said,
'Brother, arise and bid me farewell.
Let me embrace you and say goodbye.
    Everyone in the world knows that the pain of parting is
        unbearable.
    May no one have to endure separation's sorrow, the
        greatest suffering of all.'

520. When he heard this, Prince Manohar
ran and touched Tārācand's feet.
They hugged each other with love,
and as they did so they cried.
'On the day God brought us together,
we did not know this grief would befall us.'
The two Princes embraced and wept,
asking why fate was separating them.
Such love abounded in their hearts
that they could not bear to let each other go.
    They wept and wept, embracing each other, and their
        tears became a torrent,
    for they knew with certainty they'd never meet again
        while they lived in this world.

521. The two Princes, embracing and weeping,
could not bear to part out of love.
Madhumālatī went and pulled them apart,
separating the still weeping Princes.
'You are masters of men, of vassals,
how can you weep like women?
Men who are truly brave and resolute,
never grieve over such a small matter.

We are helpless women, with far less intelligence—
we go crazy over the slightest thing.'
Madhumālatī separated them gently, with compassion for their great grief.
Still their tears flowed like torrents, as they recalled the love they had known.

522. 'Look at us. We are helpless women,
steeling ourselves to bear this separation.
Never in our lives had we known suffering,
but when it fell on our heads suddenly
we learnt full well how to suffer.
We even used to cry, on lighting a fire,
when smoke welled up from the flames.
Our mothers and fathers gave us birth,
but still we have to endure
whatever destiny has written for us.
You are men, crying like this,
then how can we weak women be brave?
You are lords of the earth, and your hearts must be resolute and strong.
Just see how we helpless women have coped with the infinite pain of separation!'

523. Madhumālatī's eyes filled with tears.
She fell at Prince Tārācand's feet.
The Prince raised her up affectionately,
and, mindful of their parting, embraced her.
Madhumālatī said through her tears,
'You restored me to life in this birth.
My parents gave me birth and rejected me;
but you, my brother, protected me.
I had given up all hope of meeting Manohar,
but you brought us together again,
and delivered me safe to my home.
For my sake you abandoned your kingdom—now where can I find the water
to extinguish the fire of love for you that burns in my heart at this parting?'

524. 'How can I drag out my long life,
when you are slaying my soul
by leaving for your own city?
The moment I was given wings,
I should have flown away somewhere
and died unhappily in my madness.
I wouldn't have returned to my parents' home,
but lost my life somewhere or other.
It was you, my brave brother,
who brought me to my home again
and changed me from a bird to a human.
My soul remained in my body
because I used to see you.
Today the world seems a wasteland to me.
I have abandoned all my family, my brother, and now I travel to a foreign land.
You and I must bid farewell, without hope of ever meeting again.

525. 'It was my mother who transformed me
into a bird and banished me.
At that point I saw you, and my former love
was rekindled in my soul.
Then, with hope awake again,
I flew to the earth and sat down
tangling myself by force in your snare.
You showed great courage on my behalf,
gave me back my kingdom and former beauty,
and bestowed on me my blessed married state.
My heart had given up all hope,
but through your courage, my brother,
I have now achieved success.'
Crying piteously, Madhumālatī turned to fall at the Prince's feet.
Tārācand embraced her and said goodbye to her as a brother does a sister.

526. Pemā's heart was burning with love.
She wept as she hugged Manohar.

'Brother,' she said, 'you should know
how great is my pain at parting from you.
How can I pass my life without you?
From the day Rūpamañjarī banished you,
I spent the whole time weeping.
Still, I had hoped we would meet again,
and we were indeed reunited
while breath remained in my body.
Now at this parting I have no such hope.
We shall not meet again in this life.
  I did not know grief when I parted from my family,
    since I saw you were by me.
  But now, my dear brother, you are parting from me, and
    I feel total despair.

527. 'Why did the Creator make today the day
on which I have to hear of your leaving?
The day when friends and dear ones part
is a day not to be lived in this life.
I was separated from family and retainers,
but I survived, dear brother,
because I had you in my heart.
Now you are going and leaving me,
I don't see how, even for a moment,
life can remain in my body.
Seeing you near by strengthened my soul.
Today, giving you up fills me with despair.
  Everyone in the world knows well that being separated
    is to die every instant.
  O God, don't give anyone separation's agony while they
    are living on this earth!

528. 'The flesh-eating demon abducted me.
He took me to a wood, dark and enigmatic,
where even the day was black as night.
For my sake you took on this great burden
and slaughtered that mighty demon.
You killed the night-crawling demon
and brought me to be with my family

from whom I had been severed.
Brother, you are going off and leaving me.
For me, just to live will be a heavy burden.
With you and me parted, dear brother,
whom shall I look to for consolation?'
    Saying this she left the Prince, and moved on to embrace Madhumālatī close.
    Love's fire was burning in her heart as she said goodbye to her lifelong friend.

529. Crying, the two Princesses hugged each other.
As they parted, their former love reawakened.
They said, 'Today we have finished with meeting,
and now our boats will sail alone in the ocean.
Today destiny has placed us apart.
We leave our families, and now belong to another.
God, who kept us together as children,
throws us in different directions in our youth.
No sooner than we were united,
one is now going east, the other west.
    Dear friend, those days of play, of childhood love and happiness have gone.
    We part today, and I can't see how we shall ever meet again as long as we live.

530. 'We used to meet one day a month.
From today we cannot even hope for that.
Our lives were attached, each with the other,
and we used to long to be together.
Sometimes we played on the palace roof,
and sometimes in the picture-pavilion.
How hard is the human soul that it can bear
this harsh separation between you and me?'
The Princes came and drew them apart,
and seated them weeping in their palanquins.
    Then Madhumālatī departed for Kanaigiri and Pemā set off for Pavaneri.
    With their new lords they left their parental homes, and went to their parents-in-law.

The Arrival

531. Tārācand looked towards Pavaneri.
Manohar turned his caravan to Kanaigiri.
He was two years on the path
before his journey neared its end
and he approached the fortress of Kanaigiri.
Its palaces were all adorned with gold leaf
and shone and sparkled most beautifully.
The castle had fifty-two thousand battlements,
each studded and inset with jewels.
When the rays of the sun fell on them,
they glittered and shone even more brightly.
The fort wall enclosed twenty four miles, an expanse which was fully populated.
The torches burning bright on the palaces could be seen ten *yojana*s* away.

532. Meanwhile the King's Chief Provisioner,
a treasure-house of virtues called Tivārī,
had taken leave of King Sūrajbhānu.
He was making a trip to the Gaṅgā
to bathe on the occasion of a festival.
He was going down the very road
on which the Prince was arriving.
As soon as they saw one another,
each recognized the other instantly.
They both dismounted and embraced.
The Prince enquired how his parents were,
and asked after the welfare of the whole family.
Hearing that his mother and father were well, his heart exulted with happiness.
He was so happy to hear the good news that no other desire remained in his heart.

533. The Chief said to the Prince:
'Since you left for foreign lands,
the King has ceased to rule the kingdom.
He has had nothing to do with royal affairs,

and those of us in authority have run everything.
The King now dresses in black clothes,
and all his subjects and retainers remain sad.
The whole city has been dejected,
and nobody listens to music any more!
From the day you left the kingdom,
no musical instruments have been played.
From the very day, O royal Prince, you departed for foreign lands,
the King, Sūrajbhānu, has completely forgotten he rules this realm.'

534. The Chief stayed there that night.
In the morning he addressed the Prince,
'With your leave, I shall go to the King
and tell him that you are safe and well.'
The Chief took his leave and went at once,
speedily covering seven *yojana*s
in just one watch of the day.
He went in to the King and announced
that the Prince was well and on his way.
The King and Queen heard this news,
and revived like fish in agony in the air
who had just returned to water.
He also told them that the Prince had married and brought home with him
Madhumālatī, the lovely daughter of the Queen of Mahāras and King Vikram.

535. Hearing the news of the Prince's arrival,
there was joy and celebration
in each and every house of the city.
Musical instruments were brought
and placed at the palace doors.
Kettle-drums were beaten everywhere.
When the drums rang out loudly,
they sounded like clouds thundering in the sky.
Queen Kamalā could not sleep,
but spent the night in games and laughter.

Sūrajbhānu, in anticipation of seeing his son,
was like a parched and thirsty man
looking forward to a drink of water.
    The best singers with the sweetest voices were singing
        at the palace doors.
    Dancers, accomplished actors, and mimics gave fine
        poetic performances.

536. The royal elephants were adorned
and brought to the palace doors,
with seats on their backs studded with gold.
Horses worth a fortune were made ready,
looking as if they were set to run
with the speed of the wind.
All was decorated by the town's people,
each according to his own responsibility.
All the palaces were freshly whitewashed.
Sandalwood incense was burned in each one.
Inside and outside, on gates and ramparts,
silken hangings made everything colourful.
    All Manohar's palaces were inlaid with gold, and
        studded with shining gems.
    Each was polished and cleaned to be fit for the royal
        Prince to live in.

537. As morning broke, the Prince came home,
bearing with him all the presents
he had been given by his father-in-law.
With him was Madhumālatī in her palanquin,
with priceless jewels hanging down all around.
The Prince ran and fell at his father's feet,
who was like a blind man recovering his sight.
Then Manohar went to touch his mother's feet,
and the Queen embraced her darling son.
She kept the Prince in her embrace,
like a fish in torment finding water again.
    When Kamalā hugged Prince Manohar and held him
        close to her chest,

spontaneously, a stream of milk gushed out from the
Queen's breasts.

538. In this world no one can become immortal,
but death cannot destroy the one
who has died himself before his death.*
Whoever suffers the burning fire of love,
escapes from death in his life on earth.
He who has saved himself
by taking refuge in love,
will never die no matter who kills him.
Once he has found his life by dying,
death will never come near him again.
Death has become the fruit of life,
through it, one's body becomes immortal.*
O soul, if you are afraid of death, then follow the path
of taking refuge in love.
Now and hereafter, fear of death disappears, for love is
the sanctuary of the world.

539. The elixir of immortality will fill love's sanctuary, wherever
it is found.*
As long as poetry is cultivated on earth, so long will our
lovers' names resound.

APPENDIX

The Symmetry of *Madhumālatī*

It is hoped that readers will have enjoyed the symmetry of the plot of *Madhumālatī*, with the two couples interacting and coming together in a beautifully balanced conclusion, as well as the circularity of the story which returns to its starting point though at a higher level. Unless, however, they were unusually perceptive, they may not have noticed that the narration of the story, the manner of its unfolding, is also in my reading symmetrical.[1] What suggestive clues has Manjhan left that might justify this claim of narrative symmetry? Consider the following: the point referred to as the turning point of the story, when Manohar heard about the life-giving tree and became certain that God would give him victory over the demon, comes exactly halfway through the story; the shipwreck and the introduction of Pemā come exactly a third of the way through the narrative and the introduction of Tārācand and his capture of the bird Madhumālatī come exactly two-thirds of the way through; the episode with the fairies occupies precisely the second eighth of the story and ends exactly a quarter of the way through the narration; Manohar and Madhumālatī's ultimate union occurs at exactly five-sixths of the way through the story and the leave-takings begin at eleven-twelfths of the way through. In addition, the end of the first meeting of the couple at verse 135 is exactly 180 verses, a third of the text, from their second meeting at 315. The full union at verse 450 is exactly 270 verses (half of the text) from Manohar's shipwreck and total aloneness in verse 180. Finally, Pemā's story to Manohar in the forest is exactly 270 verses away from the story of Tārācand's falling in love and marrying her and spread over exactly the same number of verses. Such precision and proportionality cannot have been accidental and must have been deliberate on Manjhan's part. What is the explanation?

1 The symmetry has been discussed in two studies: S. C. R. Weightman, 'Symmetry and Symbolism in Shaikh Manjhan's *Madhumālatī*, in C. Shackle and R. Snell (eds.) *The Indian Narrative: Patterns and Perspectives* (Wiesbaden: Harrassowitz, 1992), 195–226, and Weightman, 'Symbolism and Symmetry: Shaikh Manjhan's *Madhumālatī* revisited', in L. Lewisohn and D. Morgan (eds.), *The Heritage of Sufism,* iii: *Late Classical Persianate Sufism (1501–1750)* (Oxford: One World Publications, forthcoming).

The story is circular and a brief scrutiny of other Shaṭṭārī works reveals that the circle was their favourite and most persistent symbol, used in expressing the cosmology of the Order as well as in many other applications. When the poem is plotted round a circle, it becomes clear what is going on. The poem in the critical edition, which has good manuscript support, has 539 verses. Around a circle; verse 1, in praise of God and beginning with the word Love, become verse 540, like a serpent swallowing the tip of its tail. Taking 540 to be the basis of the proportionality, the clues given by Manjhan and identified above can be entered on the circle, as in Fig. I. The turning point of the battle with the demon comes precisely at the bottom of the circle. Nine separate points around the circle are given by these clues, which enables one to deduce that the complete design has twelve points with an interval of 45 verses between each point as shown in Fig. II, which reveals the full symmetry in all its complexity.

What is the purpose of this design? At the very least, it would have provided Manjhan with a model on which to plan his writing which would produce a well-proportioned and symmetrical story and narrative. Closer examination, however, reveals that it is far more than just

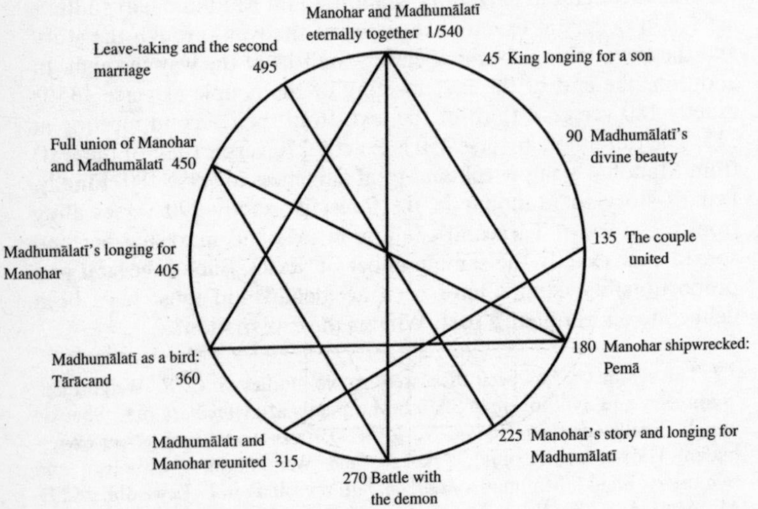

Fig. I. Manjhan's Clues

an author's preliminary sketch. It will be shown how it embodies the Shaṯṯārī Order's cosmology and that the symmetry's various systems reinforce and further elaborate the symbolism, thus making *Madhumālatī* even deeper and richer than is at first realized, and that much more of a masterpiece in consequence. First, however, it will be helpful to review the twelve points on the circle that the symmetry emphasizes. The first, at the top of the circle, is verse 1/540 discussed above which is both the end and the beginning of the story and in which Manohar and Madhumālatī are eternally together. The second is verse 45. The Prologue ends at verse 43 and the story begins at 44, which introduces the King and his longing for a son. Verse 45 elaborates on the reasons why having a son is desirable. In that sense it is the true beginning of the story of *Madhumālatī* and, symbolically, perhaps it is suggestive of the causes for Creation itself. The third is verse 90, which is part of the description of Madhumālatī and so highlights Divine Beauty. The fourth is verse 135, which marks the end of the lovers' first meeting and partial union. The fifth is verse 180, which marks the beginning of the next phase of Manohar's story after the shipwreck when he is totally alone immediately prior to meeting

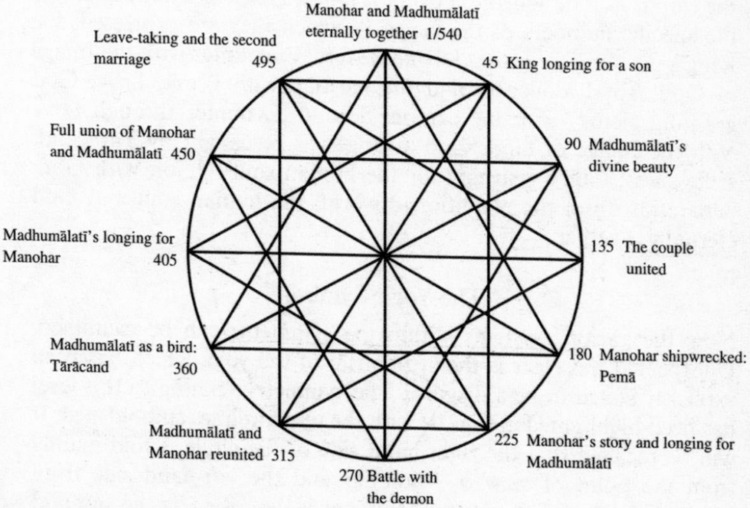

Fig. II. The Full Symmetry

Pemā. The sixth is verse 225, which is the beginning of Manohar's story of meeting Madhumālatī and their separation and his suffering. The seventh is verse 270, the halfway point both of the story and of the battle with the demon. The eighth is verse 315, at the start of Manohar's second encounter with Madhumālatī. The ninth is verse 360, which is at the point where Madhumālatī allows herself to be caught by Tārācand. The tenth is verse 405, which is part of Madhumālatī's *bārahmāsā*, her account of the suffering she had felt in separation from Manohar throughout the twelve months of the year. The eleventh is verse 450, in the middle of the description of their full married union. The twelfth is verse 495, in which the four decide to leave and the final leave-takings begin.

Although the emphasis given by the symmetry appears to be specific to these twelve verses, in fact it is better to consider the emphasis to be rather to the point in the narration, to what is going on over say three or several verses rather than to a single verse. Although numbers and the numerical value of letters formed an important part of Shaṭṭārī practice, it is not thought here that the symmetry was numerological. As far as can be divined what seems to matter to Manjhan is the overall shape and design and the precise proportionality rather than that any particular number should be exemplified. This suggestion would not effect the symmetry but would mean that the emphasis is designed to be on the following themes rather than on the specific numbers of the verses in which they are expressed: the King's yearning for a son; Divine Beauty; Encounter with the Image of God; Total aloneness and the meeting with Pemā, Love; God granting victory over the demon; Second encounter through Love with the Image of God; God arranges to be caught by Tārācand, selflessness; God's yearning for the human soul; Union with God: Separation from the conditioned world; the human soul and God eternally together.

The Yogic Symbol

Now the various systems within the symmetry can be examined. Unexpected but clear is the symbolism of the yogi, which has been explicitly stated to be a disguise. The symmetry relating to this level has been highlighted in Fig. III with the relevant lines emboldened. It will be recalled that the right-hand side of the circle is told mainly from the point of view of Manohar and the left-hand side from Madhumālatī's point of view. Manohar is described as the sun and Madhumālatī as the moon, which would be interpreted in yogic terms

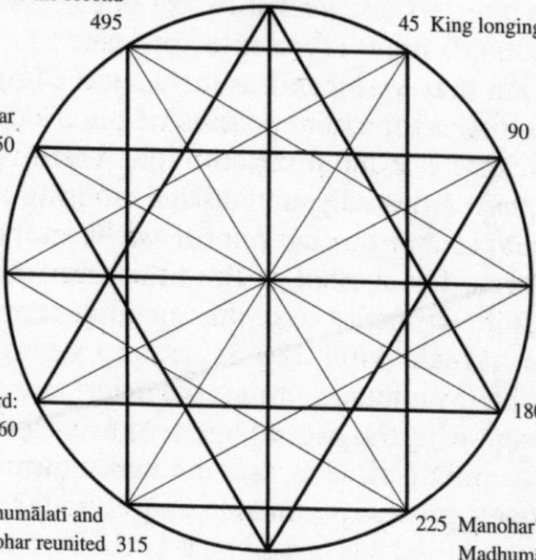

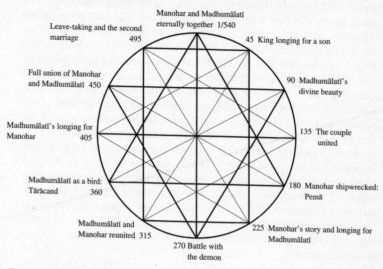

Fig. III. The Yogic Symbol

as the *iḍā* and *piñgalā nāḍī*s, the two main psychic veins which run up either side of the spine and which connect at both the top and the bottom with the central psychic channel, the *suṣumnā*, which runs up from the base of the spine to the top of the head. It is possible to locate the *iḍā nāḍī* on the right side as line 45–225, and the *piñgalā nāḍī* on the left as line 495–315. In this way the line 270–540 becomes the *suṣumnā nāḍī* and it is quite obvious what is implied. The battle to release Pemā from the demon is none other than the battle every Tantric yogi undertakes to set free the force of *kuṇḍalinī* so that the *śakti* or energy can travel up the *suṣumnā* bringing to life the various *cakras* it passes through until it reaches the *sahasrāra cakra* at the very top where it brings about the highest state of *sahaja* and the Union of Śiva and Śakti. It is also possible to read from the diagram the different *cakras:* the *mūladhārā cakra*, where the *kuṇḍalinī* is detained, is at the base of *suṣumnā* represented by verse 270; the *svādhiṣṭhāna cakra*, which is essentially the sex centre, is the intersection of the *suṣumnā* by the line 315–225; the *maṇipūra cakra*, the navel, is represented as the intersection of *suṣumnā* by line 360–180; the *anāhata cakra*, the heart *cakra*, is the intersection of *suṣumnā* by the line 405–135, which is significantly exactly at the centre of the entire diagram; the *viśuddha* or throat *cakra* is the intersection of *suṣumnā* by the line 450–90; the *ājñā cakra*, situated between the eyebrows, is the intersection effected by the line 495–45 and the topmost *cakra*, the *sahasrāra*, is represented by verse 540/1. Read in this way, it can be seen that Manjhan has included a complete model of the Tantra yogic psycho-spiritual process within his design and integrated it well with his symbolism. But the yogic symbolism is a disguise, as has been repeatedly emphasized, and what is particularly significant is that the heart *cakra* appears in the very centre of the design. In Tantrism, the symbol of the heart, the *anāhata cakra*, is two interpenetrating triangles and this again is represented in the diagram by the triangle 540/l–180–360 interpenetrated by the triangle 450–90–270. Manjhan situates the heart *cakra* at the very centre of his design with the two interpenetrating triangles, the symbol of the heart, around it. It is as if he was indicating that in his eyes the whole yogic process is valuable only in so far as it sets Pemā free to awaken the heart to Love, which is the real means of mankind's salvation.

The *Coincidentia Oppositorum* of Love

In Fig. IV the six lines that pass through the centre of the diagram are emboldened so that the twelve points on the circle are seen as the end of twelve spokes radiating out from the centre of the circle. At 540/1 the lovers are together; at 45, apart; at 90, together; at 135, together; at 180, apart; at 225, apart; at 270 apart; at 315 together; at 360, apart; at 405 apart; at 450, together; at 495, together. For each of the six lines, the lovers are together at one end and apart at the other. While this might be accidental, since so little is accidental in this work it is worth considering what it might mean if it were deliberate. The overall symbolic value of the circle for the Shaṭṭārī Order was that there was Unity at the centre represented by the point and the circumference of the circle represented all the different manifestations of the phenomenal world. In placing the lovers apart at one end of the *radii* and together at the other end, it is as if Manjhan were saying that togetherness and separateness are only phenomenally opposites. In the Unity of Love in the centre these two states do not exist, there is only Love. Love is the true *coincidentia oppositorium*, a proposition endorsed by many other of the great Sufi writers.

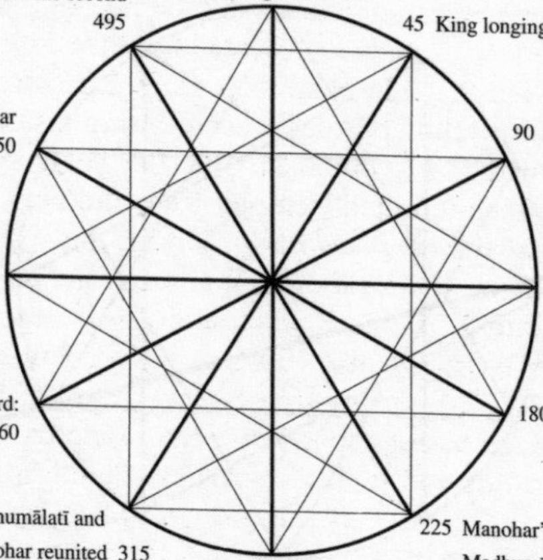

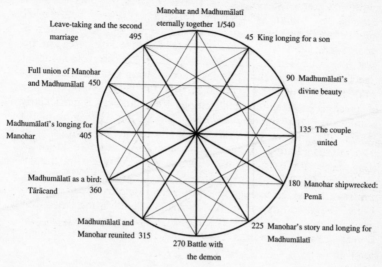

Fig. IV. The *Coincidentia Oppositorum* of Love

Inner and Outer Quaternities

At its most obvious the diagram shows the story falling into four quarters produced by the lines 270–540 and 135–405. While not particularly sophisticated, this fourfold division of the story, allowing for a small degree of overlap, does correspond to the four stages of the 'universal' spiritual path given by Underhill and discussed in the Introduction. The first quarter is concerned with Awakening, the second quarter with Purification and Struggle, the third quarter with Illumination and the Dark Night of the Soul, and the final quarter with Union. That is coincidental but, when put into Manjhan's terms, it becomes a valid categorization, although for Manjhan it would be more appropriate to speak of Initial Union, Descent, Ascent, and Re-Union along classic Neoplatonic Shaṭṭārī lines.

It is, however, in the utilization of the four triangles within the circle that the symmetry and intermeshing symbolism become highly sophisticated. This can be seen in Fig. V, where the four triangles are emboldened.

The first triangle, formed by verses 1/540–180–360, could be designated **The Triangle of Outer Narration**. It can be regarded both statically and dynamically. Statically, it represents the major characters in

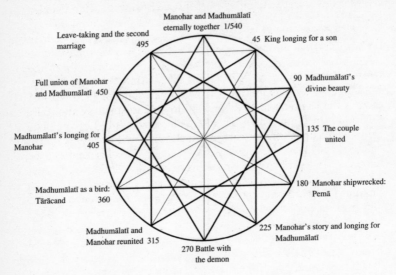

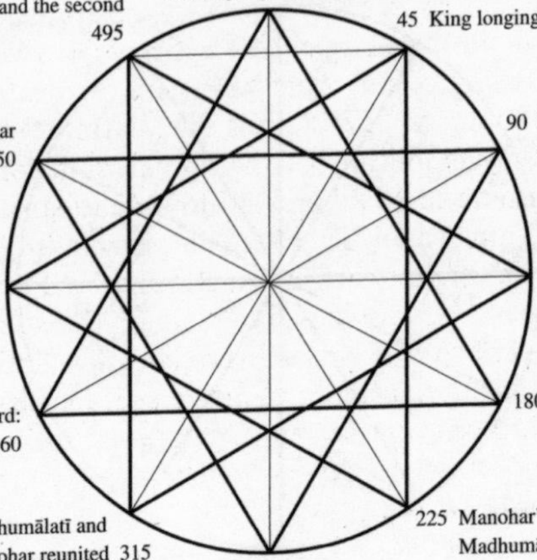

Fig. V. The Four Triangles

the story; Madhumālatī and Manohar at 1/540, Pemā at 180 and Tārācand at 360. Dynamically, it represents the three mutually dependent processes that make up the story. The first process is the story of Manohar and Madhumālatī, which begins at 1 and ends at 539. The second process is the story of Pemā, which truly begins at 180 as Manohar heads off into the forest and finds her in the hut. This process continues until almost the poem's end. The third process is the story of Tārācand, which begins at 360 and continues almost to the end. These three processes or stories, each beginning at their indicated places, interreact to produce the total dynamism of the work on the literal outer level.

The first triangle, that of outer narration, is interpenetrated by the triangle 90–270–450, which can be designated **The Triangle of Inner Narration** because it gives the inner, *bāṭin*, meaning to the outer, *zāhir*, story. The three points are Manohar's first contact with Divine Beauty (90), the descent and struggle with the demon to set Love free (270), and the full Union of Manohar and Madhumālatī (450). The inner narrative is that of the Shaṭṭārīs' inner path—putting oneself at the point of Divine Beauty, descending to the phenomenal world, struggle and ascent until full Union. It is specifically Shaṯṯārī but also shared by all spiritual paths that are informed by Neoplatonism.

The third triangle, 45–225–405, provides the motivations that drive the story and can thus be designated **The Triangle of Yearnings**. At 45 there is the yearning of the King for a son or symbolically of the Creator for creation. At 225 there is the yearning of Manohar for Madhumālatī or symbolically of the human soul for God. At 405 there is the yearning of Madhumālatī for Manohar or symbolically of God for the human soul. These are the yearnings of Love in all its forms which drive the story and much else besides. Finally, the fourth triangle, 135–315–495, provides the goals of the story and can be designated **The Triangle of Union and Unification**. 135 gives the first Union, partial, neither real nor unreal, but the first goal of the Shaṯṯārī *sālik*. 315 gives the second Union, that of Illumination, and 495 gives the final state of Unification before leaving the conditioned world altogether.

These four triangles form a tetrad along the lines of Aristotle's *aetiae*, which had long before become part of Islamic philosophy. The Triangle of Outer Narration, the literal story and its characters which provide the ground, the actual material in need of transformation, is Aristotle's material cause. The Triangle of Inner Narration provides the ideal pattern of the descent from God to the phenomenal world and the ascent back again to God which constitutes Aristotle's formal cause. The Triangle of Yearnings which provides the instrumentality of the tetrad is Aristotle's efficient cause and The Triangle of Union and Unification, which is the intentional term, the aim of humanity, Union, is Aristotle's final cause. All of this is implicit in the symmetry of Manjhan's masterpiece.

Manjhan's Shaṯṯārī Cosmology

Finally, there is Manjhan's cosmology, which will be shown to be foundational to his story-telling, his imagery, and his symbolism at every level. This was a cosmology which derived ultimately from the Great Shaikh Ibn al-ʿArabī but which reached Manjhan through a number of intermediaries and interpreters as the received Shaṯṯārī cosmology. In his work the *Jawāhir-i Khamsah* Shaikh Muḥammad Ghauṡ discusses six worlds or levels of manifestation of the Absolute. These are represented by Manjhan as a hierarchy of six levels into which the circle is divided as shown in Fig. VI, where the relevant lines are emboldened.

When Manjhan's narration and symbolism are examined in

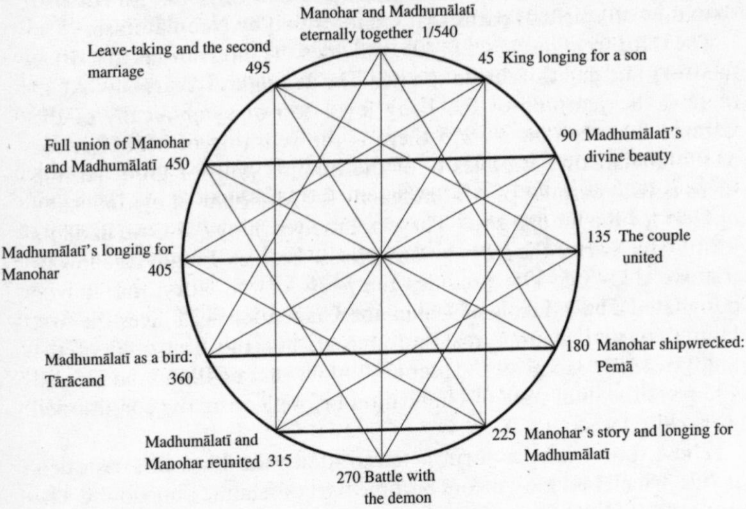

Fig. VI. Manjhan's Cosmology

relation to these six levels or worlds, it is clear that he made every attempt to respect the characteristics of each cosmological level as far as was possible given the constraints of telling his story. The first world, called the *Martaba al-Aḥadiyyat*, or the Level of Oneness, which is beyond all attribution and determination, is represented by everything in the circle above the line 495–45. The whole of the Prologue is contained here, that is, this unconditioned undetermined world of Absolute Oneness is prior to the beginning of everything. The King appears on both sides of the circle, which confirms the correctness of regarding him as an important symbolic figure, especially as it is the King whose yearning in this world leads to the birth of Manohar in the world below, and it is to him that Manohar returns with Madhumālatī. The story from 495 is taken up with leave-taking from the conditioned world of relationships. Even Pemā and Tārācand have separated from Manohar and Madhumālatī before the last leg of the journey home. In this world the Divine Absolute is non-determined (*lā taʿayyun*), beyond all attributes and absolutely One (*al-Aḥad*).

The second level, the *Martaba al-Waḥdat*, the Level of Unity, is the first degree of manifestation (*tajallī*) or determination (*taʿayyun*). It occupies that segment of the circle contained between line 495–45 and line 450–90. In the cosmology, this is the world in which the Absolute manifests in the form of light, unity, and the archetypal reality of Muḥammad; and the Divine Names and Attributes exist in the Divine Presence and are identical to it. In the narration, this level contains the greater part of the head-to-foot description in which Madhumālatī's body is unveiled in terms indicative of the Divine Names and Attributes. Here too Manohar, sometimes suggestive of Muḥammad and Adam, is born and brought up and educated particularly in names, as Adam was by God. On the left of the circle, the first full union of Manohar and Madhumālatī takes place, which is followed by the marriage and union of Pemā and Tārācand. Thereafter all four live together and their harmony and unity is constantly stressed. In this way, as with the first level, Manjhan respects the specific characteristics of this world in his narration.

The third level, the *Martaba al-Waḥdāniyya*—Comprehensiveness perhaps gives the flavour of its meaning—is the second determination or self-disclosure of the Divine Absolute. It is represented by the segment of the circle between the lines 450–90 and 405–135. On this plane, Divine Unity is manifested in the eternal Names, the *aʿyān al-ṣābita*, the fixed entities which are the prototypes for the multiple forms of creatures in existence. This is the plane where the forms are determined and distinguished one from another, although they never come into concrete existence except through their shadows on the more material planes of the divine descent. It is also the plane on which Love (*ʿishq*) comes into being. This plane is therefore one of plurality, identities, and interrelatedness. Manjhan reflects this in his narration by having the greater part of the discourse on the right hand of the circle devoted to the conversation between Manohar and Madhumālatī in which they tell one another their names and identify themselves fully. The left hand side contains most of the main characters of the story who converse and exchange letters, the final outcome of which is the arrangement and performance of the marriage ceremony, although Union itself occurs in the world above. The marriage is also the culmination of the oath of eternal fidelity which the couple swore to one another at their first meeting, which in turn is suggestive of, and symbolizes, the covenant made between God and humanity and the arising of Love between them. Although the greater part of Madhumālatī's *bārahmāsā* appears in this segment of the narration, in fact, it strictly belongs in the worlds below given it is a description of her suffering throughout the year spent there searching for Manohar.

The fourth level, the *Martaba al-Arwāḥ*, is the Level of Souls, which is the third level of determination. It is the plane of souls or spirits who can recognize one another and who acknowledge the *'ayān al-ṣābita*, the prototypes, as their masters. It is represented by the segment of the circle which is contained within the lines 405–135 and 360–180. This is the world in which the human soul and God are aware of their separation and suffer the pain of Love in consequence. In fact, it is the primary characteristic of this world that the human soul, becoming aware of its separation, should suffer *viraha*, the pain of Love, which Manjhan describes as the sole hope for mankind since it is the only way that the soul can become conscious of itself. Manjhan begins to experience this grief from the very beginning of this section of narration when he wakes up to find he has, as it were, fallen out of paradise. Reason and human intelligence in the form of doctors cannot cure him because they do not know Love. He ends the section totally alone, cast up on an unknown shore, with only the name of Madhumālatī and the Mercy of God. On the left-hand side of the circle, the narrative of this section begins with Madhumālatī allowing herself to be caught and to be put in a cage. The bird in the cage is one of the Sufis' most persistent symbols for the soul imprisoned in the body; Rumi uses it at one point to refer to the soul in the body and at the same time to refer to people locked in the iron cage of 'reputation'.[2] Madhumālatī's mother turned her into a bird in the first place to protect her family's reputation, so there are echoes here of Rumi's double usage. When her mother sees Madhumālatī in the cage she is overcome with remorse and weeps, immediately restoring her to her proper form. Tears of remorse, as Rumi constantly insists, are the soul's certain way of attracting the Mercy of God. But in this section it is Tārācand whose selflessness and selfless love is perhaps indicative of *'ubūdiyya*, servanthood, who shows the way for the soul to ascend to higher worlds. Finally, it is here, on this plane of souls, that Madhumālatī begins her *bārahmāsā* expressing poignantly the Love and yearning that God has for the human soul.

The fifth level, *Martaba al-Imṣāl*, the Level of Imaginal Forms, is the level of determination of the subtle and imaginal forms which are

[2] This occurs in the story of the Merchant and the Parrot, and the preceding few lines of the story of 'Umar and the Ambassador, in Book One of the *Maṣnavī* of Jalālu'ddīn Rūmī. See R. A. Nicholson, *The Mathnawī of Jalālu'ddīn Rūmī* (London: Luzac 1926), 85–102.

the shadows of the prototypes and have a type of subtle materiality. This plane of almost astral forms is represented by the segment of the narration between the lines 360–180 and 315–225. This is a world symbolized by picture-galleries, gardens reminiscent of Paradise, and young and beautiful unawakened maidens. It is in the picture-gallery that Manohar and Madhumālatī meet for the second time and where she tells him her beauty cannot be seen with ordinary eyes. It was when coming out of the picture-gallery that Pemā was captured by the demon. Pemā means Love, but here is the shadowy love called *ʿishq-i majāzī*, metaphorical love, in contrast to *ʿishq-i ḥaqīqī*, real love, which belongs to a higher world. Madhumālatī is transformed into a bird in this world, flying everywhere in search of Manohar, beautifully expressive of the insubstantiality of this imaginal plane.

Finally, there is the sixth level, *Martaba al-Ḥiss*, the Level of Sense Experience, also known as *ʿālam-i ajsām*, the world of bodies. This is the world in which Pemā, Love, is detained and incarnate. This is the world in which Manohar has to fight his demon and to which the Shaṭṭārī Sufi has to descend before beginning his ascent. In conclusion, this is significantly the world in which Manohar and Madhumālatī never meet.

Manjhan has clearly made his cosmology foundational to the symmetry of his narrative and his symbolism. There are other possible interpretations that could be mentioned with regard to the six levels just discussed, such as the six days of creation, but sufficient has been shown to demonstrate conclusively that for Manjhan the symmetry of his narration was as important to him as the symbolism it reinforces and deepens. It is hoped that this Appendix has added further to the understanding and appreciation of the poem. *Madhumālatī* was well known and highly regarded in Indian Sufi and literary circles and was translated into Persian several times as well as producing a particularly renowned version in Dakkhani Urdu, the *Gulshan-i ʿishq*, by the Sufi poet Nuṣratī. But in these later renderings it was the beauty of the story that was captured not the symmetry. In so doing a considerable portion of Manjhan's genius and achievement was lost. It is that which this Appendix has sought to restore.

SIMON WEIGHTMAN

EXPLANATORY NOTES

3 *two worlds in the one sound Oṃ*: the two worlds are this world and the next, and could refer here either to the Muslim *ʿālamain* or the Hindu *ihaloka* (lit.'this world', Skt.) and *paraloka* (lit. 'other world', Skt.). The term *ekoṃkāra*, the one sound, is a reference to the *Qur'ānic* account of creation, in which God said 'Be' and 'It was.' Here the poet translates God's word (*kun fayakun*) into the Hindavī word for the *nāda* or sound which sets the universe in motion.

three worlds: this is the Hindu *tribhuvana*, the three worlds of heaven (*svarga*), earth (*manuṣya-loka*), and hell (*naraka*).

four ages: the four ages (*yuga*, Skt.) are the four Hindu periods of time into which the aeon is divided, namely, the *Kṛta*, *Dvāpara*, *Tretā*, and *Kali yuga*s (these Sanskrit terms refer to four throws of the die in gaming, with *Kṛta* considered the lucky or winning throw and *Kali* the losing). The first three have already passed and we are now in the *Kali yuga*, marked by particular degeneracy.

Absolute: the word used to denote the Absolute Reality (*al-Ḥaqq*) is the Hindavī Brahma.

He came as Death . . . come: this half-line is somewhat puzzling. It is possible that Death (Yama) translates the Arabic *qaẓā*, or fate, which is one of the attributes of Allah in His capacity as the apportioner of fates according to His divine will. For Yama, see note to p. 59 below.

One Light . . . worlds: this line refers to the famous Light verse of the *Qur'ān*, in the Sūrat al-Nūr, 24: 35: 'Allah is the Light of the heavens and the earth. The parable of His Light is as if there were a Niche and within it a Lamp: the Lamp enclosed in Glass; the glass as it were a brilliant star: lit from a blessed Tree, an Olive, neither of the East nor of the West, whose Oil is well-nigh luminous, though fire scarce touched it: Light upon Light! Allah doth guide whom He will to His light: Allah doth set forth Parables for men: and Allah doth know all things.' (A. Yusuf Ali, *The Holy Qur'ān*: *Text, Translation and Commentary*, Beirut: Dar al-Qur'ān al Karīm, 1934, 1993).

Countless are the forms . . . names: this refers to the *ạ'yān al-s̱ābita*, the eternal hexeities or patterns, and the divine Names, which are so important in the account of creation given by Ibn ʿArabī (AD 1165–1240), which had itself become more or less the accepted version of creation for Indian Sufis after the fourteenth century. The divine Names were the basis of Shaṭṭārī letter mysticism and cosmology, and were used extensively by the Shaṭṭārīs to inculcate God's qualities or attributes in the being of the practitioner.

4 *Invisible*: Alakh, an epithet frequently by Sufi poets to describe Allah.

whatever exists, exists in Him: this refers to the doctrine of *waḥdat al-wujūd*, the unity of existence, which is the key term in the highly influential ontological monism of Ibn ʿArabī. Within Ibn ʿArabī's paradoxical formulation, the world is an unfolding of God's essence and therefore shares in that essence, yet is not identical with God's being, which is beyond human comprehension.

ten directions: the ten directions are the four cardinal points, halfway between each cardinal point, and above and below.

the Creator shows His hidden nature: in a variant reading, the Rampur MS of the *Madhumālatī* reads *āpa dikhāvā* ('discloses himself'), not *guput dikhāvā* ('discloses the secret').

5 *He has neither beginning nor end*: we have followed the Ekadala manuscript in reading the second half-line as *ādi na bhau anta na āhi*.

Creation itself is the mirror of Your face: the *ḥadīs̤ qudsī* to which this refers is the famous, 'I was a hidden treasure, and longed to be known. So I created the world in order that I may be known' ('*kuntu kanzan makhfīyan fa aḥababtu an uʿrafu fakhalaqtu al-khalqa lika yuʿrafu*'). A *ḥadīs̤ qudsī* ('divine saying', Ar.) is a traditional saying or story which relates a revelation from God in the words of Muḥammad and is not found in the *Qurʾān*.

This lamp of creation: this refers to the *nūr-e muḥammadī*, the light of Muḥammad, an association of the Prophet with the light of the first manifestation of the divine essence which developed early and was much used by the Sufis.

For him, the Deity fashioned the universe: the *ḥadīs̤ qudsī* to which this alludes is *laulāka mā khalaqtuʾl-aflāka*, 'If you had not been, I would not have created the heavens.'

The moon split in two at the pointing of his finger: Sūra 54: 1 reads, 'The Hour of Judgement is nigh, and the moon is cleft asunder.' It was a much later tradition that developed attributing this as a miracle performed by Muḥammad to convert unbelievers, but it was one lacking authority either in scripture or *ḥadīs̤*. None the less, this 'miracle' became established as part of Sufi lore and is often alluded to in Sufi poetry.

Manifest, the name is Muḥammad . . . He: this concept of the *ḥaqīqat muḥammadiyya*, the reality of Muḥammad or the archetypal Muḥammad, was developed by Ibn ʿArabī as homologous with the manifestation of the divine essence in the form of light, and was much used by the Shaṭṭārīs and other Indian Sufis.

6 *of his four companions*: these were not, of course, companions of the Prophet, but were in fact the four righteous Caliphs. See notes below.

Abū Bakr: Abū Bakr ibn Abī Quhāfa, father of ʿĀʾisha, youngest wife of Muḥammad; Abū Bakr reigned as Caliph for two years (AD 632–4) before dying.

ʿUmar: ʿUmar ibn Al-Khaṭṭab was pre-eminent among the early Caliphs for contributing to the spread of Islam. He reigned for ten years (AD 634–44) before his assassination by Fīrūz, a Persian slave.

ʿUs̱mān: ʿUs̱mān Ibn ʿAffān commissioned the second and final version of the *Qurʾān*. He ruled for thirteen years (AD 643–56) before being slain by the son of Abū Bakr.

ʿAlī: ʿAlī ibn Abū Ṭālib was Muḥammad's cousin and married Fāṭimah, the Prophet's daughter. He was the father of Ḥasan, who was poisoned, and Ḥusain, who was martyred in the battle that decisively split Islam into the sects of Sunnī and Shīʾāh. ʿAlī followed ʿUs̱mān as Caliph from AD 656 to 661.

Salīm Shāh: Salīm or Islām Shāh Sūrī, the son of Sher Shāh Sūrī, ruled from Agra after his father's death from an exploding cannon at the siege of Kalinjar in 1545. He was the patron of Shaikh Manjhan, who formed part of the coterie of poets and learned men at his court. Manjhan, a disciple of the great Shaṭṭārī Shaikh Muḥammad Ghaus̱ Gvāliyārī, has often been confused with another Manjhan, also a disciple of Shaikh Muḥammad Ghaus̱. This second Manjhan was the *qāẓī* of the town of Chunar and is mentioned in Ghaus̱ī Shaṭṭārī's *Gulzār-i Abrār*. That the two are different personages is clear from the account of Muḥammad Kabīr in the *Afsānah-i Shāhān*, British Library MS Add. 24409, fo. 105b.

Indra's throne: god of rain and thunder, Indra was considered the king of the gods in the Vedic period, but later became secondary in importance to Śiva and Viṣṇu. His weapon is the thunderbolt (*vajra*) and he is famous for his excesses in drinking and womanizing. His court is supposed to be populated by celestial musicians (*gandharva*) and heavenly nymphs (*apsaras*), who are exquisitely beautiful and excel in music and dance.

Through the nine regions and the seven continents: the nine regions refer to the Indian cosmology of the nine divisions of the earth, i.e. Bhārata, Ilāvarta, Kiṃpuruṣa, Bhadra, Ketumāl, Hari, Hiraṇya, Ramya, and Kuśa. The seven continents are traditionally depicted as islands each surrounded by a sea of a particular fluid. Thus, Jambūdvīpa has the sea of Lavana (salt), Plakṣadvīpa, the sea of Ikṣu (sugarcane juice), Śālmalidvīpa, the sea of Surā or Madya (liquor), Kuśadvīpa, the sea of Ghṛta (clarified butter), Krauñcadvīpa, the sea of Dadhi (curds), Śakadvīpa, the sea of Dugdha (milk), and Puṣkaradvīpa, the sea of Jala (fresh water). Jambūdvīpa lies in the centre of all the continents and the golden mountain Meru stands in the middle of it. For a more extensive treatment of this cosmological scheme in Hindavī Sufi poetry, see Malik Muḥammad Jāyasī, *Padmāvat*, ed. M. P. Gupta, verses 150–8. Jāyasī uses the convention to suggest seven stages through which the seeker must pass in order to reach the Mānasa lake, the true home of the soul.

Laṅkā: the island ruled by Rāvaṇa and where he imprisons Sītā, the wife of Rāma, in the epic, *Rāmāyaṇa*. The mythic Laṅkā is believed to be a reference to the island now known as Sri Lanka, located off the southern tip of India.

the fourteen sciences: the fourteen *vidyā*s or sciences are usually listed as the four Vedas, the six Aṅgas, Dharma, Mīmāṃsa, Tarka or Nyaya, and the Purāṇas.

Hanumān's bridge: son of Vāyu the Wind-God, and general of the monkey army, Hanumān is a central character in the *Rāmāyaṇa* and is noted for his enormous strength and absolute devotion to Rāma. During Rāma's rescue of Sītā, from the prison of Rāvaṇa, Hanumān, along with an army of monkeys, built a bridge of stone between India and Laṅkā.

7 *Yudhiṣṭhira*: eldest of the five Pāṇḍava brothers of the epic *Mahābhārata*, and king of Indraprastha, Yudhiṣṭhira is famed for his virtuous and righteous behaviour and his skill at kingship.

Harīścandra: a king famous for his liberality, honesty, and unflinching adherence to the truth. In a trial devised by two sages, Harīścandra stood by his word even though he had to lose his kingdom, to sell his wife and son, to become a slave of a low-caste man and to agree to put his own wife to death under the charge of being a witch.

Karṇa: the half-brother and enemy of the Pāṇḍava brothers in the *Mahābhārata*. Karṇa was the son of Sūrya, the sun-god, and received divine armour and earrings from his father at birth. In an act of legendary generosity he gave these away to the wily Indra who, disguised as a brahmin, asked him for a boon.

Ḥātim: a Christian Arab nomad who lived before Muḥammad, Ḥātim al-Ṭaiy is remembered chiefly for his hospitality, often slaughtering as many as forty camels at one time for his guests and for the poor.

Bhoja: the eleventh-century king of Ujjain and Dhar. Bhoja was a legendary patron of the arts and reputed to be the author of numerous works including the famous *Śṛngāra Prakāśa*, a Sanskrit work on aesthetics.

Bali: the emperor of the *asura*s (demons). Bali granted a boon to Viṣṇu in his incarnation as a dwarf. Viṣṇu asked to be given all the ground he could cover in three steps, and when Bali agreed, he grew to cosmic size, then stepped over heaven and earth. Out of respect for Bali's kindness, Viṣṇu stopped short of stepping over Pātāla, the underworld, and gave it to Bali to rule.

Vikrama: also known as Vikramāditya, this emperor of ancient India (generally believed to have ruled in the first century BC, although his existence in not an established fact) is famed for being an extraordinarily just and righteous ruler, and for subduing the 'barbarians' who had invaded the kingdom.

8 *Shaikh Muḥammad Ġhauṣ*: Shaikh Muḥammad Ġhauṣ Gvāliyārī (d. 1563) was the spiritual guide of Shaikh Manjhan, the poet, and famous for devising the Shaṭṭārī method of *da'avat ul-asmā'* or the invocation of the Names of Allah. He and his brother Shaikh Phūl were especially close to the Mughal emperors Bābur and Humāyūn, and after the Sūrī victory over the Mughals in 1540 the Shaikh escaped the armies of Sher Shāh Sūrī and fled to Gujarat. After Sher Shāh's death in 1545, his son Islām Shāh made amends with the Shaikh and accepted Manjhan as one of the group of poets he patronized at his court.

The one whom his gaze touches is protected: here the poet uses the Hindavī *disṭi* to suggest the Persian *tavajjuh*, the absorbed attention of the Shaikh which transforms the consciousness of the disciple.

washes out the stain of death!: a reference to the Sufi experience of *fanā*, self-annihilation on the path. The triumph over death refers to the stage of subsistence after annihilation, *baqā*.

over seven oceans: see note to p. 6 above.

the secret syllables of spiritual power: a reference to Shaṭṭārī letter-mysticism, in which the Arabic letters of the ninety-nine Names of Allah encode a system of visualization and interior discipline.

9 *Kali age*: last and worst of the four *yuga*s or ages, the Kali *yuga* is characterized by widespread sin and degeneracy as well as social, political, and environmental chaos. At the present time the Kali *yuga* has been in effect for approximately 5,000 years and will continue for another 425,000 years, at which time Śiva will destroy the universe and then begin a new cycle of *yuga*s. See note to p. 3 above.

it's simplicity: this verse also makes extensive reference to the Shaṭṭārī system of interior discipline, in which the letters of the alphabet signify particular divine Names. The disciple has to empty his self of all worldly emotions and fill it with the qualities embodied in the Names, gradually transforming his body into a mirror for the divine Essence.

leave aside all the mind's arguments; know him!: among the Shaṭṭārīs, as among other orders of Sufis, annihilating one's being in the teacher (*fanā fi-'l-shaikh*) was an important step along the Sufi path.

but few recognize his secret nature: here, as elsewhere, the Sufi distinction between the interior (*bāṭin*) meaning and the exterior or literal (*ẓāhir*) meaning of the *Qur'ān* is invoked to comment on the double reality of the spiritual guide. The Shaikh has a visible worldly form and an invisible significance in the spiritual cosmos of the Shaṭṭārīs, where he serves as the conduit of divine grace and mercy and enables the disciple to achieve closeness to God.

10 *All the pandits . . . shaved their heads to learn from him*: a pandit (<*paṇḍita*, 'learned', Skt.) is a scholar learned in scripture and law. It is customary for pandits to shave their heads.

11 *and imbibed the nectar of pleasure, enlightenment*: this line makes clear the link between Shaṭṭārī austerities and the ultimate pleasure (*mahāras*) of divine union in the *Madhumālatī*. The term *mahāras* refers simultaneously to the fruit of Sufi austerity, the goal of erotic mysticism, and the aesthetic pleasure of reading the text. In the Sufi poetics of the text, divine grace can grant the same plenitude as the years of self-mortification along the Shaṭṭārī path, and both these can be appreciated only by the connoisseur (*rasika*) who understands the multiple meanings of the erotics of union.

Khiẓr Khān: Khiẓr Khān was a prominent noble at the Sūrī court and *muqṭa*ʿ (governor) of Bengal. He revolted against Sher Shāh Sūr in 1540 and was disciplined by him, but was subsequently reinstated in royal favour. On Khiẓr Khān Turk and his temporary rebellion against Sher Shāh, see I. H. Siddiqui, *History of Sher Shāh Sūr*, 107.

flees like mice: our translation is only an appromixation for the Hindavī phrase *mūsa udāsā*, which remains a puzzle for us.

12 *In Praise of the Word*: the 'word' which is the subject of address in the following three verses is simultaneously the sacred word which set the world into motion in the Qur'ānic narrative of creation ('*kun!*') and the word which makes up human language and is the unit of speech and story. The doubleness or paradoxical nature of the word, its place in the human heart as well as its divine imperishability, represents a view of language which contains the identity-in-difference of human and divine nature which is fundamental to Ibn ʿArabī's theory of *waḥdat al-wujūd*. The word is also the basis of the poetics of double meaning which is at work in the *Madhumālatī*, since events in the story are understood to have multiple significances through the allusive power of words.

Hari's mouth: 'Hari' is one of the epithets of the god, Viṣṇu. Viṣṇu is one of the supreme deities of Hinduism, and is characterized as the sustainer of the universe. In his numerous incarnations on earth (including as Rāma and as Kṛṣṇa) he acts as the saviour and protector of humanity.

13 *then the world came into existence*: this refers to the famous tradition popular among Sufis, 'I was a hidden treasure, and longed to be

known.' From God's love for seeing His own beauty, the universe came into being as a mirror for God's face (cf. v. 6). Love and beauty are also central to the aesthetics of the *Madhumālatī*, in which the heroine becomes an exemplification of the process of the self-disclosure of the divine. Her beauty incites love within the seeker, while *viraha*, the condition of being separated from his beloved, drives him onwards along the Sufi path. The narrative logic of the romance hinges on this polarity between love (*prema*) and separation (*viraha*), as the hero and heroine try to consummate their desire by overcoming their separation and uniting in love.

the simple mystery: *sahaja bheda*, here used to represent the easy internalization of the Sufi paradox of the identity, yet radical difference, of the being of God and man.

14 *To the Soul*: this verse plays ambiguously on the paradoxical identity between God and the soul to refer to the Sufi notion of the reality of man (*ḥaqīqat-i insānī*) as encompassing all of creation in microcosm. Man contains within himself all the stations and ranks of created things, the divine Names, the planets and stars and angels. Within Shaṭṭārī cosmology, man acts as the second intermediate state or *barzakh* between God and the world, analogous to the *nūr-e muḥammadi* (the light of Muḥammad), the first visible manifestation of God's self-disclosure.

Why do you destroy yourself with pride?: a reference to the *nafs-i ammārah* or lower soul, the seat of pride and carnal desire, which it is part of the Sufi's quest to destroy.

15 *Some Spiritual Advice*: the following two verses use the imagery of Nāth-yogic practice to refer to the Shaṭṭārī appropriation of Indian yoga into their own Sufi practice. Thus, Shaikh Muḥammad Ġhauṣ Gvāliyārī translated the Sanskrit *Amṛtakuṇḍa* ('The Pool of Nectar') into Persian under the title *Baḥr al-Ḥayāt*, and this manual was widely circulated among Shaṭṭārīs and other Sufis. See Carl Ernst, 'The Pool of the Water of Life' (forthcoming), for a translation of the text.

sound: the *dhuni* or *nāda* referred to here is part of the Shaṭṭārī theory of the human body as a microcosmic universe. The practitioner has within him an analogue of the sacred sound which sets the world in motion (*Oṃ*, *kun*), and has to tune his inner ear to that sound in order to move along the Sufi stages of ascent and descent.

That is the light of your inner heaven: the inner heaven (*kabilāsa*) referred to here is an internal bodily analogue to the Islamic paradise (*jannat*), which is later represented as the mango grove in which Pemā (Love) plays with her companions.

He dwells . . . in the circle of emptiness: in the *Baḥr al-Ḥayāt* and other Shaṭṭārī texts on spiritual practice, the *śūnya-maṇḍal* ('circle of emptiness') is an inner stage on the yogi's path close to the pool of nectar between the eyes, at the head of the spinal column.

In Praise of Carnāḍhi: Carnāḍhi or Çhunār was the Bihari town outside which Shaikh Muḥammad Ġhauṣ meditated for twelve years, until he moved to Gwalior in 1523.

16 *It must be seen to be appreciated*: a reference to the mystic body, which contains within it a symbolic geography wherein the three rivers Gaṅgā, Jamunā, and Sarasvatī flow. Conquering this fort signifies the Sufi conquest of the self, which the verse implies is above the power of any earthly king.

O lustful parrot . . . many birds!: this is a reference to the tradition that the *semala* or silk-cotton tree (*Salmalia malabarica* or *Bombax heptaphyllum*: *śālmali,* Skt.) attracts birds with its beautiful red flowers, but its pods only produce a worthless cotton. The silk-cotton tree is thus used as a metaphor for anything that is sensually attractive but of no lasting spiritual value.

17 *the man of truth abandoned this Kali age*: a reference to the accidental death in 952/1545 of Sher Shāh Sūr, the patron's father, by an exploding cannon on the battlements of the fort of Kalinjar. The date of the accident is supplied by the Persian chronogram, *z̓ātish murd* ('he died by fire').

19 *Only a fool hears exquisite verse in silence*: since the Hindavī mystical romances were written to be read aloud to select audiences at courts and Sufi hospices, the listener's pleasure was an important part of the poet's aesthetic purpose. A particularly good verse would be appreciated by the audience verbally, and poets and performers would take such accolades as proof of their success. Manjhan implies here that only a fool would fail to appreciate exquisite verse by not praising the poet aloud.

Such juicy matters only connoisseurs know: *rasa* is the pleasure which listeners or readers take in stories as well as the lovers' consummation of desire in the savour or juice of love (*prema*). The transcendent dimension of *rasa* allows the *premākhyān* narratives to refer allegorically to the relation of mirrored desire between God and creatures. This verse indicates the importance of *rasa*, a term adapted from Sanskrit aesthetics to support a triple aesthetic purpose: to allude to the circulation of desire between divinity and humans, to characterize the narrative/erotic consummation of desire between the lover and beloved of his story, and to construct the relation between his poetic text and its audience. *Rasa* thus signifies the allusive interplay of these three kinds of desire and their transformation into a divinely sanctioned love, *prema* or *'ishq*, which is the goal of Sufi practice as well as the central symbolic value of the Hindavī *premākhyāns*.

Dvāpar: third in the degenerative cycle of *yuga*s or ages, the Dvāpar *yuga* is the time period when many mythological and literary events are believed to have taken place. See note to p. 3 above.

20 *who gives rice-balls for the ancestors?*: this is a reference to the *sapiṇḍikaraṇa* ritual which is a form of *śrāddha* (ritual for the spiritual welfare of deceased family members) to be completed on the 12th day after death. The son of the deceased must make an offering of balls of rice (*piṇḍa*, Skt.) mixed with water and sesame in order to ensure the entry of the spirit of the deceased (*preta*, Skt.) into heaven. Only sons are allowed to perform this ritual and so having one is necessary for the soul's eternal happiness.

22 *God of Love*: Kāmadeva, the Indian god of love, is portrayed as a beautiful youth riding on a parrot and armed with a bow of sugar cane, which is strung with a row of bees, and arrows tipped with flowers. Once he caused Śiva to have amorous thoughts of the goddess Pārvatī while he was meditating. Furious, Śiva incinerated Kāmadeva with fire from his third eye, and thereafter Kāmadeva was known as *anaṅga*, the 'bodiless one'. It is significant that although Manjhan feels free to invoke the traditional Indian God of Love in telling his story in polished and conventional imagery, he nowhere mentions Kāmadeva when he is defining his notion of love in the Prologue (verses 27–30). There, he prefers to recast the Sufi notion of divine love into a Hindavī aesthetics and metaphysics of *prema-rasa*, the juice or savour of love.

23 *On the sixth night . . . birth*: this is a reference to *ṣaṣṭi*, the ceremony on the sixth day after the birth of a child. The child is given a name and it is believed that Brahma, the god of creation, writes the child's fate on his forehead on this day.

all thirty-six serving castes: traditionally, the low-caste servants (divided into thirty-six groups, such as barbers, dhobis, and shoemakers) connected to a household receive gifts upon festive occasions, such as marriages and births.

bodies anointed with sandal and aloes: the word used for the unguent in the original is *catursama*, a traditional perfume made of: (1) sandalwood (*Santalum album*, *candana*, Skt.), the oil extracted from the sweet-smelling wood of the sandal tree; (2) aloes (*Aloe perfoliata*, *sthūlādalā*, Skt.), a fragrant wood much used in incense-making and cosmetics; (3) musk, a fragrant substance extracted from the scent glands of the musk deer (*Moschus moschiferous*, *kastūrī*, Skt. and Hind.); and (4) saffron, from the Arabic *zaʿfarān*, which comes from the stamens of the crocus flower (*Crocus sativus*, *keśara*, Skt., *kesar*, Hind.), which yields a brilliant yellow colour when used as a spice o a cosmetic. These four substances were mixed into a paste and then smeared on the body as a cosmetic.

lips stained with betel: *betel* is a preparation of leaves, areca nut, and spices which is chewed as a stimulant. Betel juice leaves a red colour on the lips, and beautiful women are frequently described as having lips tinted red from chewing betel.

vermilion on their heads: red lead or vermilion powder is known as *sindūr*. Husbands first put it in the parting of their wives' hair during the marriage ceremony, and thereafter women apply it to their partings as a sign of their married status.

Dhrupada and Dhruva: a particularly rich and stylized courtly mode of singing songs in Hindi or Braj, popular during the sultanate and Mughal periods and distinct from the lighter style of *khyāl* singing that was invented by Sultan Ḥusain Shāh Sharqī of Jaunpur in the late fifteenth century. The name is derived from the Sanskrit *dhruva-pada*, 'fixed verse'. The introductory stanzas of the *dhrupada*, sung repeatedly as a fixed refrain or chorus, are called *dhruva*.

24 *five well-born nurses, and seven maids to play with the baby*: the numbers five and seven have a special significance in Shaṭṭārī practice, there being five jewels of discipline on the *mashrib-i Shaṭṭar*, and seven stages/planets/faculties in the Shaṭṭārī self, matching the six *cakras* ('wheel', Skt., a nerve centre in the body) and the *amṛtkuṇḍa* ('pool of nectar', Skt.) of the yogic self. See note to p. 15 above for *amṛtakuṇḍa*.

25 *that each word had several meanings*: the position which Manjhan advances as a fundamental of knowledge, the multiple meanings (*artha*) of each word (*bacana*), is a view of language which is basic to the polysemy of the text. Later in the verse, the levels of mystery of scriptural texts are taught to the Prince as a basic interpretative strategy. This *ʿilm-i bāṭin*, or knowledge of the inner secrets of Being, is fundamental to the Sufi poetics of the *Madhumālatī*, since the text may be seen as the translation of divine mystery into a concrete, culturally specific poetics. The process of signification which is thematized here allows for polysemy as a condition of meaning.

the true meanings: this half-line introduces the term *sat-bhāva* ('true meaning/essence', Skt.), which works as a structuring principle for reading and referring to double or multiple meanings in the text of the *Madhumālatī*. The 'true meanings' of the literal events of the ... are obliquely referred to by the poet, and the Shaṭṭārī ...cal manuscripts provide the larger ideological framework ...h elements are taken and adapted into the text's poetics of ...erence.

... a philsophical text composed in the second century BC by

Patañjali, the *Yogasūtra* is a manual explaining the disciplined mental and physical activity required for the practitioner to attain perfection and eventually liberation from existence.

Amarakośa: the most celebrated and authoritative lexicon in the Sanskrit language, it was compiled in the first century BC by Amarasiṃha, a scholar in the court of the legendary king Vikramāditya (see note to p. 7 above). Indisputably the most memorized dictionary in the world, a study of it was considered essential for a mastery of Sanskrit.

Kokaśāstra: another name for the *Ratirahasya*, composed in the twelfth century AD by Kokkoka, a royal pandit. Richard Burton describes in his edition how the pandit came to recite the *śāstra* before the king: 'A woman who was burning with love and could find none to satisfy her inordinate desires, threw off her clothes and swore she would wander the world naked until she met with her match. In this condition she entered the levée-hall of the Raja upon whom Koka Pandit was attending, looked insolently at the crowd of courtiers around her and declared that there was not a man in the room. The king and his company were sore abashed, but the Sage [Kokkoka], joining his hands, applied with due humility for royal permission to tame the shrew. He then led her home and worked so persuasively that well-nigh fainting from fatigue and from repeated orgasms she cried for quarter. Thereupon the virile Pandit inserted gold pins into her arms and legs, and, leading her before his Raja, made her confess her defeat and solemnly veil herself in his presence. The Raja was, as might be expected, anxious to learn how the victory had been won, and commanded Koka Pandit to tell his tale, and to add much useful knowledge on the subject of coition. In popular pictures the Sage appears sitting before and lecturing the Raja, who duly throned and shaded by the Chhatri or royal canopy, with his harem fanning him and forming tail, lends an attentive ear to the words of wisdom.' (Quoted by Alex Comfort, in *The Koka Shastra: being the Ratirahasya of Kokkoka and other Medieval Indian Writings on Love*, pp. 54–5.)

Gītā: the *Bhagavad Gītā* ('Song of the Lord', Skt.) is a section from the epic *Mahābhārata* relating a conversation on the battlefield between Arjuna, one of the Pāṇḍava brothers, and his charioteer, the God Kṛṣṇa. Arjuna has been paralysed by remorse at the thought of the impending battle when he will be required to fight and kill his teachers, friends, and kinsmen. Kṛṣṇa explains to Arjuna in a series of arguments how he can fulfil his duty and still remain morally virtuous, namely by devoting himself to the ideal of selfless action. Kṛṣṇa then reveals himself to be God by appearing to Arjuna in his cosmic form. Arjuna, duly impressed, accepts his duty and enters the battle. The *Gītā* is one of the central sacred texts of India and is commonly read and quoted.

26 *the month of Caitra*: this is the lunar month corresponding to March–April. Kāmadeva is also called *Caitrasakha* (friend of Caitra) as he is associated with the season of spring.

27 *the sixteen adornments*: these are the traditional Indian *solah siṅgār*, the sixteen ways that a woman could adorn herself to look beautiful. The sixteen kinds of make-up are: (1) *dāntan*, 'tooth-brush'; (2) *manjan*, 'tooth-powder'; (3) *ubṭan*, 'cosmetic paste' made of gram flour or barley meal for softening and cleaning the skin; (4) *sindūr*, 'vermilion' for the forehead and parting of the hair; (5) *kesar*, 'saffron', also for the forehead; (6) *anjan*, 'antimony' or 'collyrium', kohl for the eyes; (7) *bindī*, 'dot, mark, or spangle ornamenting the forehead'; (8) *tel*, 'hair-oil'; (9) *kaṅghī*, 'comb'; (10) *argajā*, 'perfume'; (11) *pān*, 'betel' for reddening the lips; (12) *missī*, 'dark paint for the teeth and lips'; (13) *nīl*, 'indigo' for tattooing; (14) *meṅhdī*, 'henna' for the hands and feet; (15) *phūl*, 'flowers' for the hair; (16) *āltā*, 'red dye' or 'lac', an insect-based extract used to paint the feet red.

29 *Sleep can be both good and bad . . . the difference*: this verse and the following one play on the Sufi idea of the world as a state of sleep for its inhabitants. In the *Favā'id al-Fu'ād* of Shaikh Niẓām-al-dīn Auliyā', one of the discourses of the master explains the point, 'Saints on the verge of death are like a person having a dream, and it is as if the beloved is lying in bed beside him. At the moment that that sleeper departs this life, it is as if he is suddenly startled awake from his dream, and that Beloved for whom he had searched throughout his life, he sees lying beside him in his own bed. Imagine the joy and delight that he experiences!' (Translated by Bruce Lawrence as *Morals for the Heart* (New York: Paulist Press, 1992), p. 134.) Only when the seeker ascends to the stages which are outwardly seen as sleep can he awake to true selfhood. The 'true sleep' is here distinguished from the sleep of negligence (*ġhaflat*) of the last line of the verse, 'which kills a man as he lives'. The Rampur manuscript (Rā) reads '*pema surā*' (the wine of love) rather than the printed *parama nidrā* (the great sleep) and the Ekadala MS (E) reads *parama sukha* (the great happiness). We have preferred the Rampur MS reading in preparing our translation.

Sleep to the world is a lesser death: the 'lesser death' (*fanā*) thus involves falling asleep to worldly things in order to awaken to the spiritual cosmos within.

sweet sleep: a coded reference to the seeker's falling asleep to the world and into a state of readiness for spiritual awakening. The nymphs, as we shall see, take him to have a transformative vision of a beautiful divine heroine.

30 *Saurāṣṭra and Gujarāt . . . Isle of Singhala*: Saurāṣṭra and Gujarāt are western provinces of India, and the Isle of Singhala refers to a half-mythical island in the eastern sea, somewhere beyond Laṅkā.

the city of Mahāras: the city of Mahāras ('the great *rasa*'), the home of Madhumālatī, signifies simultaneously the abode of divinity and the mystical state which is the ultimate goal of the seeker. The use of the term *rasa* indicates the conjunction of aesthetic pleasure and religious meaning which informs the poetics of the *premākhyān*.

31 *both were perfect in beauty*: the word used for beauty, *rūpa*, lit. 'form', indicates the Shaṭṭārī distinction in their discussions of the body between form/appearance (*ṣūrat*) and its underlying reality (*ḥaqīqat*). As we shall see in the description of Madhumālatī's form, the manifestation (*tajallī*) of her divine beauty before Manohar is described in terms which refer simultaneously to her body and to a Shaṭṭārī theology of divine self-disclosure.

To look upon them . . . in the state of mystical union: the equivalence which is here drawn between the union of Manohar and Madhumālatī and the ultimate goal of mystical practice, between the path of asceticism and the vision of divine beauty, is fundamental to the narrative grammar of the *premākhyān*s. These two paths both converge in the taste of love's savour (*prema-rasa, lazzat-i ʿishq*), the central aesthetic/religious value of the text.

He is the sun and she the moon. She is the sun and he the moon: the paradoxical unity of being between the two lovers is the mystical secret to which the romance refers through its poetics of suggestion.

the last trump would sound through the triple world: i.e. the world as we know it would come to an end, creation's ultimate purpose (divine love) having been fulfilled.

God Himself incarnated these two: the poetics of incarnation, of embodying the invisible divine within a visible form is the focus of the next section of the poem.

32 *Pleiades*: this constellation of six stars is known as the *Kṛttikā Nakṣatra* in Sanskrit and is frequently depicted as surrounding the moon. In mythology, the Kṛttikās are nymphs who became the nurses of the god of war, Kārttikeya. The poet here uses the Hindavī *kacpaciyāṉ*, a word that suggests both the glittering beauty of the stars and their warm allure.

34 *gem-bearing snakes*: it is traditionally believed that a cobra carries a priceless jewel in its hood, and that snakes in general are the protectors of the jewels hidden in the body of their mother, the earth.

scent of sandal: this verse and the one previous imply a comparison between Madhumālatī's perfumed tresses and Mount Malaya or the southern mountain, which is renowned for its sandal trees and its snakes. Snakes are supposed to prefer to live entwined around sandal trees, and the breeze from the south, like Madhumālatī's fragrant yet deadly tresses, carries the scent of sandal with it.

35 *the moon had fallen into the demon Rāhu's power*: in the traditional Indian explanation of the eclipse, when the gods first produced *amṛta*, the nectar of immortality, Rāhu assumed a disguise and began to drink it. The sun and moon detected his deception and informed Viṣṇu, who threw his *cakra* (discus) and severed Rāhu's head. As the *amṛta* had only got to his throat, the head remained immortal and was placed in the sky, where it periodically swallows the sun and the moon.

Love happily took in his hands his bow: Kāmadeva is armed with a bow and arrows: the bow is of sugar cane, the bowstring is a line of bees, and each arrow is tipped with a distinct flower. He is usually represented as a handsome youth riding on a parrot and attended by Nymphs, one of whom bears his banner displaying the Makara, or a fish on a red ground (John Dowson, *A Classical Dictionary of Hindu Mythology and Religion, Geography, History, and Literature* (London: Kegan Paul, Trench, Trubner and Co., Ltd., 1928), 146.

36 *wagtail's wings*: the wagtail or *khañjana* (*Motacilla indica* or *alba*) is a small, dainty bird which darts about wagging its tail up and down and its head back and forth. It is often described as moving like a pony or dancer and is a favourite subject of comparison with a woman's eyes.

like fish playing face to face: fish-shaped eyes are considered a mark of beauty.

Udayācala: the eastern mountain or hill from behind which the sun is supposed to rise.

Her nose is the channel for the sun and moon: reference is here made to the two channels of the sun and the moon in the yogic body (*piṅgalā* and *iḍā*), which feed the body with airs. The practitioner strives to control his breath (*ḥabs-i dam*, *praṇāyāma*) in order to gain spiritual power. The image here connects Madhumālatī's body with the yogic body, establishing a correspondence between the divine self-disclosure and the Shaṭṭārī notion of the human body.

37 *Lord Śiva*: one of the principal deities of India, Śiva destroys the universe at the end of the cycle of *yugas* (see note to p. 3 above). He is represented as the ideal ascetic, spending thousands of years meditating and practising austerities.

bimba: a tree (*Monmordica monadelpha*) bearing bright red gourds, very frequently used as an illustration of the scarlet colour of a woman's lips.

39 *Viṣṇu*: see note to p. 12 above.

Rāhu . . . would surely have devoured this moon: see verse 81 and note p. 35 above.

to sacrifice his life on the saw at Prayāg: Prayāg, at the meeting of the Gaṅgā, Jamunā, and Sarasvatī rivers, is considered one of the holiest places in India. At this confluence, a saw was supposed to be laid down for devotees on which they could sacrifice themselves as a demonstration of their devotion. This was considered a meritorious act and attracted large crowds of spectators. Women anointed the partings of their hair with the blood of the victims, in the hope of having a long and happy marriage. Apparently the saw was destroyed by order of the Mughal emperor Shāh Jahān.

40 *the triple crease of her neck*: a common attribute of a beautiful woman, possibly also a veiled reference to the *triveṇī*, or the three rivers Gaṅgā, Jamunā, and Sarasvatī, which come together at Prayāg.

Viśvakarman, the All-Maker: the architect of the gods and the maker of all their ornaments, weapons, and aerial chariots.

her flawless palms . . . filled with deep red vermilion: having palms stained red is considered a traditional mark of beauty.

wood-apples: a woman's breasts are frequently compared to the fruits of the *bel* or *bilva* tree (*Aegle marmelos*), which are very hard and round. Lakṣmī used to make a daily offering to Śiva of a thousand lotus buds. One day she found her supply of lotus buds was short by two. She then remembered that Viṣṇu used to compare her breasts to lotus buds. She then cut off one breast, and Śiva, satisfied with her sacrifice, appeared before her and said that her severed breast would become the wood-apple.

44 *Seven circular paths lead to this chamber*: a coded and suggestive reference to seven levels of spiritual practice, or seven planetary stations or stages of ascent. The poet here suggests that Manohar has gone through the *brahma-randhra* or heavenly door that is located between the eyes in the symbolic yogic body to reach the *amṛtakuṇḍa* or pool of nectar that lies within. The maiden's bedroom is located, it will be recalled, in the city of Mahāras, the 'great *rasa*'.

Seeing her beauty . . . his eyelids refused to open: this is a reference to the blinding of Moses when he looked upon the glory of God in Sūra 7: 143, 'When Moses came to the place appointed by Us, and his Lord addressed him, he said: "O my Lord! Show (Thyself) to me that I may look upon Thee." Allah said, "By no means canst thou see Me (direct); but look upon the mount; if it abide in its place, then shalt thou see Me." When his Lord manifested his glory on the mount, He made it as dust and Moses fell down in a swoon. When he recovered his senses he said: "Glory be to thee! To Thee I turn in repentance, and I am the first to believe."'

45 *Rāghava line*: the solar dynasty descended from Raghu, to which Prince Rāma of the *Rāmāyaṇa* also belonged.

Prayāg: lit. 'place of sacrifice', Prayāg is the celebrated place of pilgrimage at the confluence of the Gaṅgā, Yamunā and Sarasvatī rivers, each of which is also considered holy. The modern city of Allāhābād is situated at Prayāg. For the saw, see note to p. 39 above.

47 *his body's eight limbs*: the eight limbs (*aṣṭāṅga*) of the body are the hands, chest, forehead, knees, and feet, and the term denotes the totality of Manohar's response.

48 *God mixed the pure water of your love*: the author suggests through this imagery the primordial scene of creation, in which Creator and created being, lover and beloved, are one. In this and the following verses, many of the suggestive terms which suggest the Shaṭṭārī Sufi theology of the unity of existence (*waḥdat al-wujūd*) are employed, adding a transcendent level of meaning to this encounter in the flesh. The terminology used in the Prologue to delineate the poetic universe of the romance is thus translated here into a narrative poetics of Sufi love.

From my former lives . . . the Creator formed this body: this passage is a reference to the description of the creation of Adam in Sūra 23: 12–14, 'Man We did create from a quintessence of clay; then We placed him as a (drop of) sperm in a place of rest, firmly fixed. Then We made the sperm into a clot of congealed blood; then of that clot We made a (foetus) lump; then We made out of that lump bones and clothed the bones with flesh; then We developed out of it another creature. So blessed be Allah, the best to create!'

Before life even . . . to me: a reference to the Sufi notion of separation (*hijr*) from God from the first moment of creation; the separation is blessed because it keeps the creature mindful of the Creator and yearning to return to God from the embodied world.

49 *the lotus of Brahma*: before the universe existed, Viṣṇu, in the form of a baby, was lying on a banian leaf and floating in the endless ocean of milk (*kṣīra sāgar*). A lotus began to grow from his navel, and in the lotus Brahma was sitting. Brahma then began to create the universe.

the bird of love was released to fly: This motif is found commonly in Islamic mystical literature, in which the divine in the form of the Universal Spirit moves through the world in the form of a dove after creation. See, for instance, Muhyi'ddín Ibn al-'Arabí, *The Tarjumán al-Ashwáq: A Collection of Mystical Odes*, tr. R. A. Nicholson

(London: Royal Asiatic Society, 1911), pp. 20, 72–3. The bird moving out on the primordial waters could also be a reference to the divine 'breath of the merciful' or *nafas al-raḥmān*. Here the motif foreshadows Madhumālatī's later transformation into a bird in search of Manohar, and fits in with the general Sufi viewpoint of God creating the world because of His own desire to see His beauty mirrored in it. For the theological definitions of these notions, see the Prologue, especially verses 27–30.

50 *You are the sun . . . lights the world*: in this and certain other images, a theological hierarchy is set up in which Madhumālatī is the divine source and Manohar is the individual soul which has left God to come into the world. His yearning for her refers allegorically to the longing of the creature to return to God. It can also be interpreted as the overwhelming erotic longing of two lovers for one another, and this ambiguity of reference is characteristic of the poetics of the Hindavī Sufi romances.

This is the beauty . . . concealed: the images that follow link Madhumālatī's beauty to the theology and self-disclosure of the Shaṯṯārī Sufi godhead. Each image adds another echo to the resonant terms for divine beauty: God is a 'hidden treasure', the soul of the three worlds, revealed in countless forms, the beginning of all things and the end beyond all things. In this entire passage, the aesthetics of poetic beauty are made into theology through the ambiguity inherent in the word *rūpa*, which means both beauty and form. Here it marks the play between bodily form and divine essence in the Sufi's moment of recognition in which the soul in the lower world recognizes its reality, its true source from which it has come and to which it has to return. Shaṯṯārī cosmology was based on the point of divine essence which is manifested in successive *dā'irahs* or circles of divine manifestation. In terms of Manjhan's narrative poetics, this moment marks the acolyte's first taste of the divine essence; when he is separated from it, he has to make his way back around the circle to the point of absorption in divinity.

Śiva and Śaktī: in this ancient concept, Śaktī (lit. 'energy') is the female personification of power, while the male Śiva represents inert matter. Manjhan is not suggesting a doctrinal similarity to Sufi ideology, but that the divine and the human, in their indissoluble union, create and control the whole of the universe.

51 *Contemplation of this beauty is true meditation*: again, an ambiguously theological half-line which links love and the ascetic path, as does the second line of the *dohā*, which makes clear that man has to annihilate himself (*fanā*) in order to see God.

52 *your body is its mirror*: a reference to the famous Sufi tradition that God created the world as a mirror for divine beauty. Thus, for Sufi

audiences, Madhumālatī embodies divinity in this encounter, and Manohar the worldly seeker who has been granted a glimpse of God.

54 *even if he is on the path of sin . . . heavenly fruit of immortality*: here the poet refers to the *sharʿiah*, the right path, translated as *dharam-panth* in Avadhi, which he suggests is the foundation of Sufi self-transformation. The erotic poetics of mysticism presented in the *Madhumālatī* do not constitute an open invitation to sin. Instead, the seeker has to be true to *sat* (a gloss for the Arabic *ḥaqq*), to be mindful of God rather than a worldly beloved, and to remain within the bounds of the Islamic code of conduct.

essence of truth: the word used for 'the essence of truth' is *sat-bhāva*, which the poet has used before for the 'true meaning' of the poetic text (cf. verse 57). Employing it here suggests that the 'true' referent of the Princess's reticence is the need for the mystic to keep to the bounds of the *sharʿiah* in order to advance on the Sufi path.

our glances should meet: the meeting of glances is significant in Sufi practice because the Sufi *pīr*'s glance or *naẕar* often causes the spiritual awakening of the disciple. In the narrative poetics of the romance, Manohar is the novice whose inner being has been stirred up by this meeting with the divine Madhumālatī.

55 *They swore the oath . . . with Rudra, Brahma and Hari bearing witness*: *Rudra* and *Hari* are used here as epithets for Śiva and Viṣṇu, respectively. The significance of the oath, which is brought up when the Prince and Princess meet again, is the avoidance of public disgrace through right action, following the strictures of the *sharʿiah*, and adherence to true love. Madhumālatī, as a well-born Princess, cannot afford to link her name publicly with a lover's, so presumably part of Manohar's duty is not to reveal her name for fear of disgrace—only then will God protect their love in all their births. This implies that there is a narrative silence being imposed on the Sufi novice—he cannot speak openly of the secret of mystical love, the identity of being between lover and beloved (*waḥdat al-wujūd*). Similarly, concrete forms and events in the narrative contain allusions to Sufi mysteries which cannot be discussed openly, necessitating a poetics of suggestion and resonance.

Lovers' Play: in the following section there is a heady ambiguity of reference as erotics and theology inform one another in the encounter between the lovers. The text works both as a courtly poem in which the erotic body of the heroine is presented for the male reader, as well as a Sufi mystical poem of the soul's awakening to the love of God, and the suggestive allegory between these levels of meaning lends the next few verses their appeal. On a slightly less heady note, readers will recall that the Prince is supposed to be only fourteen on this night of vision. He must subsequently prove himself a spiritually aware man through an arduous quest and many ascetic ordeals before he can see Madhumālatī again.

57 *red betel*: see note to p. 23 above.

59 *Yama*: Yama is the personification of death in the Indian tradition. When the lifespan allotted to each being by Brahma (see note to p. 49 above) is at an end, Yama sends his minions to bring the soul to *Yamapurī* (lit. 'city of Yama'). There, the souls are judged and sent to either *naraka* (hell) or *svarga* (heaven).

60 *Who has ever found nectar without a snake?*: a reference to fragrant sandalwood, whose sweetness is supposed to be guarded always by poisonous snakes coiled around the perfumed tree-trunks and branches.

61 *Sahajā*: the spontaneous, natural, simple mystical state, to which Manohar's nurse awakens him. She impels him to embark on a difficult ascetic quest to gain the beautiful Madhumālatī. The placement of Sahajā as Manohar's mystical guide in the narrative implies that without proper spiritual instruction and nurture, no one can realize the simple or 'self-born' mystery of the human identity-in-difference with God (*waḥdat al-wujūd*).

65 *Sahadeva*: one of the five righteous Pāṇḍava brothers (see note to p. 7 above) in the epic *Mahābhārata*, who was famous for his knowledge, particularly of astronomy.

66 *unite the cakora bird with the moon*: the *cakora* bird, or Greek partridge (*Perdix rufa*), is said to long for the moon without hope of its love being requited. Since an immense distance separates the bird from the moon in the sky, the image is commonly used to express the hopeless longing of lovers for one another.

67 *Śeṣa*: the serpent companion of Viṣṇu, Śeṣa is also called *Ananta*, 'endless', on account of his infinite length. In his form with one thousand heads, Śeṣa is the couch and canopy of Viṣṇu when the God sleeps in the intervals between the cycles of *yuga*s (see notes to pp. 3 and 12 above).

Sumeru: also known as *Mahāmeru*, this mountain is a dazzling golden peak in the Himalayas and is the seat of Śiva. All the gods dwell on the sides of this mountain, which is covered with precious gems and rare plants, birds, and animals. Sumeru keeps the heavens in place by supporting their weight.

silk-cotton tree: see note to p. 16 above.

nīm tree: the *nīm* or *margosa* tree (*Azadirachta indica*) is famed for its bitter but medicinal leaves and fruit.

If woman's behaviour . . . 'snake' in the Turkish tongue: the word used in the Hindavī text is *mār*, which means 'snake' in Turkish. 'Snake' is a common derogatory term for a seductive and deceitful woman in Turkish culture.

68 *thorn on the ketakī blossom*: the *ketakī* or fragrant screw pine (*Pandanus odoratissimus*) has particularly lovely and sweet-smelling blossoms, as well as spiky leaves.

Vāmā: *vāma*, the left side, refers to the belief that women control the left-hand side of creation. The left side holds negative connotations in the Indian tradition.

69 *Borax transforms gold in separation's fire*: borax (*suhāgā*) transforms gold in the alchemist's fire, making it shine with greater purity. The Prince implies that he has similarly been transformed in the fire of separation.

70 *mantra*: an inspired utterance with an esoteric meaning that frequently possesses special powers.

71 *Śravaṇa*: this is a reference to an episode in the *Rāmāyaṇa*, where King Daśaratha, the father of Rāma, accidentally kills Śravaṇa, a hermit-boy who was so devoted to his blind and lame parents that he carried them everywhere on his shoulders in two baskets. The blind parents cursed Daśaratha to die longing for his own son, so that he would also know the pain that he had inflicted on them.

72 *Daśaratha*: in the epic *Rāmāyaṇa*, King Daśaratha suffered terribly when his son, Rāma, was exiled to the forest for fourteen years. This was the result of the curse discussed in the preceding note.

begging bowl: this bowl (*khappar*) is traditionally made from a coconut shell and is where the yogi collects the food, drink, or money offered by followers.

yogi's staff and crutch: the staff is made from bamboo or *timur*, a stick covered with knots, or is a trident of metal, and is used for walking or as a weapon. The crutch, or *ãcal*, is made of a horizontal stick about sixteen inches long fastened to a short vertical support. It is used as a rest for the chin or arms during meditation.

He marked his forehead with a circle: marking the forehead with pigment or ashes acts as a symbol of a devotee's specific faith or spiritual path.

smeared his body with ashes: it is a very common custom among ascetics in India to rub ashes on their skins, either over the entire body or in specific marks. As ashes are associated with the cremation grounds, this signifies the yogi's acceptance of death and his abandonment of the world. The god Śiva, the supreme ascetic, always covers his body with ashes from the cremation ground itself.

hung shining earrings in both his ears: while it was customary for men in pre-modern India to wear earrings, yogis wore particularly large and heavy ornaments as a sign of their asceticism. This led to their being called also the *kān-phaṭā* or 'split-ear' yogis.

ascetic's viol: the *kiṅgarī* or *ektārā* is a stringed instrument of medium size with a box-like frame carried by yogis, who use it to accompany their recitations of devotional poetry.

Letting down his matted locks: a characteristic mark of the yogi is not to wash or to comb his hair, but to let it become dirty and matted.

patched cloak and the girdle of rope: a special rope (*ārband*) made of black sheep's wool to which the yogis fasten a loincloth (*laṅgoṭī*).

Gorakh yogi: a follower of the rigidly austere tantric cult also known as the Nāth yogis. Their founder, Gorakhnāth, is believed to have lived between the ninth and twelfth centuries in eastern India. He was born a Buddhist but converted to Śaivism (worship of Śiva). The Nāth yogis practised a complex mix of austerities and alchemy in order to attain a state of perfected immortality that they believed to be the *sahaja* or natural state of a human being. Manohar's assumption of the yogic disguise implies, in the narrative code of the Hindavī Sufi romances, his going on an ascetic quest to seek Madhumālatī. In this way the Hindavī Sufi poets adapt the symbolic vocabulary of a local religious group towards their own goal of expressing Sufi terms and concepts in a local Indian language. In conjunction with the yogic disguise of the hero, the Sufi poets also use many yogic terms for practices and states of being that Manohar essays on his way to Madhumālatī. See also notes to p. 15 in the Prologue.

basil-bead necklace: the rosary made of basil-beads or *rudrākṣa* berries (of the tree *Elaeocarpus ganitrus*) is worn by all ascetics devoted to Śiva, and is used to count recitations of the names of God or prayers. The word *rudrākṣa* means 'eye of Rudra (Śiva)', and is believed to be a reference to the third eye of Śiva, which will be opened during the destruction of the universe at the end of the Kali *yuga*.

horn whistle: the whistle (*siṅgnād*) of the Nāth yogis is made of deer or rhinoceros horn, is about two inches long, and is blown before meals and before morning and evening worship.

75 *The one who remembers the Creator . . . bed of flowers*: this is a reference either to the trial by fire of Abraham or the ordeal of Prahlāda. Abraham, revolted by the worship of idols which his people practised, went into a temple and desecrated the statues. King Nimrod then ordered him to be burnt alive. Allah intervened and miraculously Abraham was not harmed by the flames. Sūra 21: 66–9 reads, '[Abraham] said, "Do ye then worship, besides Allah, things that can neither be of any good to you nor do you harm? Fie upon you, and upon the things that ye worship besides Allah! Have ye no sense?"

They said, "Burn him and protect your gods, if ye do (anything at all)!" We [Allah] said, "O fire! Be thou cool, and (a means of) safety for Abraham!"' Prahlāda was the son of a *rākṣasa* (demon) king, Hiraṇyakaśipu. Hiraṇyakaśipu hated Viṣṇu because the god had killed his brother. Prahlāda was always completely devoted to Viṣṇu and thus enraged his father, who decided to torture the boy until he renounced his devotion. Every attempt Hiraṇyakaśipu made to destroy Prahlāda, including throwing him into a pit of fire, was rendered harmless by the boy's prayers to Viṣṇu. Hiraṇyakaśipu finally gave up his terrible efforts and accepted his son again.

76 *grove of plantain trees*: the *kadalī vana* or plantain forest (*Musa sapientum*) in Indian *siddha* traditions, from where this image is borrowed, signifies a place of self-mortification and ultimately, self-transformation. See David G. White, *The Alchemical Body: Siddha Traditions in Medieval India* (Chicago: University of Chicago Press, 1996) for a detailed account.

he gave his head, then set foot: a reference to the *namāz-i maʿakūsa* or *ulṭī sādhanā* practised by Sufis in imitation of Nāth yogic practice.

zikr: a reference to the technical movements of head and mouth which are attached to the Sufi practice of *ẕikr* (lit. 'remembering', Ar.), recalling the Names of God. The Shaṭṭārī Sufis were particularly adept at the practice of invoking the Divine Names (*daʿavat al-asmāʾ*), which is here evoked allegorically as a necessary stage on the seeker's path towards union.

Having lost his love, he could not recognize himself: a reference to the famous Sufi *ḥadīs̱*, 'He who knows himself, knows his Lord.' Manohar has forgotten himself because he has lost his love, and he has now to awaken and train himself through ascetic practice in order to reach God/his love.

77 *the moon of the second night*: the moon of the second night is supposed by the poets of this genre to be spotless and unblemished because of its smaller size, hence a better simile for the purity and radiance of the beloved's face than the full moon. See v. 81, p. 35.

The soles of her feet were red with dye: it is a traditional Indian mark of beauty to have the soles of the feet and the palms of the hands painted or dyed red with lac, an insect extract.

78 *a heavenly nymph banished to earth by the curse of Indra*: Indra frequently sent celestial nymphs to earth to excite the passions of holy men and to distract them from gaining ascetic power. See note to p. 6 above.

yojana: a measure of distance roughly equal to eight miles.

As she stretched out her lovely arms . . . began to shine: the image suggests that her two breasts, which are round like the orbs of the sun and the moon, come into view when the maiden extends her arms. In the mystical or allegorical imagery of the poem, the sun and the moon could also refer to particular wind-channels in Manohar's subtle body that began functioning at this stage in his transformative interior journey.

79 *truth is the essence of this world*: a reference to the central value of the 'true essence' (*sat bhāva*) of the romance, which is the ultimate identity-in-difference of God and the world, lover and beloved, seeker and sought.

Brahma's cosmos: a reference to the yogic notion of the macrocosmic universe within the symbolic body, the *brahmāṇḍa* (lit. 'Brahma's egg'). This is entered through the gateway between the eyes, the tenth door or *daśama-dvāra,* and is supposed to contain within it all the planets and stars, the sky and ether, and all the cosmic stations on the ascetic path.

82 *Tell me carefully . . . through you*: here the poet anticipates the maiden's place in the narrative, to act as a guide on the path of love for Manohar.

Pemā: another allegorical character who functions as Manohar's helper on his quest. Her name means Love, here a reference to the Sufi notion of ordinate love and not to the Indian God of Love, Kāmadeva.

My home is the city of Ease-of-Mind: Citbisarāuṉ, the name of Pemā's city, could either mean Ease-of-Mind (*citta-viśrāma*) or Forgetfulness (*cit-bisarāuṉ*). In either case it is a paradisaical city with a garden around it, where consciousness is lost. In the suggestive passage that follows, Pemā and her friends suggest unmanifested souls at play in the garden of paradise. Love's incarnation in this mortal world is allegorically described as the demonic kidnapping of Pemā (Love) and her imprisonment in a dark and dreary forest, guarded by a demon who signifies the lower or carnal soul, the seat of lust, greed, and egotism.

84 *haṃsa birds*: the bar-headed goose (*Anser indicus*), which breeds on the lakes of Central Asia and in the winter migrates to India. The *haṃsa* is used very commonly as a poetic device. It is famed for its snow-white beauty and grace and its flight to Lake Mānasa at the beginning of the rainy season to unite with its beloved. It also possesses the unique ability to separate milk from water when the two have been mixed, which is evidence of its great wisdom.

85 *the fifth note of the scale*: the leading or regnal note or *vādī svara* that establishes the general character of a *rāga*. It is supposed to be so called because its tone is produced by air drawn from five parts of the body: the navel, breast, throat, heart, and forehead.

86 *Entering the picture-pavilion*: the *citrasārī* or picture-pavilion, a gallery with pictures painted on the walls, is a reference to the *ʿālam al-imṣāl* or world of images, an intermediary stage between paradise and the mortal world. The allegorical reference is heightened in the next verse by the girls' (or unmanifested souls) inability to speak when they emerge from the pavilion; language itself is inadequate to describe the higher levels of mystical experience.

87 *They could not open their mouths . . . spoke through gestures and signs*: only signs and gestures can communicate the new stage of manifestation, signifying the radical breakdown of language as one strips away the veils that cover divinity.

88 *Without life my body lives on . . . fire of separation*: Pemā's condition is therefore just like the Sufi's, who lives in the world away from God's paradise. The condition of separation keeps the Sufi perpetually mindful of his divine source, from which he has been incarnated into this mortal world. Similarly, Pemā's kidnapping by the demon suggests her mortal incarnation. Manohar's task in the following sections will be to kill the demon and take Pemā back to her native land, the paradise-like realm of Citbisarāuṉ.

91 *ghee*: ghee is butter clarified over a flame until it is free of all impurities. It is poured over a fire during many rituals and makes the flames leap up with greater intensity.

Pemā's Sorrow: readers will recall that Pemā means Love, so that in the following allegorical passage it is the abstract value of love that is being held captive by the demon in the plantain forest. The demon, who signifies the ego or the carnal soul, will have to be killed by the seeker Manohar in order to release the Princess Love.

Vāsuki: one of the seven great *nāga*s (serpents) who hold up the earth.

Kubera: the god of riches and treasure, he is the regent of the northern quarter of the earth.

92 *mahuā*: the *mahuā* (*Bassia latifolia*) is a tree bearing sweet flowers that are used for preparing liquor. Elephants are much addicted to *mahuā* blossoms.

caper bush: the caper or *karīl* bush (*Capparis aphylla*) is a thorny and leafless shrub which grows in deserts and is eaten by camels.

henna: the henna plant (*Lawsonia inermis*; *mehndi*, Hind.) forms a very dense, thorny bush, with sprays of fluffy, gold flowers which have a heavy fragrance. The leaves are crushed into a paste which is used to create red designs on the hands and feet or to dye hair.

jasmine flower: the jasmine (*Jasminum auriculatum*; *jūhī*, Hind.) has very small and extremely fragrant white flowers.

flame-of-the-forest: also known as the parrot tree because it is attractive to parrots (*Butea frondosa*; *ḍhāk*, Hind.). Between January and March it blooms in a riot of reddish-orange flowers covering the entire crown, and the sight of *ḍhāk* trees blossoming in a grove is said to look like a forest fire, hence its English name.

rose-apple: the rose-apple (*Eugenia jambos*; *gulāb jamun*, Hind.) is a middle-sized tree with greenish-white flowers and small, pear-shaped, yellow or pink edible fruit.

the green jack-fruit wrapped itself in a thorny sari: the jack-fruit tree (*Artocarpus integrifolia*; *kaṭahal*, Hind., *panasa*, Skt.) bears the largest edible fruit in the world, up to a hundred pounds in weight. The light-green skin of the fruit is covered in spiky growths.

ghunghuci berry: the *ghunghuci* tree (*Abrus precatorius*) bears red berries with a characteristic black dot.

The baḍahal fruit turned yellow: the *baḍahal* tree (*Artocarpus lakoocha*; *vaḍaphala*, Skt., 'large fruit') bears sizeable yellow fruit from which a yellow dye is made.

the tamarind grew twisted: the tamarind tree (from Persian *tamar-i Hindī*, meaning 'Indian date'; *Tamarindus indica*, *amblī*, *imlī*, Hind.) has a short, strong trunk, with black bark covered in deep fissures and horizontal cracks. The flowers are small, creamy or yellow, and scented. The brown, twisting pods contain hard seeds and sour pulp which is used in cooking.

The wishing-tree left this world altogether: the wishing-tree or *kalpataru*, is one of the five trees in *Svarga*, the heaven ruled by Indra, and is reputed to grant all wishes.

93 *green pigeon*: the green pigeon (*Bucula aenea*; *hārila*, Hind.) is believed to avoid all contact with the earth. It hangs upside down from twigs to drink from streams and if killed it will continue to grasp the twig rather than fall to the ground.

The drongo lost its own voice . . . many tongues: the common black drongo (*Dicrurus adsimilis*; *bhṛnga*, Skt.; *bhujaṅga*, *bhujan*, Hind.) has black plumage and a long forked tail. It rides on the back of grazing cattle to eat the insects disturbed by the animal's movement. It is known for coming very close to fires to catch the insects roused by the smoke, which gives it two other Sanskrit names, *dhūmyāt*, 'smoky', and *kolasā*, 'black like charcoal'. It has a very wide repertoire of sounds and is an accomplished mimic.

94 *kosas*: a measure of distance roughly equivalent to two miles.

explaining its true meanings: the 'true meanings' (*bhāva*) are the suggestive cues which are part of the love-play of Manohar and Madhumālatī.

95 *like a pair of wagtails on the wing*: see note to p. 36 above.

a thief's drugged sweets: the *ṭhag*s or deceivers, robbers who would roam about central and northern India and befriend travellers, often deceived them by feeding them drugged *laḍḍū*s which made them fall asleep temporarily or permanently. The term *ṭhag-laḍḍū* is idiomatic for losing one's wits under deception. The *ṭhag*s could then loot the travellers' worldly goods, leaving them without anything. In the same way, Manohar is complaining about the vision of Madhumālatī leaving him bereft of all his senses and his soul.

97 *elephant-gems in every elephant*: this is a reference to the belief that pearls and other precious jewels can be found in the temples of rutting elephants, if one dares to come close.

98 *The man who chooses this path . . . death*: here 'death' is a reference to the Sufi value of *fanā* or annihilation of self. Pemā, instead of becoming the seeker's wife in the manner of the other *premākhyān*s, becomes Manohar's spiritual guide and gives him instruction on how to attain the great *rasa* of love.

Whoever takes separation . . . clear: the spiritual eye or 'eye of the heart' (*chashm-i dil*) is a reference to the inner illumination granted by an accomplished Sufi master to a seeker.

The man who can dive in . . . diver: the Hindavī word for diver, *marjiyā*, contains a pun, for if split into *mar* and *jiyā* it can also mean 'the one who has died while alive', i.e. one who has attained annihilation by diving into the ocean and is therefore blessed with the pearl of everlasting subsistence in love of God (*baqā*). The image occurs also in Kabīr's poetry, as well as in other Hindavī Sufi poets such as Malik Muḥammad Jāyasī, *Padmāvat*, ed. M. P. Gupta, verse 33.

99 *does not turn head over heels, cannot traverse this path correctly*: a suggestive reference to the *namāz-e maʿakūsa* or *ulṭī sādhanā* of the Sufis, in which the practitioner hangs upside down (frequently in a well) for specified periods in order to mortify himself while reciting inwardly the Divine Names.

100 *The five elements*: the five elements (*pañca-bhūta*) are earth, fire, water, air, and ether (*ākāśa*).

Phāgun: the Indian month of spring corresponding to February–March, see note to p. 171 below.

101 *dhamār*: a kind of lively dance accompanied by singing, done during the spring festival of *Holī*, or the Sufi practice of jumping into or running through fire in order to mortify the body.

102 *As Lakṣmaṇa was struck . . . the life-restoring herb!*: this is a reference to an incident also recounted in the *Rāmacaritamānasa* of Tulsīdās,

the great Avadhi version of the epic *Rāmāyaṇa* of Vālmīki. Lakṣmaṇa was wounded by Meghanāda, the son of Rāvaṇa, with the javelin Śaktibān and had to be treated before daybreak or he would die. Hanumān then flew to the Himālayas and searched for the magical herb Sañjīvanī. As he could not be certain which of the many plants it was, Hanumān simply uprooted the entire mountain and flew with it back to Laṅkā. The herb was identified and Lakṣmaṇa's life was saved.

104 *catursama paste*: see note to p. 23 above.

gandharva: the *gandharvas* are the celestial musicians of the gods, and are frequently depicted in art as flying through the air and making music.

110 *Sāvan*: *Sāvan* (*śrāvana*, Skt.) is the month of the rainy season in the Indian calendar, corresponding to July–August. See note to p. 168 below.

white gourd-melons: the long white fruits of the plant *Benincasa cerifera*, here meant to suggest the demon's lines of teeth.

112 *in it lives the demon's soul*: Manjhan's suggestive use of this common folkloric motif suggests that the root of egotism is pleasure, here signified by a dense and shady forest laden with ambrosial fruit. Manohar's struggle with the demon is thus an allegory of the seeker's struggle with the egotism and lust that pervade his carnal soul.

113 *karṇikāra tree*: the *karṇikāra* (*Pterospermum acerfolium*; *kanakchampa*, Hind.) is a large tree with fragrant, small white flowers in March to June. Its fruit ripen in the cold season.

117 *cakī bird*: *cakī* birds (*Anas Casarca*; *cakravāka*, Skt.) mate in couples. They are supposed to be separated at night and to mourn until they meet their mates in the morning.

the lotus had blossomed . . . rays: a possible reference to the blossoming of the *sahasra-dala-kamala* or thousand-petalled lotus, a site in the esoteric yogic body.

papīhā who caught the raindrops . . . Svātī: the *papīhā*, the hawk cuckoo or brain-fever bird (*Cucculus varius*, also *cātaka* in Skt.) is a grey-brown, pigeon-sized bird which is supposed to live on raindrops dripping from the sky when the constellation Svātī is overhead. It is silent in the winter, but with the approach of the hot season becomes increasingly noisy. Its distinctive call is a loud shriek repeated five to six times rising in crescendo, rendered in Hindi as *pī-kahāṉ* or 'where is my love?'

120 *second incarnation of Rāma . . . set Sītā free*: see notes to pp. 6, 71, 72, and 216 for information about Rāma.

123 *the picture-pavilion in the garden*: an allegorical reference to the world of imaginal forms (*imṣāl*), to which the seeker has to ascend in order to have another vision of the divine. This is the same pavilion or *citrasārī* from which Pemā was carried off by the demon, and to which the virginal souls (Pemā's girlfriends) in paradise descend on their way to the world of corporeal forms (*ajsām*).

127 *how could there be love between the two?*: this is a coy way of suggesting a meaning (*vyaṅgyārtha*) opposite to the expressed sense of the couplet, the *abhidhā* or denotative meaning. The beauty of the line is that while on the surface the poet emphasizes the unlikeness and distance between the moon and the lotus, covertly the moon is understood to be the lover and lord of the lotuses (*kumudīśa*) and able to make them open and close through showing and hiding himself. In other words, of course there is a relation between the white lotus and the moon: she longs for him and will only blossom when he is shining in the sky.

131 *Rāhu*: in astrological terms, Rāhu represents the ascending mode which causes both the solar and lunar eclipse. For the mythological connotations of Rāhu, see note to p. 35 above.

ratti: a jewellers' weight, equal to eight barley-corns.

132 *courageous perfection*: the Hindavī *sāhasa-siddhi*, evidently a reference to a spiritual station of successful awakening.

136 *. . . the sun's brilliance . . . your radiant face*: a suggestive reference to the blinded Moses in front of the burning bush, unable to bear the shock of God's radiance.

that special vision: a reference to the *chashm-i dil* or 'eye of the heart', Pers., that is opened in the seeker's spiritual awakening under the guidance of a Sufi Shaikh. The passage suggests a process by which the seeker is immersed in a vision of the spiritual guide's beauty and annihilates his selfhood in him (*fanā fi'l-shaikh*). In this process, the seeker needs to borrow special sight from his guide and use it to have a vision of the Shaikh's beauty, thereby gaining the power of mystical insight or gnosis (*ma'arifa*) himself.

139 *Ratī and fish-bannered Kāmadeva*: Ratī (lit. 'pleasure', Skt.) is the wife of Kāmadeva, the God of Love. Kāmadeva is known as '*makara-ketu*' or 'the one who has a fish on his banner' because of his incarnation on earth as the son of the god, Kṛṣṇa. A sage named Śambara was cursed to die soon after the birth of the son of Kṛṣṇa. When the baby was born to his queen, Rukmiṇī, Śambara stole the baby and threw him into the ocean, where a fish swallowed him up. A fisherman caught the fish and presented it to Śambara, who cut open the fish and gave the baby to Māyāvatī, his kitchen maid. Māyāvatī raised Kāmadeva as her son, until a visiting sage informed

her that she was actually Ratī reborn on earth. As Kāmadeva grew into a youth Māyāvatī began to make advances toward him, which horrified him as he thought of her as his mother. Māyāvatī then told Kāmadeva their true identities and advised him to kill Śambara and take her to Kṛṣṇa's court in Dvārkā. Kāmadeva did so and then presented her as his wife to his parents, Kṛṣṇa and Rukmiṇī.

142 *pool of nectar*: besides the sexual reference to Madhumālatī's virginity, the term signifies also the *amṛta-kuṇḍa* or pool of nectar, in Shaṭṭārī terms the *ḥauẓ al-ḥayāt* or water of life between the eyes. The seeker could only immerse himself in this pool of nectar after performing hard austerities and crossing all the chakras or stations below the eyes in the geography of the subtle body.

143 *The rains of Svāti . . . oyster shell*: it is a common belief that pearls are produced from drops of rain which have fallen from the constellation Svāti.

Sometimes she seemed amazed . . . the pain of separation: many of these traditional signs of love-sickness are familiar from Sanskrit, Persian, and Arabic erotologies, the classical sources from which the Sufis drew many ideas and conventions for their Hindavī romances. The signs of love-sickness include loss of concentration and appetite, weeping blood, wasting away, having delusional fantasies, and an obsession with the object of desire.

144 *dharma*: a Sanskrit word signifying the righteous law or social duty, the principle of cosmic and natural order that underwrites the structure of social relations in traditional Brahminic ideology.

royal happiness: the term used is *rāja-sukha*, a reference to Manohar's tasting the savour of love, the *rāja-rasa* of the Prologue. It is also allegorically significant that he had to ascend to his inner heaven (*Kabilāsa*) to taste the 'royal savour' of love. See verse 43 in the Prologue above.

145 *Bharaṇi*: a constellation containing three stars, which is visible during the rainy months of July and August.

Bhādoṉ: Bhādoṉ (*bhādrapada*, Skt.) is the sixth month of the Indian calendar, corresponding to the middle of August to the middle of September. It is marked by heavy rains, storms, and dark clouds.

147 *siddha yogi*: a perfected and spiritually advanced adept, which Manohar has become through his defeat of his carnal soul and rescue of Love. The manuscripts differ on the second *ardhālī* in this couplet, but each reading is problematic. We have preferred the Ekadala manuscript (E), which reads *siddha jogī tau āpura jāpā*.

Madhumālatī Transformed: the entire section that follows is an allegory of the divine descent into the world of forms in search of a lover. God seeks a mirror to reflect divine beauty back to itself, as would happen in a loving relationship.

148 *Kadalī forest*: the *kadalī vaṇa* or plantain forest (*Musa sapientum*) in Indian *siddha* traditions, from where this image is borrowed, signifies a place of self-mortification and ultimately, self-transformation. See David G. White, *The Alchemical Body: Siddha Traditions in Medieval India* (Chicago: University of Chicago Press, 1996) for a detailed account.

Godāvarī river: a very deep river in south India, Godāvarī is glorified in Indian texts for its power to bring prosperity to anyone who bathes in it.

Mathurā: the birthplace of Kṛṣṇa, Mathurā is located south of Delhi in north-central India, on the banks of the Jamunā river.

Gayā: a holy site located in the modern state of Bihar, Gayā or Bodh Gayā is renowned as the place where Gautama Buddha attained *nirvāṇa*.

Prayāg: see notes to pp. 39 and 45 above.

Jagannāth: the source of the English 'juggernaut', a famous temple located at the site of the modern city of Puri in the eastern state of Orissa. Jagannāth is famous for its yearly *ratha-yātra* or 'chariot-trek'. At this festival, enormous figures of Kṛṣṇa, his brother Bālarāma, and their sister, Subhadra, are wheeled through the city on carts and then immersed in the ocean.

Dvārkā: the legendary city ruled by Kṛṣṇa, Dvārkā is believed to have been on the far western edge of northern India, off the coast of what is now Gujarat.

Tārācand: Tārācand as an allegorical or emblematic character signifies selfless and devoted service, the *khidmat-i khalq* of the Sufi discourses on practice.

the Citadel of Winds, Pavaneri: a reference to the place of the mystic winds or airs of the subtle body.

fair Fortress of Respect, Māngaṛh: another allegorical reference to a mystical station. Unfortunately, there is no single generalized Shaṭṭārī cosmology within which these allegorical places can be located. Rather, the allegory of the *Madhumālatī* works piecemeal, with certain details containing symbolic references and certain passages working as allegories in little. It is necessary to place the Hindavī imagery within the Persianate literary culture that surrounded the local Sufi shrines, if one is to imagine the response to these works among *desī* (indigenous) Muslim and non-Muslim audiences.

149 *So very like was he to Manohar*: here and in the next few verses the poet makes a sly reference to the notion of the exemplum, allegory,

or likeness, *misl*. The suggestive implication is that for God, the devoted servant is the likeness of the lover for whom the divine beloved longs so passionately, a longing that is the root cause for creation.

compassion and affection awoke in his heart: a reference to the idealized virtues of the Sufi path that the seeker sought to inculcate within his own self. Hence Tārācand's response signifies the spiritual awakening that leads to his undertaking selfless and devoted service to the world (*khidmat-i khalq*). Tārācand, in his newly compassionate state, will resolve to restore Madhumālatī to her former shape.

Can one who wants mangoes be sated with sour berries?: the verse plays on the likeness of sound between *āṃba*, mango, and *āṃvlā*, sour gooseberries.

150 *pearls*: here a reference to the pearls of gnosis, *maʿarifa*. The bird, which signifies the divine spirit roaming the world in quest of a lover, feeds only on the pearls of gnosis fostered in the consciousness of spiritually aware men.

152 *I simply do not know my future . . . on my forehead?*: this line is a reference to the belief that the Creator Brahma inscribes each person's fate in invisible letters on his or her forehead.

153 *Jambu, island of the rose-apple tree*: see notes to pp. 6 and 92 above.

156 *poor fire-cracker*: the Hindavī word is *tūṃbī or tūmaṛī*, the small gourd *Lagenaria vulgaris*, often used in a hollowed-out state to carry water by mendicants. The word can also refer to a kind of firework, a small earthen pot filled with gunpowder and other explosives and topped by a wick that leads into the pot. When lit, it produces a fiery rain of sparks.

for the sake of another's happiness: here Tārācand grows into his function as an allegorical character, as his awakened compassion leads him to sacrifice himself and to suffer hardships in order to serve Madhumālatī with devotion.

163 *great path of dharma*: here a reference to the path of mystic practice, and the component of selfless service that Tārācand embodies.

168 *Everything I shall reveal to you . . . dear friend*: the following twelve stanzas, which describe in detail each month of Madhumālatī's journey, are an example of a standard Indian poetic convention, the *bārahmāsā* (lit. 'twelve months'). This is a set of verses in which a reference to each month illustrates a single theme. *Bārahmāsā*s are classified into various types such as religious, agricultural, and the *viraha-bārahmāsā*, which describes the sufferings of a woman separated from her lover during the twelve months of the year. They are often employed by poets as set-pieces in larger literary works such as the *Madhumālatī*, but briefer lyrics are also popular among village

women, who compose and sing them even today. For a brief scholarly treatment and examples of the form, see Charlotte Vaudeville, *Bārahmāsā in Indian Literatures: Songs of the Twelve Months in Indo-Aryan Literatures* (Delhi: Motilal Banarsidass, 1986).

Sāvan: Sāvan (*śrāvaṇa*, Skt.) corresponds to July and August and is the height of the rainy season (*varṣā*). Its stormy atmosphere of dark clouds and lightning is thought to produce an erotic and passionate mood. Since travel comes to a standstill because of the rains, Sāvan is an opportunity for lovers to stay inside with each other. However, it is also a time of potential separation, as the returning lover can be stranded somewhere else until the flooded roads are clear.

169 *Bhādoṉ*: this month (*bhādrapada*, Skt.) corresponds to August–September, and it is the darkest month of the year, being the end of the rainy season.

Maghā: this constellation is the tenth lunar mansion (*nakṣatra*), consisting of five stars, and is prominent during the month of Bhādoṉ.

Navarātra: literally 'nine nights', Navarātra is the nine days of worship done in the month of Kuṃvār, dedicated to the goddess Durgā. Each day requires the offering of water in a consecrated pitcher and of nine kinds of plants: *rambhā*, *kaccvī*, *haridrā*, *jayantī*, *bilva*, *daḍima*, *aśoka*, *mānaka*, and *dhānya*. One of the nights of Navarātra is the *kumārī-pūjā*, when young girls are worshipped as pure manifestations of the goddess.

Kuṃvār: this month, also known as Kvār (*aśvina*, Skt.), corresponds to September–October and is the first month of *śarada*, or autumn. It marks the end of the rainy season and the beginning of cool weather.

170 *Kārtik*: Kārtik (*kārtika*, Skt.; *kātik*, Hind.) is the month sacred to Viṣṇu, and corresponds to October–November. It was the traditional time of departure for husbands and lovers going on trading or martial expeditions or on ascetic pilgrimages. The 'festival of lights' referred to is the holiday of Dīvālī or Dīpāvalī, which is dedicated to Lakṣmī, the goddess of wealth. Dīvālī is celebrated with the lighting of many lamps and the giving of presents.

Aghan: the month of Aghan (*āgrahāyaṇa*, Skt.) begins the season of winter (*hemanta*) and corresponds to November–December.

Pūs: the month of Pūs (*pauṣa*, Skt.) is the equivalent to December–January, and is a very cold time in north India.

171 *Māgh*: Māgh (*māgha*, Skt.) corresponds to January–February, and is the month of winter, the cold season (*śiśira*, Skt.).

Phāgun: Phāgun (*phālguna*, Skt.) heralds the beginning of spring and corresponds to February–March. The spring festival of Holī falls during the ten days prior to the day of the full moon in Phāgun.

One of the most widely and exuberantly celebrated holidays in India, Holī is characterized by the singing of ribald songs and the throwing of coloured water and powder. A bonfire is always kindled in each village and a doll-like effigy of Prahlāda's stepmother Holikā is burnt (see note to p. 75 above). Normally strict social distinctions are overturned and everyone joins equally in teasing, chasing, and splashing each other with coloured water.

172 *Caita*: Caita (*caitra*, Skt.) is the first month of spring (*basanta*) and corresponds to March–April. The land grows green again in this month and it is thought of as the romantic season.

Baisākh: Baisākh (*vaiśākha*, Skt.) corresponds to April–May, and is a verdant and colourful season in north India, but the heat of summer is beginning to build.

Jeṭh: Jeṭh (*jyeṣṭha*, Skt.) May–June is the height of summer (*grīṣma*, Skt.), and is the hottest month of the year. Traditionally it is also the favoured month for weddings.

173 *my lord*: here the poet uses the word *sāīṉ* (<*svāmī*, Skt.), which signifies master and can also mean the Lord of the universe.

Asāḍh: Asāḍh (*āṣāḍha*, Skt.) falls in June–July, and is the 'month of clouds', as it is the beginning of the monsoon. It is thus considered a month of return and reunion, as husbands who had been travelling would try to return home before the rains began. The image of a woman watching the approaching dark clouds while waiting anxiously for her husband's return is frequently evoked in Indian literature.

174 *life*: another allegorical reference to the divine spirit. The word used by the poet is *jīva*.

Every concern fled . . . anxious for you: a reference to *tark-e duniyā*, the Sufi value of giving up the world for the sake of the beloved.

177 *patchwork cloak*: a reference to the *dalq-i muraqqaʿ* or patched cloak of the Sufis, the rough garment signifying their status as travelling mystics.

Gorakh's path: here, as elsewhere, a reference to asceticism in general rather than specifically to the path of the Nāth yogis. The usage is characteristic of the poet's strategy of using vernacular imagery to approximate Persianate Sufi ideas, emptying the *desī* word of its specificity and employing it to signify a notion in Sufi ideology.

181 *syces*: a syce (*sais*, Hind., originally from Arabic, *sā'is*, 'groom', a loanword from Syriac *sausī*, meaning 'to coax') is a common Indian term for a groom or ostler.

like the full moon of Caita . . . Viśākhā, Anurādhā, Jyeṣṭhā: a reference to the moon of the spring month of Caita, when everything begins to turn green again. For a description of Caita, see verse 410 above. Viśākhā, Anurādhā, and Jyeṣṭhā are the names of lunar asterisms through which the moon travels in this month.

183 *Queen's palace, where all the women were staying*: reference is here made to the *ranivāsa* or women's quarters that were a characteristic part of royal palaces in India.

Anurādhā: a constellation considered particularly auspicious. See also note to p. 181 above.

184 *orange*: the word used is *kusumbhī*, bastard saffron or safflower, *Carthamus tinctorius*, from the flower of which a red or orange dye is made.

unguent: here the poet uses the word *ubṭan*, a fragrant paste made of gram flour or barley meal that softens and cleans the skin before the application of cosmetics. See also note to p. 27 above.

185 *white kite*: the 'white kite' or black-winged kite (*Elanus caeruleus*; *kapāssi*, Hind.) is a dainty grey and white hawk with black patches on its wings. The sight of it is thought to bestow good luck.

187 *Āratī*: a common religious ritual of circling a tray of lamps clockwise in front of an object to be worshipped.

190 *The Secret of Love*: the following passage plays charmingly on the mystery to which the seeker has to awaken, namely the identity of being between lover and beloved and their coincidence as subject and object of desire within the human being. At all costs, the mystic must not disclose this secret publicly.

191 *Manṣūr*: Ḥusain bin Manṣūr al-Hallāj was a Sufi mystic hanged for blasphemy AD 26 March 922. He publicly proclaimed the words *anāʾl-haqq* or 'I am the Truth', which is one of the names of God. al-Hallāj was '. . . a man who deeply influenced the development of Islamic mysticism and whose name became, in the course of time, a symbol for both suffering love and unitive experience, but also for a lover's greatest sin: to divulge the secret of his love' (Annemarie Schimmel, *Mystical Dimensions of Islam* (Chapel Hill: University of North Carolina Press, 1975), p. 64).

195 *dhamār*: see note to p. 101 above.

nilgai: the nilgai (*Bosephalus tragocamelus*) is a wild antelope-like creature, 130–40 centimetres tall, with a tawny or grey coat, a dark mane, and short horns among the males of the species. It is found only in the Indian subcontinent, ranging from the Himalayas to the southern elevations of Mysore.

201 *The psychic channels . . . in his body*: the psychic channels of the moon (*iḍā*) and the sun (*piṅgalā*) are nerve conduits that flow from the nose to the base of the spine. A balance between their masculine

(*piṅgalā*) and feminine (*iḍā*) energies is necessary for good health. See also note to p. 36 above.

202 *bimba fruits*: see note to p. 37 above.

207 *five nectars*: *pañcāmṛta*, a mixture of milk, curds, ghee, honey, and sugar, served to the bridegroom and guests as a special food at the wedding.

betel leaves: betel leaves are chewed after eating as a digestive aid. See note to p. 23 above.

The marriage knot . . . seven times: this is a reference to the *saptapadī* (lit. 'seven steps'), a marriage ritual in which the bride and groom go seven steps around a sacred fire with the ends of their garments tied together. This is a symbol of their future co-operation in married life.

209 *between the lovely lily and the moon*: this is a reference to a kind of water-lily or night-lotus which closes during the day and opens at night. It is thus believed to be in love with the moon as it opens only to see its beauty. See also note to p. 127 above.

Canopus: a bright star in the southern constellation of *Argo navis*, particularly noticeable in the cool autumnal nights of Kuṃvār.

The Rite of Departure: the following section uses the *gavanā* or *gaunā*, the child-bride's departure to her husband's house after the consummation of the marriage, to present an allegory of the soul's departure for the heavenly kingdom of the beloved. The idea is commonly found in Indian Sufi poetry, which often celebrates the death-anniversary of a Shaikh as his nuptials (*ʿurs*) with the divine lover. The mystic is depicted as a woman longing for the husband's house, to which he has gone after death. It will be noted that here the poet makes the married Madhumālatī subject to her lord's wish, rather than the divine maiden who was the object of his quest.

212 *You must serve your lords wholeheartedly*: this verse and the following verses employ a cunning extended reference to the mastery of God through the mothers' presentation of advice to the new brides: of serving the husband, and by implication, God. In Sufi terms, God is like the master of the house into which the novice goes like a new bride. The image is carried through several parts: the husband is like the Lord, he must be served like God, he takes the bride/the soul to a paradise-like realm where He is the master (the foreign land which is mentioned repeatedly in the text).

216 *She had given up all illusory attachments*: here the poet makes clear that the new marital home is an implied reference to heaven, the true home of the soul which has been sent into this world, and now leaves it as the bride of God. All her attachments to her natal home are illusory, and must be abandoned if she is to attain eternal happiness.

216 *Vibhīṣaṇa left Laṅkā . . . untroubled by what might happen*: this is a reference to the incident in the *Rāmāyaṇa* concerning Vibhīṣaṇa, who was the younger brother of the demon-king Rāvaṇa. When Rāvaṇa kidnapped Sītā, Vibhīṣaṇa advised Rāvaṇa to return her and beg forgiveness from Rāma. Rāvaṇa was furious with Vibhīṣaṇa and expelled him from Laṅkā. Vibhīṣaṇa became an ally of Rāma and told him all of Rāvaṇa's military secrets. When Rāma won the battle and killed Rāvaṇa, he crowned Vibhīṣaṇa the king of Laṅkā.

219 *took hold of their ears humbly*: holding the ears with both hands is an Indian gesture of humility and remorse.

225 *yojanas*: a *yojana* is a traditional Indian measure of distance, equal to eight miles.

228 *who has died himself before his death*: this entire verse plays with the immortality of love despite the perishability of the human body. In this first couplet, dying before death refers to *fanā*, the annihilation of the carnal soul that is necessary if the seeker is to meet the divine beloved.

one's body becomes immortal: death itself is celebrated as the fruit of life, for although formless, it allows humans to live on through love.

The elixir of immortality . . . wherever it is found: the text for this line of the final couplet is not very clear, as the poet uses *so ṭhāṉva* or 'the place' but does not clarify the poetic reference any further. In context, we have taken it to mean the place where immortality abounds and is therefore, by extension, the sanctuary of love.